CW01019569

Fish & Fishers
of the
Lake District

Fish & Fishers
of the
Lake District

KEITH HARWOOD

THE
MEDLAR PRESS
ELLESMERE

Published by The Medlar Press Limited,
The Grange, Ellesmere, Shropshire SY12 9DE
www.medlarpress.com

ISBN 978-1-907110-52-8

*The author and publisher would like to thank all those who
have given permission for copyright material to be reproduced in this book.
if any have been inadvertently overlooked they will be
pleased to make the necessary arrangements.*

Designed and typeset in 11½ on 13½ point Bembo Roman.
Produced in England by The Medlar Press Limited, Ellesmere, England.

Contents

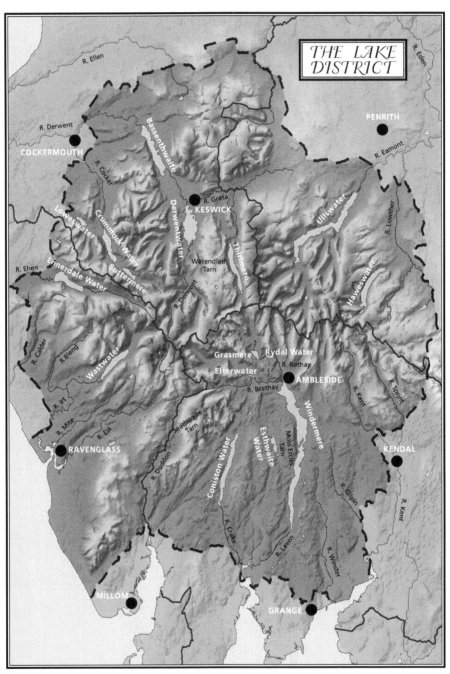

THE LAKE DISTRICT

R. Ellen

R. Eden

R. Derwent

PENRITH

COCKERMOUTH

R. Eamont

R. Cocker

Bassenthwaite

R. Greta

KESWICK

Ullswater

R. Lowther

Loweswater

Crummock Water

Derwentwater

Watendlath Tarn

Thirlmere

Haweswater

R. Ehen

Ennerdale Water

Buttermere

R. Derwent

R. Calder

R. Bleng

Wastwater

Grasmere

Rydal Water

R. Rothay

Elterwater

AMBLESIDE

R. Kent

R. Sprint

R. Brathay

R. Irt

Windermere

R. Mite

R. Esk

Seathwaite Tarn

Moss Eccles Tarn

Esthwaite Water

RAVENGLASS

R. Duddon

Coniston Water

KENDAL

R. Gilpin

R. Kent

R. Crake

R. Leven

R. Winster

MILLOM

GRANGE

—∾∾∾—

Helenae
uxori carissimae

—∾∾∾—

ACKNOWLEDGEMENTS

A number of people have helped me in the preparation of this book by lending books or providing photocopies of material in their collection, or simply by answering my many queries. First of all, I would like to thank my publisher, Jon Ward-Allen, who first suggested that I write a book on the history of angling in the Lake District, following the publication of my articles on Wordsworth, Charles Gough and Beatrix Potter in *Waterlog* magazine. I owe a debt of gratitude to angling historian, John Austin, a mine of information on North Country angling, who not only allowed me access to material in his collection but also read through my draft manuscript and made many valuable suggestions. I would like to thank the librarians at Kendal Public Library and the Harris Library at Preston for their help in locating and photocopying material. I would also like to thank the staff of the Museum of Lakeland Life at Kendal for permission to photograph material in their collection, Andrew Herd for photographing the material on Adlington & Hutchinson, and Fred Buller and Phill Williams for permission to use copyright material. Dudley Green, a former colleague, and bookseller Paul Morgan kindly provided me with photocopies of material in their possession. Michael Turner willingly gave permission to use his photograph of Philip Hutchinson.

My greatest debt of gratitude is to my wife, Helen, an expert in genealogy who greatly assisted in researching the family backgrounds of a number of anglers portrayed in this book. In addition, her knowledge of computing and IT has saved me from many pitfalls.

Keith Harwood
Clitheroe, October 2014.

INTRODUCTION

There is more to fishing than simply catching fish and, as I grow older, where I fish is just as important as the fishing itself. The Lake District is an area of outstanding natural beauty with a wealth of lakes, rivers, becks and tarns, enough to satisfy even the most fastidious of anglers and over the last fifty years or so I have been fortunate to fish many of its waters. Looking back at my fishing diary I can vividly recall autumnal days trolling for pike on Windermere, balmy summer evenings fishing the same lake for wild brown trout, bringing to the net a beautiful fresh-run salmon on the Derwent, worm fishing for perch on Thirlmere and casting to the wily brown trout of Easedale Tarn. Such memories are what fishing is all about.

The waters of the Lake District are home to a number of species of fish that are rarely encountered elsewhere in the British Isles and inhabit deep, cold lakes. These relics of the last Ice Age, the charr, vendace and schelly were once far more numerous than today and were even exploited commercially. Indeed, during the eighteenth and nineteenth centuries, potted Lakeland charr was famed throughout the country and spawned the manufacture of some beautiful pots, which are now highly collectable. Now, however, these species are under threat from a combination of factors including pollution and global warming.

Man has been exploiting the fish of the Lake District since prehistoric times and from the Middle Ages to the end of the nineteenth century, when sea fish became more readily available, a flourishing commercial fishery existed in the Lakes. More recently, the perch and pike of Windermere were netted to provide a valuable source of food during the Second World War. Angling with rod and line, however, is a relative late-comer to the Lake District and has developed in tandem with the tourist industry. The establishment of a fish hook manufacturing business in Kendal during the middle of the eighteenth century suggests that angling was becoming a more popular pastime around that time. At the beginning of the nineteenth century Charles Gough met his tragic fate while on his way to fish Wythburn Lake (now Thirlmere). The first half of the nineteenth century witnessed a number of anglers visiting the Lake District specifically to fish its waters, among them Stephen Oliver, who gave a vivid account of his angling forays among the Lakeland hills in *Scenes and Recollections of Fly-Fishing in Northumberland, Cumberland and Westmorland* (1834). William Wordsworth and his brother John were both keen anglers and the fruits of their labours frequently featured on the menu at Dove Cottage.

Although tourism in the Lake District began to develop towards the end of the eighteenth century, the difficulties and expense of travel meant that it was only available to a privileged few. However, following the opening of the railway line to Windermere in 1847, access to the Lake District became available to the wider public. By the end of the nineteenth century such was the popularity of perch fishing on Windermere that postcards were printed depicting the activity and over forty boatmen were employed to cater for the needs of perch fishers. The increase in the use of private cars and the development of the motorway system in the twentieth century has resulted in mass tourism in the Lake District, not always to the benefit of the angler seeking peace and tranquillity in pursuit of fish. Nowadays, many more lucrative diversions abound to part tourists from their money and, as a result, fishing on the larger lakes at least seems to have declined in popularity. The increase in commercial fisheries stocked with over-fed rainbow trout or carp has also diverted anglers' attentions away from more difficult natural waters. However, the Lake District can still provide excellent sport for the angler willing to put in a little extra effort.

Considering the size of the Lake District and the extent of its waters, the area does not feature as extensively in angling literature as the chalkstreams of southern England or the rivers and lochs of Scotland. In the chapters that follow I have concentrated my attention on the fish of the Lake District and the fishers who recorded their experiences on Lakeland waters, commencing with William Wordsworth and ending with Hugh Falkus, who passed away in 1996. I am well aware that there are a number of contemporary angling writers such as Laurence Catlow and Paul Procter who write of fishing in the Lake District but their story, as they say, must wait for another time.

1

FISHES OF THE LAKES

Perch & Perchines

The perch is a most obliging fish. The first fish I ever caught, aged seven, was a perch. I caught the fish on my local mill lodge using a rod made out of a tank aerial, a Bakelite reel and red-tipped quill float. I remember my excitement as my float seemed to take on a life of its own and began bobbing about before finally disappearing. I vividly remember striking and feeling a solid resistance at the end of my line. The perch, all of four ounces, greedily devoured my brandling worm, freshly dug from my grandfather's allotment. It was to be the first of many such fish that saw me embark on an angling career of over fifty years and still counting. One of my earliest memories of the Lake District also concerns perch. I recall sitting in a rowing boat near Lakeside on Windermere with my dad, my uncle and cousin and catching perch after perch on my new rod, made of solid green fibreglass by Milbro. We boat-fished for perch a number of times off Lakeside and it was unusual in those days (the late 1950s) not to see several other boats out perch fishing.

Such was the popularity of perch fishing on Windermere in the late nineteenth and early twentieth centuries that it formed an important branch of the tourist industry, to such an extent that in 1899 perch fishing was described as the main industry of Bowness. In 1878 around 150 boats were licensed, forty boatmen were employed and 200 rods were hired out for perch fishing. In the early twentieth century Pettitt's of Keswick produced a post-card of perch fishing on Windermere for tourists to send to their friends and families (shown opposite).

John Watson, in *The English Lake District Fisheries* (1899), describes the methods employed by the late nineteenth century tourists to catch their perch:

Perch fishing on Windermere gives great pleasure to a host of visitors, and perch fishing has been described as the chief industry of Bowness. These bold-biting fish exist in the lake in hundreds of thousands, and are mainly captured by float fishing from a boat. Minnows and small red worms are used as bait, and there is scarcely any limit to the number of fish that may be caught. The perch taken in this way are exceedingly small, and those who are ambitious to catch larger fish use a paternoster, fishing in deeper water. It needs hardly be remarked that a paternoster is a small leaden plummet with a yard of gut attached, and on which two hooks are used. The perch taken in this way are larger only by comparison; for although one of 2lbs 3oz has been taken, the over-abundance of perch in the lake keeps down the average size to an extreme degree.

Whatever mode of perch fishing is adopted, care should be taken that the bait is actually on the bottom, as a suspended worm or minnow is always an object of suspicion. The fish may be seen swimming around it, but that is as far as they will go.

Watson goes on to mention an old method of perch fishing, which he claims was still being practised by local anglers in his

645 Perch Fishing on Windermere

day. This method employed a 'beam', a stout piece of wire about a foot in length and weighted in the middle. A length of gut bearing a hook was fastened to each end of the 'beam' and a line was fastened to the weight in the middle. The device was then worked like an ordinary hand-line. An even more bizarre method of perch fishing is given by Thomas Hofland in *The British Angler's Manual* (1848 edition). Whether the method described was ever employed in the Lake District is debatable but Hofland claims it to be deadly:

I will now let my readers into a secret in perch fishing, known but to very few, and which alone ought to secure the future fame, as well as the sale, of this volume, independently of its other merits. I have known it for many years, but have never before divulged it, except to one or two friends.

Perhaps the most taking time of the year for perch is in the autumn, as they become gregarious fish, which they are not in the spring or the summer.

Procure a large glass bottle, such as may be seen in the windows of chemists' shops; the clearer the glass the better. Fill this bottle with river water, and put into it a quantity of live and lively minnows. Cover the top with a piece of parchment, having holes punctured in it. Tie a strong cord round the neck of the bottle so prepared, and sink it near a pile in a river, or in a deep hole near the bank. This should be done early in the morning, or late in the evening, when no one is about to witness the operation; conceal the cord, and leave the bottle for two days. At the end of that time drop a paternoster, baited with live minnows, by the side of the bottle, and the angler may be assured of excellent sport; as the sight of the minnows in the bottle will have attracted numerous perch to the spot . . . Wherever, however, there are perch, whether in rivers, ponds, or lakes, the results will be the same. This may be called poaching, but I do not think it is more so than using ground-bait, or any other mode of attracting fish to a particular spot.

Nowadays, although perch are still plentiful in Windermere, you are unlikely to see many tourists out on boats fishing for perch. Many more lucrative diversions now abound in the Lake District designed to tempt tourists to part with their money. Nevertheless, good perch fishing can still be had, both in Windermere and in many of the other lakes. Indeed, in recent years I have had some excellent catches of perch fishing from the bank in Thirlmere.

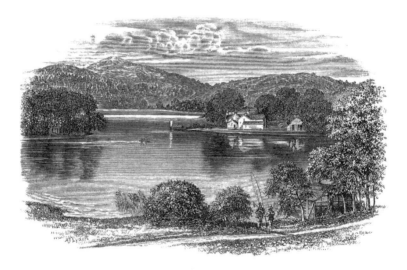

Fishing on Windermere, from British Freshwater Fishes *by Reverend Houghton.*

The perch (*Perca fluviatilis*) is the most prolific of the larger species of fish in Windermere and there is hardly a lake or a tarn in the whole of the Lake District, except those at high altitude, in which the perch is not found. Estimates of the perch population in Windermere vary and scientific study of the species in Windermere only began in the 1930s. At their peak in the late 1950s and early 1960s around five to six million perch inhabited the lake. In 1976, a catastrophic disease wiped out over 98% of the adult perch population in Windermere and thousands upon thousands of perch were washed ashore. I have witnessed a similar phenomenon at Malham Tarn in the Yorkshire Dales, where the perch population was likewise decimated. Fortunately, the species has now recovered and current estimates of the perch population in Windermere are around two and a half to three million fish.

Although very common throughout the temperate parts of Europe, the perch is undoubtedly one of the most beautiful of our freshwater fishes. It was well known to the ancient Greeks and the name perch is derived from the Greek. On larger lakes like Windermere perch have a seasonal migration, occupying shallower water (to a depth of ten metres) in the summer months and moving to deeper water (to a depth of around twenty-five metres) in the winter months. Towards the end of April the fish return to shallower water and spawning takes place in May. Female perch are capable of producing a large number of eggs, usually between 10,000 and 20,000, depending on the size of the female. Egg masses are deposited on rooted vegetation at depths of around three metres around the margins of the lake. Newly hatched perch feed on zooplankton but, as they grow, they feed on macro-invertebrates and other fish such as sticklebacks, minnows and even the young of their own species. The survival of juvenile perch is very much influenced by temperature, warmer summers producing stronger populations.

As every young angler knows, the perch is a boldly biting fish, always eager for a worm, maggot, minnow or other bait, including its own eye, as the following incident from

Cholmondeley-Pennell's, *The Angler-Naturalist* (1863) relates:

A very singular, if not unparalleled instance of the voracity of the perch occurred to me when fishing in Windermere. In removing the hook from the jaws of a fish, one eye was accidentally displaced, and remained adhering to it. Knowing the reparative capabilities of piscine organiza-tion, I returned the maimed perch, which was too small for the basket, to the lake, and being somewhat scant of minnows, threw the line in again with the eye attached as a bait - there being no other of any descrip-tion on the hook. The float disappeared almost instantly; and on landing the new comer, it turned out to be the fish I had the moment before thrown in, and which had thus been actually caught by his own eye.

A small number of the perch population become exclusively fish eating, feeding largely on a diet of juvenile perch and these fish can grow to a weight in excess of two pounds. However, the Lake District is not particularly noted for its specimen perch. A glance through the lists of notable perch captures in *The Book of the Perch* (1990) or *The Biggest Fish of All* (2011), both by The Perchfishers, reveals only one entry for a specimen perch from a water in the Lake District. However, the odd notable fish does turn up occasionally. Watson, writing in 1899 records a 4¾lb perch from Windermere, a 5lb fish from Ullswater and one of 5½lb from Bigland Tarn. James Holgate in *Reflections upon Lakeland Angling* (1989) mentions that a perch just short of 4lb was caught in Bassenthwaite in 1981 and one of 3¾lb in nearby Derwentwater in 1984. Fish over one and a half pounds turn up quite regularly, and no doubt even larger specimens occasionally turn up but go unreported in the angling press.

During the eighteenth and nineteenth centuries the Lake District was justly famed for its charr, and potted charr, in beau-tifully crafted dishes, was sent the length and breadth of the country. However, charr were not the only species to be exploited commercially. At the outbreak of the Second World War, Barton Worthington, the director of the Freshwater Biological Association, then based at Wray Castle, Windermere,

wondered how the FBA might contribute to the war effort and
help to enhance the country's food supplies. At that time Windermere contained a dense population of perch, few of which
grew larger than 200mm in length and Worthington, who had
previously worked in Africa where he had seen fish traps in use,
realised that large numbers of Windermere perch could be
caught in traps. During the autumn of 1939, trials were carried
out on various methods of catching perch: gill-nets, seine nets
and traps. In January 1940, a series of investigative traps was set
out near Wray Castle and it was discovered that perch migrate to
water of about twenty metres deep in October, while in April
they migrate to shallower water to spawn, where they could be
caught in large numbers in traps while spawning.

Worthington decided to commence a full-scale commercial
perch fishery in the spring of 1941 and 300 traps were manufactured for the purpose. The first traps were cylindrical but a
number were lost rolling down the steeper slopes of underwater
drop-offs and it was found that flat-bottomed traps were more
successful. The traps were supplied with ten-metre ropes and two
glass floats. A number of volunteers were recruited from among
local charr fishermen and boat owners to set and lift the traps.

Perch fishing by Joseph Hardman, courtesy of the Museum of Lakeland Life & Industry, Kendal.

The volunteers were assigned a beat of around twenty traps and were responsible for lifting them on certain days during the season. From the last week in April until the end of June, the traps were lifted three or four times a week. The perch were packed in fish boxes and landed at a number of centres around the lake whence they were taken to Windermere station to be transported overnight to a canning factory in Leeds. At the factory they were processed and packed in Yorkshire relish and tomato sauce and canned in sardine cans. They were sold as 'Perchines - Lakeland Perch, Britain's most lovely and tasty freshwater fish'.

Apparently, the perch, after spawning, being caught in a trap and transported to Leeds, were not as tasty as they were made out to be. However, they were relatively cheap, required few ration coupons, and proved quite popular.

The perchine experiment on Windermere proved so popular that perch fisheries were opened on other Cumbrian lakes and on several lakes and reservoirs elsewhere in England, Wales and Scotland, including Loch Lomond. However, these other fisheries proved less successful and were relatively short-lived.

Initially, perch trapping was carried out in the North Basin of Windermere but was soon extended to the South Basin and, by the end of 1942 the whole lake was being fished. Such fishing pressure on the perch population, however, inevitably had an impact and catches began to decline, so much so that by the end of 1947 it was no longer economically viable to send perch for canning. Once the trapping of perch ceased in 1947 it was expected that the number of perch would rapidly increase again, but this did not happen. In fact, the perch population remained low until 1957, when there was a spectacular rise in the year classes of 1955 and 1959, before stabilising at a moderate level until 1976, when the perch population was ravaged by disease.

In this country we seem to have an aversion to eating fresh-water fish other than farmed salmon and rainbow trout, but this was not always the case as many old angling and cookery books will testify. In countries such as Austria, Switzerland and those around the Baltic I have eaten a variety of freshwater fish species, including perch, pike and zander, and very tasty they were too. In Finland, perch is a popular fish and can be found smoked and canned in supermarkets. In these days of concerns about over-fishing in the seas around our coast perhaps it would not be a bad idea if commercial fishing on a small scale began again in some of our larger lakes and lochs - then we could all sample the delights of canned perchines!

2

FISHES OF THE LAKES

Pike

Although perch fishing in the Lake District was popular in the late nineteenth and early twentieth centuries, nowadays you are far more likely to see anglers out on the lakes fishing for pike and in recent years some large specimens have been taken. I, too, have had some success with Lakeland pike and I caught my largest pike, weighing a few ounces short of 20lb, on Rydal Water a number of years ago. Indeed, as I sit writing in my study I am overlooked by a pike in a bow-fronted glass case, caught by my son in Windermere, in 1993. The fish was caught on a trolled Shakespeare Big S lure and put up a tremendous fight.

The pike (*Esox lucius*) is the top predatory fish in the Lake District and lives on a diet of fish, including juveniles of its own species. At one time it was alleged that pike was a non-indigenous species and had been introduced into this country, like carp. However, evidence from fossils, and pike bones found in archaeological deposits, conclusively prove that the pike is native to this country and has been hunted by man for at least twelve thousand years.

In appearance the pike is like no other British fish. Its stream-lined shape, with the caudal, dorsal and anal fins set well back, combined with a muscular tail, enable the pike to dart swiftly upon its prey. Its colouring, with its brownish-green flanks and dark green back allows it to blend into the reeds or shadows of overhanging branches and ambush its unsuspecting prey. Any angler foolish enough to put his hand in a pike's mouth will soon find out that it is equipped with rows of sharp teeth that slope back to allow the easy passage of such prey as the pike may seize and, as Sir Herbert Maxwell put it, in his *British Fresh-Water Fishes* (1904):

All things considered, a more perfect predatory instrument could scarcely be devised than the mouth of a pike, especially for the capture of nimble and slippery objects.

The voracity of the pike is well documented. Numerous stories are told of pike attacking people or animals. Cholmondeley-

Rydal Water - the scene of the author's biggest pike.

Pennell, in his *Angler Naturalist* (1863) records an incident of a pike attacking a youth. The incident is related by the boy's father:

One of my sons, aged fifteen, went with three other boys to bathe in Inglemere Pond, near Ascot Racecourse; he walked gently into the water to about the depth of four feet, when he spread out his hands to attempt to swim; instantly a large fish came up and took his hand into his mouth as far up as the wrist, but finding he could not swallow it, relinquished his hold, and the boy turning round, prepared for a hasty retreat out of the pond; his companions who saw it, also scrambled out of the pond as fast as possible. My son had scarcely turned himself round when the fish came up behind him and immediately seized his other hand, crosswise, inflicting some very deep wounds on the back of it; the boy raised his first-bitten and still bleeding arm, and struck the monster a hard blow on the head, when the fish disappeared. The other boys assisted him to dress, bound up his hand with their handkerchiefs, and brought him home. We took him down to Mr. Brown, Surgeon, who dressed seven wounds in one hand; and so great was the pain the next day, that the lad fainted twice; the little finger was bitten through the nail, and it was more than six weeks before it was well. The nail came off and the scar remains to this day.

There is a sequel to this story. A few days later, a passer-by noticed something floating in the pond, which turned out to be the pike in its death throes. The pike was brought ashore and measured at forty-one inches. It was then taken to Windsor Castle. Unfortunately, its subsequent fate is not recorded.

An incident in his youth led fanatical angler and Poet Laureate, Ted Hughes, to exercise his poetical imagination and compose his often-quoted poem, *Pike*. His love of pike fishing developed while he was a student at Mexborough Grammar School, where he made friends with John Wholey, the son of a local gamekeeper. It was with John that he had his first taste of pike fishing in a local lake and it was with him, too, that Ted put three baby pike into a tank at school. During the summer holidays the boys forgot about the fish and returned to find the three fish reduced to one. This act of cannibalism is vividly recorded in his poem.

However, I suspect most anglers' first encounter with a pike is similar to that of the Swallows while out perch fishing and described so vividly by Arthur Ransome in *Swallows and Amazons* (1930). The children are contentedly fishing for perch, bringing in one after the other of the fat little fish and watching their floats bobbing together. They soon have a pile of fish at the bottom of the boat and Roger decides to count them. However, as he is in the middle of this exercise, his attention is drawn to the disappearance of his float and the odd behaviour of his rod:

Roger jumped up and caught hold of his jerking rod, which he had put down while he was counting the catch. He felt a fish at the end of his line. Just as he was bringing it to the top there was a great swirl in the water, and his rod suddenly pulled down again. Roger hung on as hard as he could, and his rod was almost bent into a circle.

"It's a shark! It's a shark!" he shouted.

Something huge was moving about in the water, deep down, pulling the rod this way and that.

"Let him have line off the reel," said John, but Roger held on.

Suddenly a mottled green fish, a yard long, with a dark back and white underneath, came to the top. It lifted an enormous head right out of the water, and opened a great white mouth, and shook itself. A little perch flew high into the air. Roger's rod straightened. For a moment the great fish lay close to the top of the water, looking wickedly at the crew of the Swallow as they looked at it. Then, with a twist of its tail that made a great twirling splash in the water, it was gone. Roger brought in the little perch. It was dead, and its sides were marked with deep gashes from the great teeth of the pike.

One wonders whether Ransome had a specific incident in mind when he wrote that passage, perhaps from a childhood fishing expedition on Coniston. I, too, like many anglers, have had similar experiences with pike, most notably when fly fishing for

Pike, from British Fresh-Water Fishes *by Reverend Houghton.*

trout on a Lakeland river. I had just hooked a lively trout when suddenly, as if from nowhere, a pike shot out and grabbed my fish. I played both fish for several minutes before the pike finally let go. The poor brown trout was mortally wounded and had to be put out of its misery.

Sadly, over the years, the pike has had a very bad press and nearly always gets the blame if the quality of fishing deteriorates. On some waters, most notably trout waters, pike are classed as vermin and a war of attrition is waged against them. Some famous anglers, too, have not had a good word to say about pike. Even the late Dick Walker, probably the most influential angler of the twentieth century, admitted that he did not like pike and regarded them as ugly brutes. Sir Herbert Maxwell, a keen game angler, was even more scathing. Writing in *British Fresh-Water Fishes* (1904) he stated that since the pike was no longer important in peoples' diets it should be regarded as an unmitigated evil that has wrought havoc among more valuable fish. John Watson, author of *The English Lake District Fisheries* (1899), claimed that pike were mainly instrumental in exterminating the vendace population of Bassenthwaite. He also stated that the pike was

such a voracious creature and was furnished with such a diges-
tion that it would consume a half-pound trout per day for twelve
months.

As a result of such attitudes pike were frequently persecuted in
Lakeland waters, as the following account from Watson shows:

*In what is primarily a salmon and trout fishery district, the pike is nat-
urally looked upon as a predatory fish, and is kept in check accordingly,
about 5,000 lbs being killed annually by the water-bailiffs in Windermere alone. These fish are mainly destroyed in the shallows in March and
April where they have come to spawn.*

Such attitudes to the pike were largely based on prejudice and
misunderstanding. Fortunately, over the last fifty years or so, the
Freshwater Biological Association at Ferry House has carried out
a great deal of research on the pike of Windermere and dispelled
most of these misconceptions. The pike does not require 180lb
of trout per year to survive, as Watson would have us believe. The
FBA's researches show that a pike of ten pounds can survive on
as little as 14lb of fish per year. However, this level of intake
would not permit any increase in the pike's weight. Generally
speaking, to survive and grow, a pike needs to eat around four
times its own body weight per year, considerably less than
Watson's 180lb!

The FBA has also shown that, although pike do prey on trout,
charr and indeed on their own species, their main diet in Windermere consists of perch. Fred Buller, the great pike expert who
worked at the FBA for a number of years, claimed that certain
Windermere pike anglers, trailing a dead perch on summer
evenings, would often scrape off the scales on the perch's flank
to expose a white patch. The idea is to make the pike think that
the perch is infected with fungus and, therefore, will make an
easy target. It seems, then, that pike may actually do a good job
in mopping up sick or injured fish.

Pike, in lakes such as Windermere, spawn in February in shallow reedy areas around the margins of the lake and initially feed

Ferry House, Windermere, home to the Freshwater Biological Association.

on zooplankton and small invertebrates. When they reach a length of just three centimetres, they become almost exclusively fish eaters. Female pike grow more rapidly than males and attain greater weights. Growth rate is often influenced by temperature and they do particularly well when the late summer and autumn months are warm.

During the Second World War, following the success of the commercial perch fishery on Windermere, the director of the FBA, Barton Worthington, decided to investigate the possibility of a commercial pike fishery. Winifred Frost, the well-known fish biologist, was assigned the task of carrying out trials. It was decided that gill-netting in winter would be the best method and trial netting was carried out during the winter of 1943-44. The nets employed had a 5-inch mesh, designed to prevent smaller fish such as trout and charr being captured. Nets measuring 30 yards long and 10 feet deep were set on the bottom in shallow water at a number of sites around the lake and were lifted every two or three days. The pike thus captured were sold on

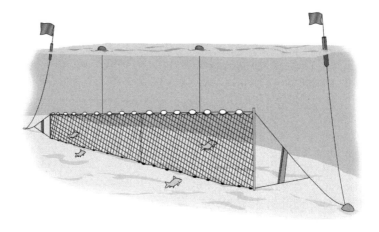

Gill-net. Courtesy of Michigan Sea Grant (www.miseagrant.umich.edu).

the fresh fish market. Pike fishing on a commercial scale proved less successful than perch fishing and was relatively short-lived.

At the end of the Second World War a culling experiment was carried out on Windermere to see if the removal of large numbers of pike would protect their prey species, especially trout and charr. In fact, the opposite proved to be the case. Large pike were caught in gill-nets and removed from the water. Although this reduced the adult pike population, numbers soon recovered and actually increased, with the population consisting of faster-growing younger fish, which put increasing pressure on the trout and charr. Over the last seventy years pike numbers in Windermere have fluctuated and declined markedly following the perch disease of 1976. Nowadays, the pike population of Windermere is estimated to be between five and ten thousand fish.

John Watson, in *The English Lake District Fisheries* (1899), pointed out that, although the Lake District has an abundance of pike, they do not compare favourably in size with fish from the Norfolk Broads and other southern waters. A glance at the big pike list in Fred Buller's, *The Domesday Book of Mammoth Pike* (1979), reveals only two entries for Lake District pike, both fish weighing in at 35lb. The first pike listed was caught on rod and line in Grasmere in 1900 by a Mr Griffin. The second fish was caught in a net in Windermere by the FBA in 1960. In more recent times, large pike of over thirty pounds have been taken in Derwentwater and Bassenthwaite. The current record Lake District pike, as far as I am aware, is a fish of 39½lb, which was taken on Esthwaite Lake, now run as a commercial trout fishery and regularly stocked with rainbow trout. The current British record pike weighed in at 46lb 13oz, and was captured by Roy Lewis in Llandegfedd Reservoir, South Wales in 1992.

During the nineteenth century, and even earlier, some fishermen, including the poet Wordsworth, employed rather unsporting methods for catching pike, especially when they were required for the table. Watson points out that trimmers, often as many as twenty at a time, were commonly employed in Lake District waters. Trimmers are basically large pike floats made out of discs of cork or wood, painted with different colours on each side. The line was wound around the disc, which had a groove to hold it in place. The hook was baited with a suitable live-bait and the groove controlled the depth at which the bait could swim. The trimmers were thrown into the water and left to swim about. A bite was signalled by the trimmer being flipped over by the pull of a pike, hence the different colours. The trimmers and pike could be dragged in with the assistance of a boat or drag-hook.

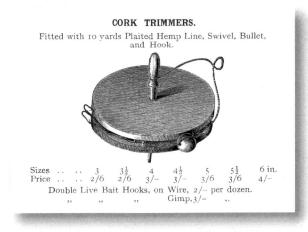

CORK TRIMMERS.

Fitted with 10 yards Plaited Hemp Line, Swivel, Bullet, and Hook.

Sizes		3	3½	4	4½	5	5½	6 in.
Price		2/6	2/6	3/-	3/-	3/6	3/6	4/-

Double Live Bait Hooks, on Wire, 2/- per dozen.
„ „ „ Gimp, 3/- „

Trimmer, as advertised in the Farlows Catalogue of 1909.

    A similar method, known as hound fishing, was recorded by
Stephen Oliver in *Scenes and Recollections of Fly-Fishing* (1834):

*Hound fishing for pike upon the lakes is most amusing when there is a
party, but affords little pleasure to the solitary angler...The following is
the mode of proceeding: a live bait, either a perch or a trout, with a short
line from two to six feet long, is attached to a piece of light buoyant wood,
or a bladder, which is then turned adrift on the lake, to float according to
the direction of the wind or current. The bait in its course down or across
the lake is frequently seized by a pike, and the resistance of the wood or
bladder, when he first attempts to make off with his prey, assists to strike
the hook. Should the hook become firmly fixed, the hound frequently disappears in the pike's attempt to descend, but after a short time, when the
wearied captive has relaxed his efforts, again mounts to the surface.*

    A much more sporting method is described by Watson in *The
English Lake District Fisheries* (1899):

*On any calm day, preferably in July, carefully select a number of the
largest minnows you can get, and place them in a minnow-can. The
minnows should be as carefully chosen as though for night-trouting.
A moderately stiff light rod of about fourteen feet is best, with reel and
dressed line. Your tackle is to be three feet of sound, round gut, not too
thick, with a small plummet at the end. Just above the lead, a small
stout hook, whipped on some six inches of gut, is to be affixed - in fact
a stout perch paternoster with only one hook. Slip the hook through both
lips of a minnow and try round the weeds, and especially in the open
spaces between the weeds. The moment you feel a bite, strike firmly but
gently, and keep your fish as much as possible out of the weeds. Lots of
jack from 1 lb to 2 lbs may be taken in this way, and sometimes a really
good fish is got . . . A pike finely hooked on gut tackle is as much unlike
the same fish taken by trolling with several large hooks in its mouth as
can well be imagined. Many a trout taken with the minnow does not
fight as well for a time as does a pike, but the pike gives in sooner than
the trout. Still, fishing for jack with what is practically perch tackle is by
no means a bad way of passing a hot July day, when most other kinds*

of angling are out of the question; and there is the satisfaction that you are thinning the number of pike.

Nowadays, pike anglers in the Lake District employ a variety of methods for catching their quarry. Dead-baiting with sea fish and fly fishing with large artificial flies are now much more popular and the pike is held in high regard as a sporting fish in its own right. This change in attitude towards pike has partly been brought about through greater scientific understanding of the species and partly through the establishment of the Pike Anglers' Club, which seeks to educate anglers about their quarry.

3

FISHES OF THE LAKES

Trout & Salmon

The brown trout (*Salmo trutta*) is a very adaptable fish and it is found in practically all Lake District waters. The species *Salmo trutta* includes the resident brown trout, migratory sea trout and the 'slob' trout, which drifts between freshwater and the brackish water of the estuary. In many other parts of the country the rainbow trout (*Oncorhynchus mykiss*), a non-indigenous species, reigns supreme and is the main quarry of the trout angler. However, in the Lake District only Esthwaite Lake and a few of the larger tarns have been stocked with rainbow trout, elsewhere the wild brown trout is the main focus for the angler.

The Lakeland brown trout has to be adaptable to survive in the many different environments found within the Lake District boundaries, from large deep lakes to high altitude mountain tarns to fast-flowing rivers and streams. In fact, few other creatures can adapt to match their environment and available food as successfully as the trout.

The trout has been around a long time. Its ancestor, *Eosalmo driftwoodensis*, was swimming around the waters of what is now North America around 50 million years ago. *Eosalmo* is the earliest known salmonid and is the ancestor of all today's trout and salmon. It derives its name, *Eosalmo driftwoodensis*, from an ancient lake bed in the Driftwood Canyon in British Columbia, where its fossilised remains were first discovered in 1977. It is believed that originally the *Eosalmo* was a freshwater fish and only learned to feed in saltwater at a later stage. This is confirmed by the fact that all salmonids, even those that spend a considerable time at sea, return to freshwater to spawn. The brown trout (*Salmo trutta*) shares the *Salmo genus* with the Atlantic salmon (*Salmo salar*). It is believed that these two species split from their common ancestor around 4.5 million years ago and that the brown trout first appeared in the area we know as the Balkans, while the salmon evolved in the Atlantic.

There is considerable variation in the brown trout of the Lake District, as Watson very clearly pointed out in his *English Lake District Fisheries (1899)* over one hundred years ago:

In colouring and several outward characteristics trout differ more widely than any other fish, and it may be said that almost every river, lake and tarn has its own peculiar trout. This is owing to the peculiar surroundings in which trout find themselves; and we can go in gradation from the black troutlets of a fell-beck tributary to the lusty trout of the same river miles below its source; and from the ill-fed fish of a bleak mountain tarn to the 6lbs and 7lbs monsters of Windermere. Yet all these are varieties of the brown trout, but varieties only; for, although differing so widely in outward appearance, they present no specific differences. In fact, I know no creature which so quickly conforms to the surroundings in which it finds itself as the common brown trout.

Not surprisingly, perhaps, since the headquarters of the Freshwater Biological Association is situated on its shoreline, the brown trout of Windermere has been the subject of greater study than trout elsewhere in the Lake District. Windermere trout, like most other Lake District trout, do not spawn in the lake itself but in the tributaries running into it. Spawning normally takes place in late November, although there is some variation and Windermere trout have been observed ascending Trout Beck as early as August. The spawning migration usually takes place during a spate and the female fish normally spawn and return to the lake within a twenty-four hour period. Male fish, however, often stay in the spawning stream for longer in order to fertilise other females. A study of the genetics of young trout in some of the tributary streams suggests that each stream has its own unique genetic stock of fish.

The young trout hatch in the spring and remain in the stream to feed for up to three years before taking up residence in the lake itself. The majority of trout, however, are two years old when they first enter Windermere. On entering the lake the young trout tend to occupy the littoral zone (the shoreline), although some trout feed in the open water of the lake. Indeed, the Windermere fish that feed around the shoreline appear physically different from the ones that feed in more open water. The shoreline fish are sometimes referred to as 'yellow bellies' on account of their yellow colouring and red spots. The trout that feed in open water tend to have silvery flanks and black spots.

The diet of Lakeland brown trout varies from month to month and from water to water. However, studies of Windermere trout show that, for feeding purposes, the year can be divided into three periods:

October-February. During this period trout largely feed on bottom-dwelling fauna, i.e. molluscs and crustaceans.

March-July. At this time of year the trout feed principally on insect larvae and pupae.

May-September. During this period the trout feed largely upon terrestrial insects found at the surface of the water.

A good knowledge of these feeding periods is very useful to the fly fisherman in pursuit of his quarry. A number of trout in Windermere and other large lakes, after reaching a foot or so in length, become exclusively piscivorous and live on a diet of minnows, perch, charr and even juveniles of their own species. These trout, often referred to as ferox trout, can grow to a large size and fish up to fifteen pounds in weight have been caught in Windermere. James Clarke in his *Survey of the Lakes* (1787) tells an interesting story concerning the voracity of these Windermere trout:

On the 28ᵗʰ of October, 1784, I was upon the shore about Cunza, when I observed a boat coming towards me, and near the same time perceived it stop and the men in it take something out of the water; on their coming ashore, they told me that in coming they saw two large trouts floating upon the surface of the lake with their bellies uppermost, close alongside each other, and seemingly dead. On laying hold of one of them they seemed to be entangled, but in lifting it out of the water the other made its escape; then they discovered that they had seized between them a small trout, and each seemed determined to lose its life rather than its prey; they had struggled till life was almost spent, and both might have easily been taken if the fishermen had believed either to be alive; the lesser, which they took, weighed about a pound and a half; the other they supposed to weigh above two pounds.

During the eighteenth and nineteenth centuries the ferox trout of Ullswater was believed to be a separate species and was often referred to by earlier writers as the 'great grey trout'. James Clarke believed it to be peculiar to Ullswater and Buttermere and stated that it could grow up to thirty or forty pounds. He even claimed that a specimen of 56lb had been killed. Since the current British trout record stands at 31lb 12oz, for a fish taken in Loch Awe in 2002, I think Clarke's 56lb fish may be nothing more than a fisherman's tale!

These larger Lake District trout are usually caught by anglers trolling from a boat using Rapala lures or similar artificial lures. Nowadays they are occasionally taken by anglers trolling for pike.

Ferox trout

Traditional charr fishers, too, catch a number of large trout as they troll the lakes. In former times, trolling with Devon minnows or natural minnows mounted on a spinning flight was a popular method of catching bigger trout. Both George Foster Braithwaite and John Watson enjoyed trolling for trout on Windermere and elsewhere. Indeed, in *The English Lake District Fisheries* (1899), Watson waxes eloquent with regard to trolling on Windermere:

Let me state that there is a great charm about trolling on Windermere, and the angler will never forget a summer night so spent. As the light fades the sounds on the lake become fewer and fewer, and by midnight one is alone on the lake. There is no sound save that of oars in the rowlocks and the soft swish of the water. The experience is pleasant enough in itself, but trout fishing, and with good sport, one realises that life is a delightful thing.

For the modern fly fisherman, used to fishing waters densely stocked with rainbow trout, fishing on Windermere or one of the other larger lakes can be a daunting prospect. Although fishing from the bank can be productive, the most effective method is to fish from a boat. Unfortunately, unless the angler has his own boat, hiring a boat at tourist rates for a whole day can be pro-hibitively expensive. The best months for fly fishing on the larger lakes are from April to June and then again in September. Again, Watson's advice on where and how to fish on the larger lakes is still as useful today as it was when it was written over a hundred years ago:

The best trout ground is along the shallow margins of the lake, and it is here that the fishing is done. A boat (not too narrow) is almost invari-ably used, preferably one with a fair amount of stability. This is kept moving slowly, the angler casting towards the shore. During the day the fish mostly lie just where the bank shelves down to deeper water, and the angler cannot do better than follow this plan. Roughly speaking, the line indicated is about forty yards from the shore. The angler should always fish with the wind - not against it - and if the boat is rowed slowly par-allel with the shore a great extent of ground can be covered . . . A long line is quite unnecessary. When a fish rises, do not snatch the flies away; it is better to be too slow than too quick. Nearly every good fish will hook itself if allowed.

With regard to flies, many of the patterns mentioned by Watson for use on the larger lakes, will serve the angler just as well today. These include: the March Brown, Orange Woodcock, Green Drake, August Dun, Blue Dun, Black Gnat, Dark Snipe, Coch-y-Bonddu, Greenwell's Glory, Zulu, Claret and Teal, and Broughton Point.

For the more energetic angler, the trout in Lakeland tarns can provide good sport and I have had a number of good days' fish-ing on Easedale Tarn, high above Grasmere. Although trout in tarns tend to be generally smaller than their cousins in the larger lakes, what they lack in size they make up for with their fighting qualities. Tarn trout rarely weigh above half a pound but, occa-sionally, larger specimens do turn up. Furthermore, due to the altitude of many of these tarns, the fish are often late in coming into condition and it is often June before they are at their best. In former times fishing with the natural bracken clock was often practised on mountain tarns. The word 'clock' is an old North Country name for a beetle and the Bracken Clock often makes its appearance at the end of May and lasts until the middle of June. Nowadays, most anglers use an artificial Bracken Clock.

Again, Watson's advice to the tarn angler is still relevant today. He believed that the angler should burden himself as little as possible since a stiff hike is often required to reach a particular tarn. I find a six or seven piece travel fly rod, together with a light reel and box of flies will readily sit in my rucksack alongside my waterproof and lunch. One of the benefits of fishing these remote tarns is that you will rarely encounter another angler and will have the place to yourself.

The Sea Trout

Sea trout and brown trout are the same species (*Salmo trutta*) but a combination of genetics and environmental factors mean that some trout go to sea to feed before returning to the river to spawn. Experiments preventing sea trout from going to sea showed that the fish subsequently lived and bred in freshwater.

Young trout from one to three years old and between five and seven inches long go through a physiological change which enables them to cope with salt water and turns them a silvery colour. These small silver trout, or smolts, shoal together to migrate to sea, usually towards the end of March and into April. Sea trout nearly always grow bigger than the resident brown trout of the same river, due to the richer feeding at sea, and specimens of up to ten kilos have been caught.

The majority of sea trout are female, and because of their size, they produce more eggs, thus ensuring future generations of fish. On average a female sea trout will produce 800 eggs per pound weight. Sea trout return to their natal river to spawn and can start returning after only a few months at sea. The majority of sea trout return to the river from June to October. During the day,

Sea trout

sea trout often lie low; they tend to move at night and the dedicated sea trout angler will often be a night owl.

Unlike salmon, the majority of sea trout do not die after spawning and around 75% of sea trout will return to sea to feed and then come back again to the river to spawn. On returning to the river, sea trout often have a silvery colour. However, once they have been in the river for some time it can be hard to distinguish them from the resident brown trout.

In the Lake District the sea trout is a popular quarry for anglers and was often referred to as a 'salmon trout' or 'mort'. The juvenile sea trout was variously known as the 'sprod', 'whiting', 'smelt', or 'herling', depending on which part of the Lake District you hailed from.

Fishing for sea trout in Lake District rivers has been popular for a long time. One of the earliest references to sea trout fishing occurs in Samuel Taylor's, *Angling in All its Branches* (1800):

In the Kent a little below Kendal I have had fine diversion with the salmon-trout which run up the river from the sea.

George Foster Braithwaite and John Watson, who were both residents of Kendal, regularly fished the Kent for its sea trout. Watson was no purist when it came to sea trout fishing as the following extract from *The English Lake District Fisheries* (1899) demonstrates:

Morts enter the river (the Kent) about the third or fourth week in June, the run lasting until October. The best and heaviest fish come first, their weight running from 1lb to 3lbs, with exceptional fish up to 5lbs, 6lbs, and 7lbs. These fish afford excellent sport on the lower reaches of the river, but once over the weirs and falls they become more widely distributed and their capture is uncertain. During the day, particularly if the water is low, it is of little use fishing for them, although a few may sometimes be taken on Pennell tackle. When the water is in flood they will bite readily at the worm . . . On the water clearing, an artificial minnow may be used. This bait, usually a quill, was for some years an excellent means of filling the pannier, but of late, for some obscure reason, it has proved ineffective. Fish will eagerly follow the minnow, but refuse to mouth it. In this state of the water morts rise well at the fly, which in this district is usually fished on the casting line by tail-fly and two droppers . . .

Another angler who enjoyed sea trout fishing on the Kent was Geoffrey Dundas Luard (1879-1956), who fished the river when staying with his cousin who lived in the area. In his *Fishing: Fact or Fantasy?* (1947) he describes a dramatic encounter with a large Kent sea trout, which eventually broke him.

The river Leven, which runs out of Windermere, and enters the estuary below the village of Greenodd, was a favourite haunt of Richard Clapham (1878-1954), author of *Fishing for Sea Trout in Tidal Water* (1950). However, the doyen of sea trout anglers must surely be Hugh Falkus (1917-1996). After a varied career and three marriages, he eventually married Kathleen Armstrong and settled down to life at Cragg Cottage in Eskdale, where he established his reputation as the father of modern sea trout fishing. His book, *Sea Trout Fishing, A Practical Guide*, first published in 1962 and enlarged in 1975, has never been out of print and is the bible of modern sea trout anglers.

Salmon

I have very fond memories of Lake District salmon. My first fly-caught salmon came from the river Derwent, as did my largest salmon to date, a magnificent bar of silver weighing in at 16½lb.

Indeed, the Lake District rivers, including the Lune and Eden, have long been noted for their salmon. According to Watson, Lake District rivers have been netted for their bounty since the fourteenth century. However, an abundance of salmon also brought an abundance of poachers, eager to cash in on nature's bounty. In 1827, over twenty illegal nets were publicly burned in the market place at Appleby. These nets, destined for use on the Eden, were brand new and belonged to a gang of poachers. Their value was estimated at between £30 and £40, an enormous sum of money in the early nineteenth century. Similar seizing and burning of nets took place in Kendal. On one occasion a portly poacher's wife hid a net about her person under her dress!

Like brown and sea trout *(Salmo trutta)*, the Atlantic salmon *(Salmo salar)* has been around for a long time and, also like brown and sea trout, is descended from *Eosalmo driftwoodensis*. The salmon is an anadromous fish, which feeds out at sea and returns to its natal river to spawn. Studies of the salmon of the river Leven, which flows out of Windermere, show that the fish spawn in the Leven itself, just downstream of Newby Bridge, in the lower reaches of the Rothay and Brathay and in Trout Beck. After spending one to three years in the spawning stream, the young salmon (parr) undergo a physiological change, which pre-pares them for life at sea. At this stage in their life cycle the fish are known as smolts. Smolts from the river Leven slowly make their way to Morecambe Bay and from there to the open sea. Smolts from the Brathay, Rothay and Trout Beck, however, have to make their way through the length of Windermere before heading out to sea. Salmon feed at sea where they grow quickly. By the end of their first year they can be twenty to thirty times their original weight. After remaining at sea for between one to three years they return to their native river to spawn.

During the last fifty years or so Lake District salmon, like most other salmon in the United Kingdom, have suffered their ups and downs. Pollution, netting at sea, salmon fish farming and global warming have all had their impact on salmon stocks. Stud-ies of catch statistics for the river Leven show a marked decline

Salmon

in catches during the 1990s, with only twenty-six fish being caught in 1999. However, riparian owners, angling associations and the Environment Agency are all working hard to reverse the decline in salmon numbers throughout the United Kingdom and there is some encouraging evidence to show that they may be succeeding.

Of all the salmon rivers in the area, the Eden is undoubtedly the queen. It is one of the few rivers with a genuine spring run of salmon, which are eagerly sought after by anglers. As well as a spring run of fish, a second migration enters the river in June and July and a third in October. One of the largest salmon taken on rod and line in the Eden weighed in at 55½lb, and was caught in the Corby Castle water by a Mr Frances of Liverpool. An even larger fish, weighing 56lb was caught in the Warwick Hall water in November 1892. One of the most famous salmon flies on the Eden was the Bulldog, which was invented at the end of the nineteenth century by Robert Strong, the owner of a tackle shop in Castle Street, Carlisle. John Watson, author of *The English Lake District Fisheries* (1899), claims to have been given the first ever specimen of this fly by Strong himself, and on it he promptly caught two spring salmon.

The Derwent, which flows into the sea at Workington, is another fine salmon river and was a favourite haunt of Arthur Ransome. Although the occasional spring salmon is taken, it is generally regarded as a late river, which fishes well from August to the end of October. According to John Watson, a salmon weighing 62lb was caught on rod and line near Cockermouth.

Unfortunately, he does not give any details. During the late nineteenth and early twentieth centuries the Silver Grey salmon fly was a favourite on the Derwent and accounted for numbers of fish. Watson himself claims to have had considerable success with this fly.

Salmon also run through a number of the larger lakes on their way to their spawning grounds. However, it seems they are rarely fished for although Watson claimed that the occasional fresh-run salmon turned up in the nets of charr fishermen.

Silver Grey salmon fly.

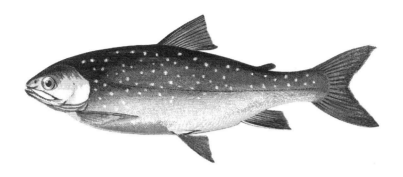

4

FISHES OF THE LAKES

Charr

If there is one fish that is synonymous with the Lake District, it must surely be the Arctic charr (*Salvelinus alpinus*), a member of the salmonid family. The word charr is often spelled with one 'r', but throughout this book I have preferred to use the older form, which is commonly employed by fishery scientists. During the eighteenth and nineteenth centuries Lakeland potted charr was sent the length and breadth of Britain and ended up on the tables of the great and good. Such was its popularity that it spawned its own distinctive type of pottery - the charr pot, the finest examples of which now command many hundreds of pounds on the antiques market.

In England, the charr is only found in the cold deep lakes of the Lake District. Elsewhere in the British Isles the species is found in some of the deep lakes in Wales, Scotland and Ireland. As its name implies, the Arctic charr is a cold-water species and has the most northerly distribution of any freshwater fish. In Britain, the populations of charr are at the extreme south of their range and are particularly sensitive to environmental change. Whether the Lakeland charr can adapt to the changes in temperature brought about by global warming only time will tell. In the Arctic, the charr is anadromous, i.e. a fish, like the salmon and sea trout, that feeds in the sea and enters freshwater rivers to spawn. It is generally believed that the charr of Britain and Ireland evolved from the migratory form but became land-locked in cold, deep lakes following the retreat of the ice at the end of the last Ice Age over ten thousand years ago.

The majority of charr in the Lake District are found in Windermere, Coniston, Haweswater, Crummock Water, Ennerdale Water, Buttermere and Wastwater. According to John Watson in *The English Lake District Fisheries* (1899), charr were common in Ullswater in the eighteenth century but became practically extinct during the 1870s due to pollution from the Greenside lead mines. The Ullswater charr used to spawn in Glenridding beck where the washing of the lead ore was carried out, which resulted in the destruction of the ova. Being a cold-water species, the charr of the Lake District is slow-growing but long-lived, some Windermere charr exceeding twelve years of age. In terms of weight, the average Lake District charr weighs between six to ten ounces, with a few larger specimens up to a pound. Very occasionally a fish weighing over two pounds has turned up. The current record for a British charr stands at 9lb 8oz, and was captured in 1995 by W. Fairbairn in Loch Arkaig, near Inverness in Scotland. However, Loch Arkaig is home to a commercial salmon farm and it is not just the salmon that grow fat on a diet of protein enriched pellets! Migratory charr grow much larger than their non-migratory cousins and fish of up to thirty pounds have been taken in Canada.

The charr is a delicate, but very beautiful fish as Patrick Chalmers remarked in *A Fisherman's Angles* (1931):

I have heard say that no man may discuss the salmon, in print, unless he has caught twelve of them for each year of his own life . . . What the ruling of charr may be I do not know, but I am confident that I now contravene it; for only once have I caught a charr, and then he was only a very little one. But he was as beautiful as a butterfly.

In overall shape the charr resembles the trout but, unlike the trout, is at its most beautiful in its spawning colours. The breeding livery can be stunning; dark sea-green back, sides with a slight silvery shade, passing into a beautiful deep red on the belly. Indeed, the charr derives its name from the Gaelic word *ceara*, meaning red.

Windermere charr are unusual in that there appears to be two distinct populations, each spawning at different times of the year. One group of fish known as the *autumn spawners* move into shallow water (one to three metres) at certain sites around the shore of the lake between October and December. Their eggs are deposited on areas of gravel that are without vegetation. One population spawns in a large pool at the lower end of the river Brathay, a main inflow to the lake. *Spring spawners*, on the other hand, lay their eggs in much deeper water of fifteen to twenty metres during January to April. Research by the Freshwater Biological Association has shown that there is a small degree of genetic divergence between autumn spawners and spring spawners. When they are not spawning the two populations appear to mix quite freely in both the north and south basins of the lake. During the summer months the fish live in the open waters of the lake, feeding on zooplankton. During the early months of the year bloodworms (midge larvae) form a major part of their diet. They are also known to feed on their own eggs during the spawning season and on perch fry and minnows.

Over the centuries charr populations in the Lake District have fluctuated due to over-exploitation or environmental reasons, as was the case in Ullswater. During the 1870s concerns were being expressed over the charr population in Windermere. Commercial fishers were employing nets with such a small mesh size that even fish half-an-inch in length were being scooped up. In 1878, new regulations were passed limiting mesh size so that no fish of less than a third of a pound could be taken and this had the desired effect of increasing the population. John Watson records that in the late 1860s a small private hatchery for the artificial propagation of salmon, trout and charr was started at Wansfell, on the banks of Windermere. Around 180,000 charr fry were hatched in boxes and turned into the lake. The experiment continued for five years and Watson regarded it as a success. Charr were occasionally transplanted from one lake to another with the object of introducing new blood, as was the case in 1892 when over a hundred Windermere charr were placed in Coniston. In 1895, attempts were made by a Major Parkin to restock Ullswater and over ten thousand charr fry were placed in the lake. Unfortunately, this experiment was deemed to be a failure although there are reports of the occasional charr being taken on Ullswater. In the period before the Second World War the number of charr running up the Brathay to spawn decreased dramatically. However, when the trapping of perch and netting of pike was introduced to increase war-time food supply and many tons of these fish were removed, the charr population once again increased.

Over the last fifty years or so, human influence has had an increasing impact on Windermere and its water quality, largely as a result of it being used as a discharge for treated sewage. This has resulted in decreased oxygen concentrations in the deeper, colder areas of the lake and the charr have been forced to occupy the shallower, warmer parts of the lake if they are to avoid asphyxiation. Furthermore, increased algal productivity has led to the silting up of areas of gravel on the bed of the lake where the charr spawn. By the early 1990s the situation was deteriorating so rapidly that there was a real danger of losing the charr population, at least from part of the lake. As a result of these concerns the bodies entrusted with the management of Windermere drew up a strategy to improve water quality and upgrade the sewage treatment plants. It appears that these improvements are beginning to have a beneficial effect and there has been a significant recovery of the Windermere charr populations. However, only time will tell whether this beautiful relic from the Ice Age will

Illustration of torgoch and charr from Houghton's British Fresh-Water Fishes.
The torgoch, meaning 'red belly' is the Welsh name for the charr.

survive global warming and increased pressures from human activity.

Unlike those other relics from the Ice Age, the vendace and schelly, the charr is of greater interest to anglers. In my long angling career I have only caught one charr, and that was by accident rather than design. I was fishing the east bank of Coniston, not far from Brantwood, when I noticed a few fish dimpling the surface about ten to fifteen yards out. I thought they were trout. However, since I did not have a fly rod with me I attached a small silver Mepps bar-spoon to my line and cast out. After two or three casts I suddenly felt a tug at the end of my line and, after a spirited fight, I landed a beautiful charr of about six ounces. After gently unhooking and admiring it, I slipped it back to live another day.

Charr are sometimes taken on the fly but the rise of a charr is unlike that of a trout. Whereas the trout will sometimes rise with a splash, the charr gently breaks the surface of the water, referred to as 'belbing' by Windermere fishermen. John Watson had this to say about his experiences of fly fishing for charr:

I have caught an occasional charr with fly in both Windermere and Haweswater - but, in the former, always when fishing for trout. When the angler is successful with trout in Haweswater, he is almost certain to have a charr or two among his catch; and, as an experiment only, the charr may be fished for here with fair prospects of, at least, some success. Almost any red or dark brown fly will do if dressed on sufficiently small hooks. Charr feed greedily upon the green drake and bracken clock in season, and in autumn they may be seen sucking down the winged ant. It is somewhat remarkable that in June, when there is the greatest quantity of flies and other surface food, that charr are then bottom feeders.

Fly fishing has come a long way since the days of John Watson in the late nineteenth and early twentieth centuries. The modern fly fisherman, especially on some of our larger reservoirs, now employs a variety of different density fly lines to cover fish at varying depths of water. Such methods have been adopted successfully by anglers fishing for charr in the Lake District. Phill Williams in an article in *Waterlog* magazine (April/May, 2000) describes how he and fellow angler, Bob Fitchie, successfully employed Hi-Di and lead core lines in search of Coniston charr:

We decided that a lead core shooting head offered the best way of max-imising meaningful time in the feeding zone. As there is little imitatable natural food to mimic, fly tying centred around red and silver, which are the main attracting colours when spinning. One problem is that charr have particularly soft mouths. Even when spinning more than half of all fish hooked invariably come adrift. To offset this, they are extremely oblig-ing fish. Bob came up with a red and silver version of Hugh Falkus' secret weapon with a size 14 flying treble in its tail. The aptly named Charr Lady was born.

Despite some rather tricky water conditions that season, success came quickly. In calm conditions it pays to get down fast then slowly work the lure back through the water column. Unfortunately, with such a short effective season you don't get much time to experiment, and feel loathe to do so at times in case it wastes precious time. But experiment we did. With a brisk wind pushing the boat along, either the drogue goes out for a slow figure 8 retrieve, or the boat is allowed to track along, trailing the lines on the down-wind side to the degree that on some days we were effectively trolling. Tackle-wise things have moved on too. Now full Hi-Di lines also form part of the kit, and smaller lures containing red marabou, squirrel hair and silver mylar have been introduced.

Elsewhere in the same article Williams describes trolling with small spinners with drilled bullets attached and employing an echo-sounder to explore the underwater contours. Whatever methods are employed in its capture it is good to see that charr can still be caught by the innovative anglers of today and let us hope that charr will be around for future generations of anglers to pursue.

5

FISHES OF THE LAKES

Vendace & Schelly

One evening in April, 2011, I was sitting on the sofa watching the local news on the BBC *North West Tonight* programme, when my attention was drawn to an item about the transportation by llama of vendace fry from Derwentwater in Cumbria to Sprinkling Tarn. I had to pinch myself to make sure that I was not dreaming! The report went on to say that, because of global warming and habitat degradation, scientists were concerned about the threat to this rare species of fish and attempts were being made to establish a self-sustaining population in Sprinkling Tarn, a small tarn in the Derwentwater drainage area. Twenty-five thousand fry, hatched from eggs stripped from Derwentwater vendace were being carried in panniers up to the tarn by llama, the most suitable form of transportation in this rugged landscape. Where the llamas had come from the report did not say!

I have never caught a vendace nor even seen one, apart from illustrations in books. According to Tindall Harris in *Here and*

Sprinkling Tarn, at the foot of Great End, which was stocked with 25,000 vendace fry in 2011.

There, An Angler's Memories (1924), a vendace was found washed up on the shore of Derwentwater in March 1924 and was subsequently set up and put on display in Keswick Museum. Another specimen, preserved in a jar, sits on the bar of the Pheasant Inn on the shores of Bassenthwaite. The vendace, the rarest freshwater fish in Great Britain, is a medium sized lake-dwelling fish, which grows to about 250mm in length and has a herring-like appearance. Its adipose fin is testimony to its membership of the salmonid family of fishes. It belongs to the genus *Coregonus albula* and is closely related to another whitefish found in the Lake District, the schelly or *Coregonus lavaretus*. Both species are survivors from the last Ice Age and inhabit cold, deep lakes. Vendace require a spawning habitat, which consists of clean gravel at depths of less than four metres. Spawning takes place from late November to late December and female vendace can carry up to 5,000 eggs. The young hatch out during March or April, depending on water temperature. Vendace are almost exclusively plankton feeders and are rarely taken by anglers. Dr John Davy, brother of Sir Humphry Davy and author of *The Angler in the Lake District* (1857), had this to say about the vendace of Derwentwater:

It is contrary to the habits of this fish to take the fly, or any of the baits commonly used here in angling. I have heard of one instance only of its having been taken with the artificial fly, and that by an old fisherman of long experience, and likewise of one only of its having been captured with the worm.

The vendace is extremely rare in the UK and, up until recently was only found in four locations: Derwentwater and Bassenthwaite Lake in the Lake District and the Castle and Mill Lochs in Lochmaben, Dumfriesshire. The naturalist Thomas Pennant recorded a local belief that vendace were introduced into Lochmaben waters by Mary, Queen of Scots, when she visited the castle in 1565. Sir Herbert Maxwell in *British Fresh-Water Fishes* (1904) is dismissive of this idea:

Rapidity was not a conspicuous feature of transport in the sixteenth century, and we have Sir William Jardine's assurance that the vendace is so delicate a fish, with such a slender hold upon life, that it will not endure a journey.

In Scandinavia and Finland, however, the vendace is relatively common and is exploited commercially. Vendace roe is regarded

Derwentwater, one of the original homes of the vendace.

as a great delicacy in Finland and is commonly served at Christmas time, whilst smoked vendace is canned and is even available for sale on the internet.

Lochmaben vendace were once considered a great delicacy, so much so that two local clubs were set up, which organised the capture of vendace and an annual feast. Sir Herbert Maxwell quotes a Mr Service of Maxwelltown on the subject:

The Vendace club was still in existence in 1869, but was wound up in 1870 or 1871 . . . The St Magdalene Vendace Club, an organisation of a very decided democratic kind, ceased shortly before the more aristocratic society. After fishing the lochs for vendace in the usual way, they held a meeting for Border games, etc., and some thirty-five to forty years ago this was rather a big annual event.

The populations of vendace in Castle Loch and Mill Loch are now extinct. Falkus and Buller in *Freshwater Fishing* (1975) state that the last vendace to have been caught in Castle Loch on rod and line was taken with worm tackle by Francis Dummit Dundas in 1937. The vendace in Mill Loch appear to have died

Tinned vendace (muikku) is considered a great delicacy in Finland.

out in the 1990s. In the case of Castle Loch, the demise of vendace was probably due to the discharge of sewage effluent, whilst in Mill Loch it was due to extreme eutrophication and the introduction of other fish species. Habitat deterioration and the introduction of non-native fish, probably by pike anglers using live-baits, have meant that no vendace have been recorded in Bassenthwaite Lake since 2001 and it was generally believed to be extinct in the lake. However, in October 2013 a survey of the lake undertaken by Dr Ian Winfield from the Centre for Ecology and Hydrology led to the discovery of a single specimen. The vendace was a juvenile fish measuring just 54mm in length. Various theories have been advanced concerning this solitary specimen. It is possible that vendace have actually survived in Bassenthwaite Lake since 2001 in very low numbers and the population may now be increasing. Secondly, it is possible that the fish entered Bassenthwaite by moving down the river Derwent from Derwentwater. The third possibility is that such downstream movement happened some time ago and the vendace have established a new breeding colony in Bassenthwaite. Whatever the reason for its presence in the lake, it is an encouraging sign that this rare fish might re-establish itself in greater numbers.

The only viable population of vendace is now in Derwentwater and even that is under threat from the arrival and increase of other fish species, most notably roach, dace and ruffe, which compete for food and prey on eggs.

Urgent action for the conservation of the species is required, hence the recent introduction of vendace fry into Sprinkling Tarn. This tarn, which lies at an altitude of 598m, was chosen following a survey by the Environment Agency of over eighty other waters and although it is only 2.34 hectares in area it fits the bill for water quality and suitable spawning gravel. The tarn is remote with no road access, hence the need for llamas to transport the fish. William Heaton Cooper, the Lake District artist and author of *The Tarns of Lakeland* (1960), regarded Sprinkling Tarn as the most completely satisfying of all the tarns of Lakeland:

I can make a list of all the reasons for this, and of all the facts I know about the tarn and its surroundings. But in the end it is the character and feel of the place itself that finally attracts so strongly.

Let us hope that the vendace find the tarn equally satisfying! However, this is not the first translocation of vendace to have taken place. During the last decade or so, several conservation projects for vendace have been undertaken by the Environment Agency, English Nature and Scottish Natural Heritage. A number of fish from Bassenthwaite (before their demise there) were transferred to Loch Skeen, a remote loch near Moffat in south-west Scotland, in 1997 and 1999. Much to the delight of conservationists the fish have survived and thrived in their new home and there are now ten times more vendace per hectare in the Scottish loch compared to Derwentwater. It is hoped that eventually, if water quality in Cumbria can be improved, they can be used to restock Bassenthwaite. Attempts to stock Daer Reservoir in Lanarkshire in 1998 with vendace fry from Derwentwater have proved less successful.

Schelly

The vendace is not the only Lake District fish to be faced with extinction. A rather dramatic headline on the BBC news website for 17th July, 2002, recently came to my attention. The headline read – 'Gunmen to guard rare fish'. The article went on to state that sharpshooters were to be brought in to the Lake District to save one of Britain's rarest fish from extinction.

The rare fish in question was the schelly (*Corogonus lavaretus*), which is found in only four Cumbrian lakes: Ullswater, Haweswater, Brotherswater and Red Tarn, nestling beneath the summit of Helvellyn. Other populations of *Corogonus lavaretus* exist in Bala Lake (Llyn Tegid) in Wales, where they are known as *gwyniad* and in Loch Lomond in Scotland, where they are referred to as *powan*. The sharpshooters were being brought in to

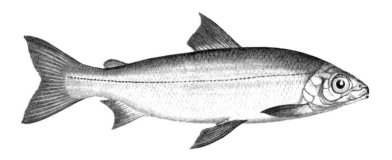

Apart from the Cumbrian populations, two other British lakes hold schelly under different names - in Bala Lake (Llyn Tegid) in Wales, they are known as gwyniad and in Loch Lomond in Scotland, as powan.

cull a colony of cormorants on Haweswater, which were pre-dating on this rare fish and threatening its survival. The schelly, or skelly, as it is sometimes known, is closely related to the vendace and is a survivor from the last Ice Age. Fishery scientists believe that both the schelly and the vendace are descended from a primitive form of migratory salmonid, which, like the salmon, entered freshwater from the sea to spawn. However, during the last Ice Age they became trapped in cold deep lakes gouged out by the ice and were forced to adapt to their new environment.

Haweswater is a reservoir in the Mardale valley, which was formed in the 1940s when a dam was built to unite the two original lakes: Low Water and High Water. Haweswater is now 6.4km long and 0.8km wide, making it one of the largest lakes in England. Over the last thirty years or so, the population of schelly in Haweswater has declined as a result of fluctuations in water level, and predation by fish-eating birds. Large fluctuations in water level occurred during the 1960s and mid-1990s, particularly during the critical spawning period from February to April, as a result of the lake being managed as a drinking water supply. During the early 1970s the schelly population of Haweswater was estimated at 200–550 fish, which by the late 1990s had declined to around twenty fish.

Drastic action was required and in 1997 schelly fry from Haweswater were introduced into nearby Blea Water and Small Water in an attempt to establish new populations. Further culling of cormorants was carried out during 2004-2006 and twenty-nine birds were shot. However, by 2010 the cormorant population began to increase again and between April 2010 and March 2011, only one schelly was caught in the fishery scientists' traps. Whether the schelly population of Haweswater will survive is debatable.

A hundred years ago, however, the schelly population of Haweswater was far more abundant as is evident from what John Watson (*The English Lake District Fisheries*, 1899) has to say:

I have frequently of late had the opportunity of observing the habits of the gwyniad [he refers to them by their Welsh name] *in Haweswater. The fish are gregarious; the shoals comprise a great number of individuals; and in fine, warm weather they frequently move and play about on the surface of the water. It has frequently been stated that the gwyniad* [schelly] *does not take the fly. It would be truer to say that it does not habitually take flies. When the fish are swimming on the surface on a warm evening they may be seen to take small flies, and I have myself taken a gwyniad* [schelly] *on a trout fly. It is also within my personal knowledge that a trout, a charr, and a gwyniad have been taken on a red-spinner* [on a No.3 hook] *on the same day.*

Up until about two hundred years ago the schelly was a relatively common fish in Ullswater and was netted and sold commercially. William Wordsworth, in his *Guide to the Lakes* (1810), recalls seeing schelly fishermen at work on Ullswater:

Friday, November 9 - In the large bay under Place Fell, three fishermen were dragging a net, - a picturesque group beneath the high and bare crags! . . . The fishermen drew their net ashore, and hundreds of fish were leaping in their prison. They were all of a kind called skellies, a sort of fresh-water herring, shoals of which may sometimes be seen dimpling or rippling the surface of the lake in calm water.

Ullswater.

The schelly in Ullswater spawn during January and February and near to the bay where they spawn is the aptly named Skelly Nab. Clarke in his *Survey of the Lakes* of 1787 describes the schelly of Ullswater as follows:

They seem to be a species of freshwater herrings; as they resemble the sea herring in both shape and size. Like the herring, they assemble in vast numbers during the harvest months, rippling the surface of the water, and are called 'Schools', or (in the country dialect) Skeguls or Skellies. When they lie in water not too deep, vast numbers are taken at one draught, sometimes ten or twelve thousands. Sometimes the schools lie so near together, and the fishermen take such numbers, that carts are employed to carry them to the adjacent market towns. They weigh about five ounces each, and 800 are commonly reckoned as many as one horse can draw. They are at these times extremely cheap, generally a penny a pound, but I have seen two Winchester pecks of them sold for a shilling.

With such large numbers being taken, it is not surprising that, by the end of the nineteenth century, John Watson notes that the Ullswater schelly is a fast vanishing species. Schelly still inhabit Ullswater and are occasionally caught by anglers

James Clarke's map of Ullswater, 1787, shows Skelley Neb, an area where schelly were netted.

ledgering for trout or perch. In December, 2007, a dead schelly was found floating near the Glenridding steamer pier and such was its rarity that it featured in the *Cumberland and Westmorland Herald*. The fish was 38cm in length and weighed 870g. It was taken to the Centre for Ecology and Hydrology for further research. Schelly tend to grow to a larger size than the vendace and the current British record for a schelly stands at 2lb 1½oz and was caught by Stuart Barrie in Haweswater in 1986.

The schelly of Red Tarn seem to be faring a little better than those in Ullswater and Haweswater and a recent search of the internet revealed a couple of video clips of anglers catching schelly in Red Tarn. However, the schelly is now protected under the Wildlife and Countryside Act of 1981 and it is illegal to fish for this species and, if accidentally caught while fishing for other fish, it must be released immediately. Let us hope that the work of the fishery scientists is successful and that both the vendace and schelly thrive in their new environments and can be successfully re-introduced into their former homes for future generations of anglers to enjoy.

Other Species of Fish

Apart from the fish already discussed, the Lake District is home to most species of freshwater fish including: eels, carp, chub, dace, grayling, rudd, bream, tench and roach. Indeed, in recent years there has been a large increase in the roach population of Windermere and what effect this will have on the resident populations of trout and charr only time will tell. However, within the confines of this book I have focused my attention on the rarer species of Lakeland fish and the fish that are the main quarry of the angler in the Lake District.

SECOND REACH, OF ULLSWATER.

6

FISHERS OF THE LAKES

The Commercial Fishers

Before the development of the deep sea fishing industry in the nineteenth century and the increasing availability of sea fish, the Lake District was an important source of freshwater fish for the domestic market. Nowadays, apart from farmed salmon and rainbow trout, we almost seem averse to eating freshwater fish. Such is not the case on the continent where various species of freshwater fish find their way on to the dining table; and in countries like Austria, Germany and Switzerland I have eaten a variety of freshwater fish, including pike, perch, zander and catfish. Many of the older cookbooks from this country include recipes for freshwater fish and Dorothy Wordsworth regularly cooked the pike caught by her brother, William, in Grasmere.

Indeed, for centuries the fish of Windermere and other large lakes in the district proved a valuable asset, and for many hundreds of years they were exploited by fisheries. These fisheries were mainly net fisheries, operated by full-time fishermen. Not surprisingly, since it is England's largest lake (10.5 miles long and

0.6 miles in width), Windermere and its fisheries have been subject to greater study than the fisheries on other lakes in the area. However, much of the information concerns disputes over fishery rights and ownership. The main species of fish in Windermere are the charr, trout, pike, perch and eel, all of which have been fished for on a commercial basis. We have already seen in Chapters 1 and 2 how the pike and perch of Windermere helped to feed the nation during the Second World War. However, the fish of Windermere have been fished for on a commercial basis for nearly eight hundred years and the earliest reference to fisheries in Windermere occurs in a document dating to 1223. This document concerns a court case between William de Lancaster 4th Baron of Kendal and the Abbot of Furness Abbey. The Abbot complained that William de Lancaster was depriving the monks of their fishery on Windermere and had broken their boat. William defended himself by stating that the monks had no right to fish on Windermere. The court found in William's favour and the Abbot was fined twenty marks. However, shortly before his death in 1246, William de Lancaster did

Furness Abbey

grant fishing rights on Windermere and Thurstanswater (an old name for Coniston) to Furness Abbey.

...And I have granted them the right to have in perpetuity two smaller boats, namely one on Windermere with twenty nets, and the other on Thurstanswater with 20 nets, for continual fishing.

It is not known how long the monks of Furness Abbey held these fishing rights but it seems they had relinquished them by the time of the dissolution of the monasteries in the sixteenth century.

During the mediaeval period the fisheries of Windermere were included in the Barony of Kendal but, following the death of William de Lancaster in 1246, the barony was divided into three sections, known as the Richmond, Lumley and Marquis Fees. Windermere, with its islands and lake were treated as part of the manor of Applethwaite and were in the Richmond Fee. However, the island of Roger Holme, now known as Ramp Holme, and its fishery came under the Lumley Fee.

By the end of the sixteenth century the Windermere fisheries were divided into three cubbles (or areas of water), the Upper, Middle and Low Cubble. The word 'cubble' seems to be a corruption of 'coble' referring to a type of flat-bottomed rowing boat and in this context appears to refer to an area that can be fished by one coble. The Upper Cubble extended from the junction of the rivers Brathay and Rothay to a line from Ecclerigg Crag to Pinstones Point. The Middle Cubble extended from this boundary to a line from Short Nab to Ash Landing, while the Low Cubble extended from this line to Newby Bridge at the southern end of the lake. Why these boundaries were chosen is not clear. Each fishery was confined to a particular cubble, although individual owners could hold fisheries in more than one cubble.

These cubbles were primarily fished by commercial fishermen using draught or seine nets. A seine net hangs vertically in the water with its bottom edge held down by weights and its top

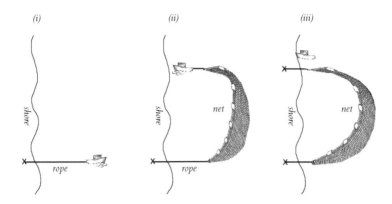

Seine or draught net.

edge buoyed by floats. When used in a lake, a rope with the net attached, is anchored to the shore and a boat is rowed around the area to be netted, paying out the rope (i), then the net (ii), and finally the rest of the rope, as the boat returns to the shore (iii). The weighted net is given time to sink before both ends of the rope are pulled simultaneously and the net is drawn on to the shore. The net was set between ten to several hundred yards from the shore at depths varying from a few feet to sixty feet and a number of hauls could be made in a day. The ropes were made out of cow or horse hair and were lightweight. Another type of net, known as the driving net, was used in Ullswater and probably in other lakes, too. The driving net was made of fine, bleached thread and has only one rope attached to it, to the end where a fixed float was secured. This float enabled the fishermen to locate the net. The net was placed parallel to the shore, at a depth of two fathoms (twelve feet) or less. Several of these nets were often set in the water at once. Before hauling the net in, the fishermen would row the boat between the net and the shore, disturbing the water as much as they could. This frightens the fish, which are generally near the shore, and makes them run towards the deeper water, where they swim into the almost invisible net and are trapped by the gills. The fishermen then haul the net into their boat and take out the fish. In addition to nets, long lines up to half a mile in length, with baited hooks every few yards, were set on the bottom and left overnight.

Research by the Freshwater Biological Association suggests that approximately three tons of charr, one ton of trout, two tons of pike, five tons of perch and two tons of eels could have been taken out of Windermere annually without damaging the fishery. However, by the middle of the nineteenth century, such was the popularity of potted charr, that excessive amounts were being netted resulting in a decline of the charr population. Around twelve charr spawning sites are known in Windermere and these proved popular targets for the netsmen.

It is difficult to estimate the economic value of the Lake District fisheries, but Clarke in his *Survey of the Lakes of Cumberland, Westmorland and Lancashire* (1787), lists the value of the fishing in a number of lakes, with the four most valuable being Ullswater £13, Windermere £12, and Coniston and Crummock Water £7 each. How he calculated these values is not known. John Watson (1899) estimated that, between 1893 and 1898, the average value per annum of charr caught in Windermere was approximately £1,200.

With regard to the fishermen themselves, the census returns of 1841, 1851 and 1861, show that fishing was very much a family tradition. At Bowness, several members of the Robinson and Kirkbride families were recorded as fishermen, while at Sawrey the Alexander family seemed to predominate.

Up until the middle of the nineteenth century, control of Windermere and, no doubt, other lakes was entirely in the hands of the owners, who regulated the number of boats on the lake and the methods of fishing. They were particularly concerned to prevent unauthorised fishing or ferrying. During the eighteenth century, the proprietors in the Low Cubble in Windermere had problems with a man, referred to only as J.B., who paid neither fishing nor ferrying rent and generally made a nuisance of himself. In 1739, they took legal advice, complaining that:

He has built a new boat and ferrys at pleasure not only within that cobble but thro' other two cobbles and often times takes and kills fish sinks timber in the draughts of the fishers whereby the fishers are hindered to draw with their nets to their great prejudice and often rows his boat into the nets of the fishers when set out in the common draughts and disappoints 'em of catching fish. The Impunity of J.B. has encouraged several other People to erect boats to carry and fish on the said Water without any Lycence contrary to Usage or Right and thereby do great Damage to the said Fishers and Fishery and Ferrying.

Unfortunately, we do not know the outcome of the case and whether J.B. was brought to justice for his misdemeanours.

The owners of the fisheries were also concerned with the protection and preservation of fish stocks. This included controlling the type and mesh size of the nets, to prevent the capture of juvenile fish. In 1798, an agreement was signed by sixteen fishery owners banning for seven years the capture of autumn spawning charr on their spawning banks during the spawning season. The same agreement also banned the use of a certain type of net, known as a case net, which was probably a type of gill net. Finally, the agreement imposed a minimum mesh size of three inches circumference. A mesh of this size would hold all charr over seven inches in length. However, around 1840, as the trade in potted charr was increasing, larger nets with a smaller mesh began to appear and these had a disastrous effect on the juvenile fish population. Around this time, too, lath or otter fishing started to become popular. The lath enabled each rod to fish several hooks simultaneously and so effective was it in catching fish that its use was banned in 1884. Plumb lining for charr (a method still in use today - see Chapter 7), which enabled the fisherman to fish at several depths simultaneously, was introduced around 1840 by a Mr Spencer from Manchester.

As a result of all this fishing pressure, catches on Windermere began to decline, to such an extent, that a committee of proprietors decided to stop all netting on the lake from the autumn of 1863. For a short while the fishing improved but in 1869 netting was resumed. During the same decade Parliament passed the Salmon Fishery Acts (1861 and 1865), which introduced a close season for trout and established Boards of Conservators for fishery districts which were responsible for administering fisheries until 1948. These Boards were mainly concerned with improving trout and salmon fisheries, while charr were of a lesser concern. However, in 1873 charr were included in the close season, which ran from October to January. This measure gave protection to autumn spawning charr but not to the spring spawners.

In 1878, there was an official inquiry into the fisheries of the Lake District, which recommended that the close season for trout and charr in Windermere be extended to 28th February. Tighter regulations on mesh size were also introduced. Further restrictions on nets and their mesh were introduced in 1884. As a result of these measures the average size of charr in Windermere increased from three to a pound to two to a pound.

By the end of the nineteenth century, no doubt due to the increasing availability of sea fish, commercial fishing for coarse fish (mainly perch and pike) became uneconomic. From around 1880 the Board of Conservators adopted a policy of renting the net fisheries and by 1902 the Board was in a position to end netting for trout on Windermere. In 1924, the Board ended all netting on Windermere, although it continued to pay rent to the fishery proprietors until 1947, and such was the demise of the commercial net fisheries of Windermere, apart from a brief resurgence during the Second World War.

However, it was not just the fish in the lakes that were exploited, the salmon in Lake District rivers provided a valuable source of income for landowners. On a number of rivers, including the Eden, Lune and Derwent, salmon coops or traps were placed at strategic positions to intercept the fish as they made their way upstream to their spawning redds. The best preserved, and the most studied, are the salmon coops at Corby Castle on the river Eden. These coops form one of the oldest functioning river fish traps in the United Kingdom and it is believed that

CORBY CASTLE, CUMBERLAND.

THE LONDON PRINTING AND PUBLISHING COMPANY, LIMITED.

The salmon coops at Corby Castle on the river Eden.

they were originally built in the twelfth century by the Bene-
dictine monks of Wetherall Priory. The present coops, however,
appear to date from the eighteenth century. The word 'coop' to
denote a fish trap appears to be unique to Cumbria.

The fishery appears to have been in the possession of Wetheral
Priory until its dissolution in 1538. After the dissolution, the
salmon coops passed to the Howard family of Corby Castle, who
still own them. The present coops comprise a series of three
sandstone piers and two abutments built into the bed and bank
of the Eden, between the east bank and Monk's Island, where
the river flows in two channels. It is believed that the monks
created the east channel especially to catch salmon, although it
could be a natural feature. Between the piers and abutments are
a series of wooden pans (boxes fitted behind sluice gates for
holding fish) and sluice gates, intended for catching the salmon
running upstream. The pans can be cleared by means of
trap-doors above, and a cat-walk extending over the piers acts as
a bridge.

Another method of catching Eden salmon and sea trout, which has been practised for centuries, is by haaf-netting in Cumbria's Solway Estuary. Indeed, the word 'haaf' is Norse for sea, and haaf-netting was introduced into this country by the Vikings who invaded the Cumbrian coast over a thousand years ago. A haaf net is mounted on a rectangular frame eighteen feet long by five feet high, supported by three legs. This frame is placed across the current by a fisherman standing behind the net in the water and holding the central upright. Fishermen walk out into the flat, shallow waters of the Solway sands and mudflats and place the haaf net in front, facing either the incoming (flood) or outgoing (ebb) tides. The net forms a bag in the water and as soon as a fish swims into the net the legs of the frame are allowed to float to the surface, trapping the fish, which is killed by a blow from a nep (wooden club). A rope is threaded through the fish's gills and tied to the fisherman's waist until he wades back to the shore.

Haaf-netting is a skill handed down through family members over many generations. It requires a detailed knowledge of the

Haaf-netting on the Solway, 1885. Courtesy Dumfries and Galloway Council.

sandbanks and tidal patterns as the fishermen often walk more than a kilometre out into the Solway to reach their fishing grounds. During the early nineteenth century, when salmon and sea trout were more plentiful, haaf-netting was common. Nowadays, haaf-net fishermen are licensed by the Environment Agency and fishing is only allowed from June to September on weekdays between 10am and 10pm. More than 200 licences for haaf-netting used to be issued but by 2008 it had been reduced to 105 and only half of these were taken up. According to the Environment Agency these restrictions were put in place to conserve fish stocks as the Solway haaf-net fishery was killing twice the number of fish as the combined rod fisheries of the Eden and Border Esk. In 2006, records show that 2,910 salmon and sea trout were caught by haaf-net fishermen compared to 1,872 caught by rod fishermen on the Eden.

Not surprisingly, the haaf-net fishermen are aggrieved by the Environment Agency's latest restrictions and feel that the Agency is being unduly influenced by wealthy estate owners who own the fishing rights further up the river. Whether the traditional method of haaf-netting will survive in the face of declining salmon and sea trout numbers is a matter for debate. However, should the reader wish to try his or her hand at this method of fishing, at least one hostelry in the area is offering its guests the opportunity to experience a day's haaf-netting.

From 1868 to 1880, the Lake District was home to another commercial fishery - the first commercial fish hatchery in the country. The hatchery, at Troutdale in Borrowdale, was established by Joseph J. Armistead in 1862. Armistead, inspired by the work, and a meeting with the pioneer of fish culture, Frank Buckland (1826-1880), carried out some experiments in hatching fish ova in his father's conservatory. This led him to build a small hatchery in the grounds of his father's house, where trout were successfully reared for several years. Finding this place and its water supply too small, he finally selected the site at Troutdale. In choosing the Lake District for his trout hatchery he was inspired by the vision of turning the area into 'An Angler's

Paradise' (the title of his book, published in 1894) by judicious stocking of its waters:

During the last few years, the facility for visiting the magnificent scenery of the Lake District has been so much increased, that many parts of it are now very accessible to the tourist, and there is a great opening for the development of its waters, which did not before exist. No part of the world perhaps possesses so many charms for the contemplative mind. It would be difficult to find one which can provide so wide a field for the imagination of the poet or for the

J. J. Armistead.

legendary fancier, or such a charming variety of tint and landscape for the artist, as the lovely glens and varied hill-sides of this beautiful country. The lover of nature invariably finds much to delight him in this romantic region, and why, now that we have the power in our hands of dealing with the water, should it not be improved, so that it may be in the future more than ever it has been in the past, in the highest sense of the word - 'An Angler's Paradise'.

In running his hatchery in Borrowdale, Armistead was assisted by John Parnaby, who had recently returned from Canada where he had been engaged in pisciculture for the Canadian Government. Whilst working for Armistead, Parnaby made several visits to America to improve his knowledge of fish culture and to bring into this country some of the more valuable food fish of that country. The first living black bass ever seen in Britain were brought over by him in 1873 and placed in the fish ponds at Troutdale. Four years earlier, Armistead and Parnaby introduced American brook trout (*Salmo fontinalis*) into this country and, according to Armistead, they did exceedingly well in the ponds at Troutdale. The brook trout were eventually distributed throughout the country and in some waters they flourished, whilst in others they disappeared. Brook trout have a strong migratory instinct and, where they had free access to a river, they simply entered the river system and disappeared. Armistead eventually came to the conclusion that, although the brook trout was a real game fish, it was not suited to our waters. Various experiments since Armistead's day seem to confirm this. The black bass, too, has never really established itself in British waters.

Following Parnaby's death, Armistead continued the work at Troutdale but, finding the available space and water supply inadequate, he began looking for a new site. Eventually, he settled on a site at New Abbey, near Dumfries, where he established the Solway Fishery, and his vision of turning the Lake District into an angler's paradise was transferred to south-west Scotland.

Brantwood, Coniston Lake. Char-Fishing.

7

FISHERS OF THE LAKES

Charr Fishers & Charr Potters

On the jetty at Bowness, where tourists wait to embark on their cruise around Lake Windermere, there is a glass display case devoted to charr and traditional charr fishing. Amongst other things, the display includes several highly polished charr spinners made by John Cooper, a Windermere charr fisher for forty years, who died in 2003. The items in the case were donated by his widow. Fifty years ago, it was not unusual to see charr fishers, with their long ash poles arcing out from the stern of their clinker built boats. Indeed, charr fishing was such an iconic image associated with the Lake District that a number of postcards were produced depicting this unusual method of fishing. Nowadays, only a handful of diehards practise this traditional method of fishing, which dates back almost two hundred years. Around a decade or so ago I, too, accompanied a traditional charr fisher on Coniston. After meeting at the lake shortly after dawn, we trolled up and down for several hours, the result being one charr of about six inches in length, which was promptly thrown back into the water to grow bigger. Such is the current state of charr fishing today. Pollution and other environmental factors, largely caused by human influence, have had an increasing impact on the water quality of Windermere and other lakes. This has resulted in a decline in the populations of charr, trout and the rarer whitefishes, such as vendace and schelly and although the Environment Agency and other official bodies are aware of the situation, and remedial steps are being taken to improve water quality, only time will tell whether they are successful or not.

According to Francis Day in *British and Irish Salmonidae* (1887), the traditional method of charr fishing using long poles, which enabled the angler to fish at several depths simultaneously, was developed around 1840 by a Mr Spencer from Manchester:

It will be between forty or fifty years ago since a Mr Spencer, from Manchester, first introduced the plumb line into the Lake District . . . his success, season after season, speedily induced imitators, and the plumb line did not take long to become established.

Before this method was introduced the majority of charr were caught by netting.

Plumb lining, as the name implies, is a method of fishing using a long line with a large plumb weight attached to the bottom. The lead weight or plumb, weighing from a pound and a half to two pounds, is cone-shaped with a fin attached to prevent it twisting the line when the boat is moving. The lead weight is suspended from a pole or spreader, about eighteen to twenty feet in length, originally made of ash but nowadays generally made of East India cane or even carbon fibre. The line connecting the tip of the pole to the rod is usually around seventy to eighty feet in length and is made from terylene; formerly it was made of braided cotton soaked in a mixture of lampblack and linseed oil. This dressing helped to preserve the line and enabled it to be used for several seasons. Six droppers are normally attached to the main line at varying depths, ranging from fifteen feet from the pole tip to the last dropper some eighty feet below. The lead is

attached some two to three feet below the last dropper. The
droppers are not tied directly to the main line but to a charr-
shackle, made of brass wire. The top dropper is normally
twenty-four feet long, with a six-foot leader, with each
proceeding dropper being three feet shorter than the previous
one.

With regards to bait, originally live minnows were used but
artificial lures were soon found to be more effective. These lures
were handmade out of sheet metal in either plain silver or a
combination of metal colours, copper on one side and electro-
plated silver on the other being a favourite. Real gold, beaten to
a thin strip from a gold sovereign, was sometimes applied to charr
baits. Some of the old-timers believed that the gold from
Australian sovereigns had special charr-catching properties.
According to Buller and Falkus in their *Freshwater Fishing* (1975),
the last fisherman to own genuine Australian gold baits was the
late Bruce Squires of Ambleside, who stopped using them at the

outbreak of the Second World War. Whatever their composition, it was believed that charr lures should be as shiny as possible in order to reflect such light as penetrated the deep water. Sheila Richardson, writing of Allan Mason, a charr fisher on Coniston in her *Tales of a Lakeland Poacher* (1993), tells of how he made his charr fishing baits:

He used sheets of thin brass or copper to cut out different shapes which varied in length from one-and-a-half to two inches. Metrication passed Allan by, he tenaciously clung to the old Imperial standards of weight and measurement. The bait was highly polished. Inserted into the two holes at either end were a three pronged hook and, at the other, a swivel. When the bait was fastened to the main line, along with about five others, it revolved round and round as it was dragged through the water, its gleaming spirals in wait for a snapping fish . . . Allan stuck to his own baits, but they echoed the same red theme, for he put a few blobs of red paint on each bait. Some also had little circles of silver soldered to the brass of the bait, which were cut from the back of his grandmother's hairbrush . . . The correct thickness of the metal bait is all important, for without it the lure doesn't travel through the water in the right manner. Allan, and his charr fishing mate Bill Dixon, have tried for over forty years to get the revolutions exactly right, making fine adjustments to the tackle to get the bait whirling through the water in a manner irresistible to the fish.

Most charr fishers developed their own tried and tested patterns of lure and kept them a closely guarded secret. Special wooden cases, often with three drawers, were made to hold sets of charr tackle. Since two poles were normally used, two sets of tackle were required, hence two drawers, the third drawer being used to store spare lures, lines, swivels and hooks.

To complete the charr fishing outfit, a bell is required, which is clipped on to the end of the pole once the tackle has been sent down into the depths and tinkles when a fish seizes the lure.

When the charr fisherman is ready to begin trolling, the heavy lead attached to the line is dropped overboard and a process of feeding out the line begins. The lead is allowed to sink until the

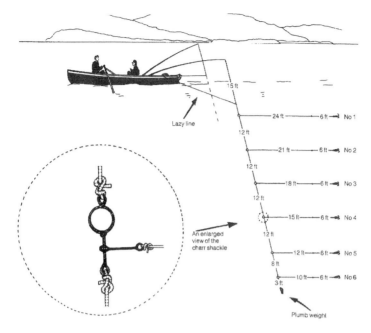

Charr fishing from Falkus & Buller's Freshwater Fishing.

first shackle is reached. The ring on the shackle is then placed over a nail on the gunwale of the boat. The sixth bait is thrown overboard and the dropper held until the bait spins freely. After a couple of strokes on the oars, the shackle is lifted off the nail and the next section of line is fed out until the next shackle is reached. The process is then repeated until all the droppers are out and the main line is secured to the top of the pole. Once this is secure, the pole is placed in one of the special rests, which are bolted to either side of the boat. The process is then repeated with the tackle on the other side of the boat. When a charr strikes the lure, signalled by the ringing of the bell, the fisherman pulls on the lazy-line (a line attached to the main line, two feet above the top shackle), which enables him to haul in the fish without moving the pole out of its rest.

Trolling speed is critical to success and most charr fishers try to keep the speed of the boat at between one and one and a half

SALMON AND FRESHWATER FISHERIES ACTS, 1861 TO 1886.

No.

Kent, Bela, Winster, Leven, and Duddon Fishery District.

LICENCE TO FISH FOR TROUT AND CHAR.

(NOT TRANSFERABLE.)

of _____ in the County of _____

having paid the sum of Two Shillings and Sixpence for this Licence, is hereby authorised to fish for Trout and Char with a single Rod and Line within the limits of the Kent, Bela, Winster, Leven, and Duddon Fishery District, at the times and places at which he is otherwise entitled to fish.

Dated this _____ *day of* _____ .

(Signed) _____

Distributor.

This Licence will expire, as to the River Bela or its tributaries, on the 31st day of August ; and as to the remainder of the District on the 1st day of October, after date of issue.

miles per hour. A good knowledge of the charrs' seasonal movements and the underwater contours of the lake are also vital to success. Much of this knowledge has been passed down from father to son over many generations, as has this method of fishing, which has changed very little over the last hundred and fifty years or so. The fishing season for charr on Windermere extends from the 1st of May to the 31st of October, with the best months being May and June. July is generally the poorest month, while catches tend to pick up again in August and September. Special licences are required by fishermen wishing to fish in this traditional manner and, apart from Windermere, the only other lakes where this method of fishing is practised are Coniston and Crummock Water. In former times, around the 12th of May, as many as twenty-five charr boats would assemble at Waterhead for the start of the charr fishing season. This meeting was known as 'The Carnival', and good catches of charr could be expected at this time in the North Basin of Windermere. John Watson, writing in 1899, states that a score of charr in a day's fishing represents a good day, while six or eight fish per day is an average take. He also mentions a catch of seventy-five fish being taken 'many years ago'. Nowadays, only a handful of fishermen fish for charr in the traditional manner and charr boats are now a rare sight.

Potted charr has long been considered a great delicacy and such was its popularity during the seventeenth to the nineteenth century that it gave rise to a cottage industry, with potted charr being exported the length and breadth of the country, especially to London. It was normally served with toast or crusty bread. Special pots or dishes were specifically manufactured to contain potted charr. These flat-bottomed pots, around eight inches in diameter and two inches deep, were often decorated on the outside with painted representations of the fish. Most of these pots were manufactured in Staffordshire, but some were made in potteries in Yorkshire, Scotland, Liverpool and Bristol. In an article on Liverpool delftware in *The Connoisseur* magazine (April, 1918), Mrs Hemming stated that Zachariah Barnes was the largest manufacturer of charr pots. Delftware, in an English context, refers to tin-glazed earthenware, and delftware charr dishes are now highly sought after by collectors and can command four-figure sums. Liverpool tin-glazed charr pots dating from the early eighteenth century are characterised by having five polychrome painted charr on them in manganese, blue, green and rust-red. Unfortunately, most charr pots are unmarked and their makers are now lost in obscurity. However, fine examples of this type of pottery can be seen in the Museum of Lakeland Life in Kendal and at the Tullie House Museum in Carlisle.

Lake District charr pot.

One of the earliest references to potted charr occurs in the work of that intrepid traveller, Celia Fiennes. Writing in 1698, Fiennes describes a visit to the Lake District:

At the King's Arms (Kendall) one Mrs Rowlandson she does pott up the charr fish the best of any in the country, I was curious to have some and so bespoke some of her, and also was as curious to see the great water which is the only place that fish is to be found in . . . the water (of Lake Wiandermer) is very clear and full of good fish, but the Charr fish being out of season could not easily be taken so I saw none alive, but of other fish I had a very good supper; the season of the Charrfish is between Michaelmas and Christmas, at that tyme I have had of them which they pott with sweet spices, they are as big as a small trout rather slenderer and the skinn full of spots some redish, and part of the whole skin and the finn and taile is red like the finns of a perch, and the inside flesh looks as red as any salmon; if they are in season their taste is very rich and fat tho' not so strong or clogging as the lampreys are, but its as fatt and rich a food.

Originally, charr pies were made of pastry with spices added to the fish but, towards the end of the seventeenth century, the use of pastry was largely discontinued and the charr were then potted in dishes. John Davy, in *The Angler in the Lake District* (1857) gives his neighbour's recipe for potted charr:

One dozen of charr, dress and wipe with a dry cloth; strew a little salt in and over them, and let them lie all night; then wipe them with a dry cloth, and season with one ounce of white pepper, quarter of an ounce of cayenne, half an ounce of pounded cloves, and a little mace. Clarify two pounds of butter. Then put them with their backs down into a pot lined with paper; and then pour the butter over, and bake four hours in a slow oven.

Davy also points out that a lot of what passed for potted charr was, in fact, potted trout and that, if the trout was of good quality, it was not inferior to charr. The Duke of Montagu, writing

to Mr Atkinson of Dalton in a letter dated 27th July, 1738, extols
the virtues of potted charr:

*I received yours of the first of this month and also Pott of Charr which
you send by the days carrier - which was the best I ever eat and I would
have you send me some of the same sort by every carrier . . . and let them
be potted and seasoned just as that Pot was, for it cannot be better.*

John Watson, in *The English District Fisheries* (1899), quotes a letter written by John Swainson of Kendal in 1819, in which he
estimates the amount of charr sold in pots from all the lakes:

*We may form some idea of the probable quantity of charr procured in one
season. I suppose, during this period, there are no less than 150 dozen
of pots used for potting charr, which makes 1,800 - and as there are
pots of various sizes, usually sold from 5s. 3d. to one guinea each, if we
average the number of fish contained in each pot at six (perhaps seven
would be nearer the truth), we shall find the number of charr caught in
one season to be 10,800, which, averaging them at a ¼ lb. each, will
amount to 2,700 lbs weight. In the above number of charr there are
900 dozens, which, at 8s. per dozen (the price the fishers sell them for),
make the sum £360, obtained for one kind of fish only, procured from
the lakes.*

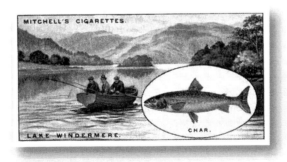

A Mitchell's cigarette card from 1928 depicting charr fishing on Windermere.

Watson also states that between 1893 and 1898, an average of
3,965lb of charr was taken annually from Windermere alone,
mainly by net fishermen. By the early decades of the twentieth
century it became clear that fishing on such a scale could not
continue and, in 1924, legislation was passed banning the netting
of charr in Windermere, which, in turn, virtually brought an end
to the commercial potting of charr and the manufacture of charr
pots. However, a few diehard fishermen still fish for the charr of
Windermere and Coniston using the traditional method of
plumb lining and let us hope that the charr will survive the
ravages of pollution and global warming for future generations
of fishermen to enjoy.

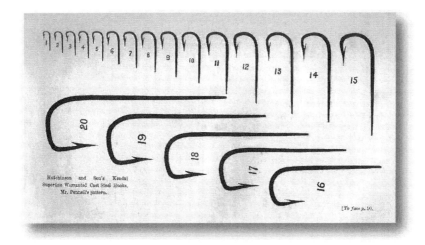

8

Adlington & Hutchinson
FISH HOOK MAKERS OF KENDAL

The term angling is derived from the Old English word 'angle' meaning a hook and, without doubt, the humble hook is the most essential part of the angler's equipment. Until the seventeenth century the angler either had to make his own hooks or had to find someone (usually the local blacksmith) to make them for him. Indeed, the earliest English book on angling, *The Treatyse of Fyshynge with an Angle* (1496), attributed to Dame Juliana Berners, gave detailed instructions on hook making:

You must understand that the most intricate and skilled part of making your tackle is making your hooks. To make them you must have suitable files, thin and sharp and beaten small; a semi-clamp of iron; a bender; a pair of small, long tongs; a hard knife, somewhat thick; an anvil; and a little hammer. For small fish make your hooks this way, of the smallest square steel needles of that you can find. Put the square needle in a red charcoal fire until it is the same colour as the fire. Then take it out and let it cool, and you will find it well tempered for filing. Raise the barb

with your knife and sharpen the point. Then temper it again, for otherwise it will break when you set the bend. Bend it like the hooks shown
below as an example. You can make bigger hooks in the same way out
of larger needles: such as embroiderers', tailors', or shoemakers' needles,
or spear points. Shoemakers' nails are particularly good hooks for big fish.
And check that they bend at the point when they are tested; otherwise
they are no good. When the hook is bent, beat the hinder end out broad,
and file it smooth to prevent the line fraying. Then put it in the fire again
and give it an easy red heat. Suddenly quench it in water, and it will be
hard and strong. (Translation by Andrew Herd, from *The Treatise Transcript*)

Hooks shown in The Treatyse of Fyshynge with an Angle *(1496).*

Early hooks were not standardised, with bends set according to
the fancy of the fisherman and their size was determined by
the needles that were to hand. One of the earliest commercial
makers of fish hooks that we know of was Charles Kirby, who set
up in business around 1650 in Harp Alley, Shoe Lane, London.
Kirby was the inventor of the hook shape (or bend) which still
bears his name and is famous throughout the world. Kirby's
reputation was enhanced by Izaak Walton's commendation of his
wares, which appeared in the second edition of the *Compleat
Angler* (1655), where Kirby was referred to as being 'the most
exact and best hook-maker the nation affords'.

As angling became more popular during the seventeenth and
eighteenth centuries there was a growing demand for fish hooks
and in 1745 Thomas Adlington set up in business as a fish hook

manufacturer in Kendal. Unfortunately, in spite of extensive research, little is known of the firm's founder. It appears that he passed the business on to his son, John Adlington, who in turn passed it on to his son, another Thomas. This Thomas Adlington died on 26th February, 1829 and, as his son George (1813-1839) was too young to take over his inheritance, the running of the business was placed in the capable hands of its foreman, Philip Hutchinson, whose mother was Elizabeth Adlington. A notice to this effect was placed in the *Westmorland Gazette*, dated 18th April, 1829:

The business will be carried on in its branches under the superinten-
dence of the executors until Mr. Adlington's son, George, (to whom the
business is bequeathed) comes of age. The executors have engaged Philip
Hutchinson, who has been foreman to Mr. Adlington for many years.
They confidently hope that 'Adlington's super-fine cast steel hooks' will
continue to merit that distinguished reputation they have so long
deservedly maintained.

Five years later, George Adlington, who had now come of age, placed the following advert in the *Westmorland Gazette*, dated 3rd May, 1834:

GEORGE ADLINGTON
FISH HOOK, AND TACKLE MAKER

STRAMONGATE KENDAL

Begs to Return on behalf of his Sisters and himself
his grateful Thanks to his Friends and the Public for
the favours conferred upon them since the Death of their Father, and
respectfully announce that he has admitted
PHILIP HUTCHINSON as PARTNER in the
above BUSINESS and that it will in future
be conducted under the FIRM of
MESSRS. ADLINGTON & HUTCHINSON.

The same advert goes on to say that, in addition to hooks, they make 'every kind of Artificial Fly and Bait, and every description of Tackle for Salmon, Pike, Trout, Perch, &c. They have now on hand all kinds of Fishing Rods, Screw, Slide and Piece; a quantity of Fine Fly and other Gut; a great variety of Flies on Gut and Hair; Trolling Lines; Reels, Plain, Hatched, and Multiplying; Landing Nets: Panniers, - and Fishing hooks of every description.'

Philip Hutchinson

The firm had clearly prospered following the death of Thomas Adlington under the careful tutelage of Philip Hutchinson. Sadly, five years later on 14th September, 1839, George Adlington died at the young age of twenty-six and the firm now became known as P. Hutchinson, Hook and Tackle Makers. In December 1854, Philip made his son, George Adlington Hutchinson a partner in the business and it became known as P. Hutchinson & Son. The census of 1861 gives us some idea of the scale of the business. In it, Philip Hutchinson is described as a fish hook maker employing three men, one woman and one boy. By 1871, Philip had retired from the business and he died on 7th March, 1873 aged seventy-six. During his life he had served for many years on Kendal Town Council where his sound judgement was highly respected. Not surprisingly, given his profession, he was a keen angler and had been a member of the Kent Angling Association since its foundation. His obituary writer in the *Westmorland Gazette* had this to say of him:

As a man of business he was very popular, and especially so to those disciples of Waltonian principles, who were naturally often brought in contact with him. In the year 1834 he entered into partnership with

Mr Adlington, and Adlington and Hutchinson's fish-hooks were soon well-known throughout England, and indeed almost in any country where angling could be followed. Notwithstanding keen competition, the firm continued to increase its business transactions, and the more the Kirby and Kendal sneck-bend hooks became known the more they were inquired for; and Kendal and Limerick shone forth before the world as the seats of the manufacture of the best fish-hooks.

The 'keen competition' mentioned in the obituary almost certainly came from Redditch, where, at the beginning of the nineteenth century a number of hook makers such as Henry Millward, Samuel Allcock and William Bartlett had set up in business. The making of fish hooks in the nineteenth century was quite a labour intensive business and a detailed account of the process is given in Richard Niven's, *The British Angler's Lexicon* (1892). The following account is an abridged summary of the main stages involved:

Stage 1 - the wires are cut by shears into the requisite length for the particular size of hook that the operator intends to make.

Stage 2 - the barb is cut by means of a hollow-ground knife, which opens the fluke to the required gauge, care being taken lest the barb be weakened.

Stage 3 - the hook points are filed to the required shape, forming either hollow, Kirby or Dublin points. All the best hooks are filed by hand, and are given either three or four knife-like cutting edges, which causes the hook to have good penetrating power.

Stage 4 - the hook is turned to give it the particular bend required. There were four distinct recognised bends made by all hook manufacturers: sneck, round, Kirby and Limerick. Springing from these four were various modifications such as Sproat, McKenzie and others.

Stage 5 - the shank is shaped by a hammer, or by the aid of a machine, to be either ringed, flatted or sharp pointed, the latter being the usual shape for flies to be tied to gut.

Stage 6 - up until now the hook has been in a soft condition and must now be hardened. This is the most difficult part of the operation as the hook should not be too hard or not hard enough. The wires are heated in a furnace until they attain a certain appearance, which a skilled workman notices with accuracy

Stage 7 - the hooks are withdrawn and plunged into oil. This converts the hitherto soft hook into a brittle condition.

Stage 8 - the brittle hooks are tempered by being withdrawn from the oil, heated in a pan over a charcoal fire and mixed with heated emery sand, with the mixture being kept in constant motion. Every now and then a hook is picked out and its temper gauged by a skilled operative.

Stage 9 - the hooks are scoured by being placed in barrels of water. The barrels are kept in motion by steam power for several days until all scale is removed from them.

Stage 10 - the hooks are now polished. They are placed in a bag containing fine emery powder and shaken until they become bright. Alternatively, they are placed in revolving barrels with an inclination of forty-five degrees.

Stage 11 - the hooks are coloured either by japanning, blueing or browning.

Stage 12 - the hooks are counted and packaged. The packages are labelled, well dried to prevent rust and sent off to the various markets.

Nowadays, when we buy fish hooks they are of standard sizes, based on the Redditch scale. However, in the nineteenth century hook sizes were not standardised and different manufacturers had their own scales. The sizes of hooks made in Kendal were the reverse of those made in Redditch. The smallest sized Kendal hooks commenced at No.00 and ran up to No.20, the largest.

Following the death of Philip Hutchinson in 1873, the business continued under his son, George Adlington Hutchinson. In the census of 1881 George, who by now was fifty years of age, is described as a fish hook maker employing four men, one boy and one girl. The business was obviously prospering and around 1878 George built a fish hook factory on Aynam Road, Kendal.

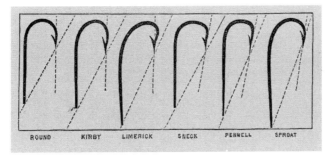

Nineteenth century hook types.

During the latter half of the nineteenth century Hutchinson & Son gained a world-wide reputation for the quality of their hooks and they were instrumental in developing new patterns. Around 1865 they developed the Sproat bend hook, at the suggestion of a local angler, W. H. Sproat of Ambleside. The shape of the bend is critical to the penetrating power of the hook and a number of different bends were developed for different fishing situations and species of fish. Sproat bend hooks were highly recommended by Francis Francis and Cholmondeley-Pennell, although Cholmondeley-Pennell did feel that it lacked depth and power in the point-side. In his *Modern Practical Angler* (1870), Cholmondeley-Pennell devoted his first chapter to a discussion of hooks and informs us that Hutchinson & Son were manufacturing a pattern under his own name:

In the pattern of hook which is now being manufactured by Messrs. Hutchinson, of Kendal, under my own name, I have endeavoured to hit the medium between the theoretical and practical requirements, and to combine as nearly as possible the advantages of the various bends referred to, and especially to the sproat and sneck bends, whilst avoiding what I believe to be their faults.

Hutchinson & Son were also instrumental in developing eyed trout hooks for chalkstream dry-fly fishing. The story of their development is told by David Beazley in a couple of articles in the *Flyfishers Journal* (Vol. 84, 1995). Although eyed fish hooks had been around for some considerable time, during the nineteenth century most fly fishing was carried out with flies dressed on blind eye hooks whipped to silkworm gut or horse hair. Flies tied on eyed hooks are found in Hewitt Wheatley's, *Rod and Line* (1849) and W. H. Aldam's, *A Quaint Treatise on 'Flees and the Art a' artyficiall flee making'* (1876), in which two mayflies are tied on turned-up eyed hooks. After seeing Aldam's eyed hooks H. S. Hall of Bristol and George Bankart of Leicester decided to experiment with eyed hooks and in a letter to Hutchinsons, dated 1st February, 1879, Hall asked if they would make some sample hooks with straight eyes added. After receiving a batch of hooks in March 1879, Hall and Bankart tried them out on the Usk. Following this experiment they decided to have the eyes turned up. Hall also suggested that the hooks would be better with a sneck bend, while Bankart decided the hooks would be better bronzed rather than blued or japanned and this, in essence, is how the form of the eyed dry-fly hook came about. Hutchinsons marketed the hooks as 'Hall's Snecky-Limerick'. Frederic Halford in his *Floating Flies and How to Dress Them* (1886) was very much in favour of the new eyed hooks for dry flies and believed that flies dressed on blind eye hooks to gut would soon become obsolete. He also favoured the upturned eye:

For attaching the flies, I am distinctly of opinion that Mr. Hall's form of the eye, inclined upwards, is more convenient and therefore preferable.

Although the manufacture of fish hooks was the mainstay of their business, Hutchinson & Son also sold a wide range of fishing tackle and artificial flies. A trade list, dating to around 1880, gives a list of the flies on offer, together with their dressings, which is very useful for the modern fly dresser. Most of the patterns listed are traditional North-country patterns although there are one or two that are peculiar to the local area, including the Windermere and the Windermere Favourite. The former is listed as a lake fly, while the latter comes under the category of sea trout and lough flies. Other sea trout and lough flies of interest include the Eden and the Malham, presumably for use on Malham Tarn in the Yorkshire Dales.

George Adlington Hutchinson retired from the family business around 1896 and was succeeded by his sons, Philip (born 1858) and Charles (born 1868). It appears that Philip looked after the hook making operations in Aynam Road, Kendal, while Charles, when he came of age in 1889, was put in charge of the retail side of the business, firstly at 43, Stricklandgate and from 1898 onwards at 43, Finkle Street and traded under the name Charles Hutchinson & Co. George died on 5th October, 1903, at his home at 86, Stricklandgate, aged seventy-two. According to his obituary writer in the *Westmorland Gazette* he had been in failing health for three or four months and the cause of death was cancer of the liver.

During the early decades of the twentieth century Hutchinson & Son began to struggle and found it difficult to compete with the larger hook and tackle manufacturers in Redditch. During the 1920s the Finkle Street premises were closed and the whole operation was moved to Aynam Road. Philip died on 11th July, 1930, aged seventy-two. His obituary writer in the *Westmorland Gazette* makes it clear that the business was in decline:

Born 72 years ago, Mr. Philip Hutchinson was the son of the late Mr. George Adlington Hutchinson, who came of a long line of fishing hook makers. This business has come down from father to son for many generations and has a world-wide reputation for the wonderful holding quality of the hooks. In latter years the business has not been quite so well-known, chiefly owing to the trade getting into the hands of larger concerns. Mr. Hutchinson never took any part in local affairs and was of a very quiet and retiring disposition. Many years ago he used to visit Spain to buy silkworm gut for the business which had a wide reputation for this angling necessity. For some time Mr. Hutchinson has been in declining health. He married Miss Blacow, who survives him.

Following Philip's death the business, now under Charles, continued to decline. In 1934, after reaching retirement age, Charles decided to close the business down and on 17th March he placed a notice in the *Westmorland Gazette* announcing a dispersal sale. It appears that it took three or four years to dispose of the entire stock but by the start of the Second World War the firm had ceased trading. Charles himself lived till the ripe old age of eighty-six, dying on 16th March, 1955.

9

William Wordsworth
POET & ANGLER

There seems to be a link between poetry and angling - perhaps it is the hours spent at the waterside, surrounded by beautiful scenery and wildlife, contemplating a float or rod tip that inspires us to verse. Ted Hughes, arguably the greatest English poet of the twentieth century and Poet Laureate from 1984 until his death in 1998, was a very keen angler. Quite a number of his poems, such as *Pike* or *Milesian Encounter on the Sligachan*, are directly inspired by fish or fishing and *River* (1983), a book of collected poems on the same topics, ought to be on the bookshelves of every thinking angler. William Wordsworth, who was appointed Poet Laureate in 1843, was also an angler. In fact, it is hardly surprising that Wordsworth was an angler when you consider that he was born and spent the majority of his life in the Lake District, surrounded by rivers, lakes and tarns.

William Wordsworth was born on 7th April, 1770, in the Cumberland town of Cockermouth. The house where he was born backs on to the banks of the river Derwent, and it was here that he developed his love of angling. Like most small boys, he was fascinated by water and, from an early age, he spent a lot of time in and around it, as is clear from his autobiographical poem, *The Prelude:*

> *Oh, many a time have I, a five year's child,*
> *In a small mill-race severed from his stream,*
> *Made one long bathing of a summer's day;*
> *Basked in the sun and plunged and basked again . . .*
> (BOOK I, LINES 287-291)

Also in *The Prelude* he talks of his early fishing adventures with his friends:

> *We were a noisy crew; the sun in heaven*
> *Beheld not vales more beautiful than ours;*
> *Nor saw a band in happiness and joy*
> *Richer, or worthier of the ground they trod.*
> *I could record with no reluctant voice*
> *The woods of autumn, and their hazel bowers*
> *With milk-white clusters hung; the rod and line,*
> *True symbols of hope's foolishness, whose strong*
> *And unreproved enchantment led us on*
> *By rocks and pools shut out from every star,*
> *All the green summer, to forlorn cascades*
> *Among the windings hid of mountain brooks.*
> (BOOK I, LINES 478-490)

At the age of nine, shortly after his mother's death, William and his brother Richard were sent to Hawkshead Grammar School, where they lodged at the home of a local woman, Anne Tyson. William loved his time at Hawkshead, and Anne Tyson very much became a mother figure to the Wordsworth boys. Lying right at the heart of the Lake District, Hawkshead gave William the opportunity to explore other rivers and lakes. A story is told

Hawkshead Grammar School.

of him persuading a local fisherman to take him fishing in the Duddon Valley, ten miles away. They were away all day and, as they came home late in the evening, William was so exhausted that he had to be given a piggy-back by the fisherman. Unfortunately, it is not recorded whether they caught any fish! The river Duddon was to remain in Wordsworth's memory and in 1820 he published a series of sonnets on the river. My favourite lines from these sonnets come in the *After-Thought* and are a poignant reminder of the brevity of human life:

> *Still glides the Stream, and shall for ever glide;*
> *The Form remains, the Function never dies;*
> *While we, the brave, the mighty, and the wise,*
> *We Men, who in our morn of youth defied*
> *The elements, must vanish; - be it so!*

During his years at Hawkshead Wordsworth spent a lot of time by the shores of Esthwaite, now run as a commercial trout fishery, but in Wordsworth's day it was noted for its perch and pike fishing. Wordsworth would rise early and wander the banks of the lake before the start of school, no doubt searching for suitable places to fish. Esthwaite is a relatively shallow lake and during the winter months, when it froze over, he enjoyed nothing better than skating on its surface.

However, fishing and the outdoor life were not the only loves of Wordsworth's life. Books and poetry sometimes took preference over fishing, as the following account from *The Prelude* of a day by the Derwent demonstrates:

> *And when thereafter to my father's house*
> *The holidays returned me, there to find*
> *That golden store of books which I had left,*
> *What joy was mine! How often in the course*
> *Of those glad respites, though a soft west wind*
> *Ruffled the waters to the angler's wish,*
> *For a whole day together, have I lain*
> *Down by thy side, O Derwent! Murmuring stream,*
> *On the hot stones, and in the glaring sun,*
> *And there have read, devouring as I read,*
> *Defrauding the day's glory, desperate!*
> *Till with a sudden bound of smart reproach,*
> *Such as the idler deals with in his shame,*
> *I to the sport betook myself again.*
>
> (BOOK V, LINES 477-490)

In October, 1787, Wordsworth went up to St John's College, Cambridge, where he spent a rather unhappy three years. He could not wait for the long vacations to come round and to be back in his beloved Lake District. Following his graduation from Cambridge and a brief romance in France, he spent several restless years contemplating his future career. Eventually, after receiving a legacy of £900 from a close friend, he settled down at Dove Cottage, Grasmere, with his beloved sister, Dorothy and devoted the rest of his life to his poetry. Between the years 1800

Dove Cottage, Grasmere.

and 1803 Dorothy kept a journal of their life together at Dove Cottage and it is from the entries in this journal that we are able to learn more of Wordsworth the angler.

Dove Cottage is almost within casting distance of Grasmere, where Wordsworth had the use of a neighbour's boat and it is here that Dorothy records their first fishing expedition:

Thursday, 29th May, 1800 – In the morning worked in the garden a little . . .Went to Mr. Gell's boat before tea. We fished upon the lake, and amongst us caught 13 bass (perch) . . . Left the water at near nine o'clock, very cold.

No doubt the bass found their way on to the menu for the next day. However, they were not always successful as the following entry records:

Friday, 9th June, 1800 - We went to R. Newton's for pike floats and went round to Mr. Gell's boat, and on to the lake to fish. We caught nothing - it was extremely cold. The reeds and bulrushes or bullpipes of a tender soft green, making a plain whose surface moved with the wind. The reeds not yet tall. The lake clear to the bottom, but saw no fish.

The pike floats mentioned above were almost certainly trimmers rather than ordinary cork floats. Robert Newton, from whom they acquired their floats, was the landlord of an inn in Grasmere, who presumably made pike floats as a side-line. Fishing with trimmers, although not exactly a sporting method of catching pike, is certainly an effective one. A contemporary account of trimmer fishing is given in T. F. Salter's, *The Angler's Guide* (1815):

Another way of laying a trimmer, or trimmer-fishing, is by winding a line on a piece of round cork, of about five inches in diameter, which has a groove to hold the line; bait the hook with a live fish, running it through the gills, or back fin: draw as much line from the groove as will let the bait swim a little below mid-water. These cork trimmers may be thrown into ponds or still waters, and left to swim about, as they may be recovered with the assistance of a boat, or your drag-hook.

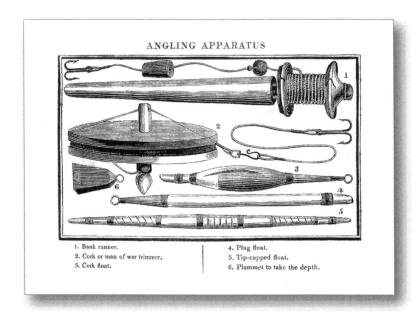

ANGLING APPARATUS

1. Bank runner.
2. Cork or man of war trimmer.
3. Cork float.
4. Plug float.
5. Tip-capped float.
6. Plummet to take the depth.

The following extracts from Dorothy's journal seem to imply
that this was one of the methods employed by her brother for
catching pike on Grasmere.

*Tuesday, 10th June, 1800 – John (the poet's brother who was staying
with them at the time) had been fishing in Langdale and was gone to
bed.*

*Wednesday, 11th June, 1800 – A very cold morning - we went to the
lake to set pike floats with John's fish . . . Went to bed in the afternoon
and slept till after six. William and John went to the pike floats - they
brought in 2 pikes.*

At Dove Cottage the Wordsworths lived a relatively simple life.
Both William and Dorothy enjoyed gardening and grew most of
their own vegetables. Meals consisted largely of porridge or pota-
toes, boiled mutton and home-made pies, giblet pie appearing to
be a particular favourite. Not surprisingly, therefore, fresh fish
provided a welcome variation to their diet and the fish that
William caught invariably ended up on the table, as the next
day's entry records:

*Thursday, 12th June, 1800 – William and I went upon the water to set
pike floats. John fished under Loughrigg. We returned home to
dinner, 2 pikes boiled and roasted.*

Elsewhere in her journal Dorothy records William catching a
pike of 7½lb and a fortnight later one of 4½lb. Apart from
Grasmere she mentions her brother fishing in Rydal Water,

Wythburn Water, Elterwater and in the Langdales. As is the case with most anglers, things do not always run smoothly, as the following incident records:

Tuesday, 27th April, 1802 – A fine morning. Mrs. Luff called. I walked with her to the boat-house. William met me at the top of the hill with his fishing rod in his hand . . . I left him, intending to join him, but he came home, and said his lines would not stand the pulling - he had had several bites.

One of Wordsworth's fishing companions during his early years at Dove Cottage was the Reverend Joseph Sympson, vicar of Wythburn. In a letter to her friend Jane Marshall, dated September 1800, Dorothy records their friendship:

We are also upon very intimate terms with one family in the middle rank of life, a Clergyman with a very small income, his wife, son and daughter. The old man is upwards of eighty, yet he goes a-fishing to the Tarns on the hill-tops with my Brother, and he is active as many men of 50 . . . and the son is an interesting man, he is about 40, manages his Father's glebe land, reads a little and spends much time in fishing.

Dorothy's journal records several fishing expeditions with the Sympsons. Unfortunately, the last entry in Dorothy's journal dates to January 1803 and for details of Wordsworth's later life we have to turn to other sources. In 1822, Wordsworth published his *Guide to the Lakes*, which includes several brief references to fishing, the most interesting of which concerns an excursion on the banks of Ullswater:

Friday, November 9th – Rain, as yesterday, till ten o'clock, when we took a boat to row down the lake . . . In the large bay under Place Fell, three fishermen were dragging a net, a picturesque group beneath the high and bare crags . . . The fishermen drew their net ashore, and hundreds of fish were leaping in their prison. They were all of the kind called skellies (schelly), a sort of fresh-water herring, shoals of which may sometimes be seen dimpling or rippling the surface of the lake in calm weather. This species is not found, I believe, in any other of these lakes; nor, as far as I know, is the chevin (chub), that spiritless fish (though I am loth to call it so, for it was a prime favourite with Isaac Walton), which must frequent Ullswater, as I have seen a large shoal passing into the lake from the river Eamont. Here are no pike, and the charr are smaller than those of the other lakes, and of inferior quality; but the grey trout attains a very large size, sometimes weighing above twenty pounds.

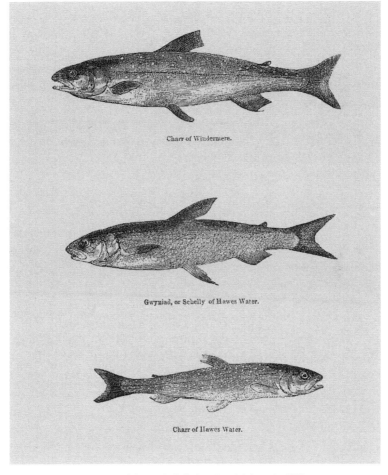

Charr of Windermere.

Gwyniad, or Schelly of Hawes Water.

Charr of Hawes Water.

Drawings of charr and schelly from Davy's Salmonia, 1828.

Nowadays, the skelly or schelly, a member of the Salmonid family, is a very rare capture in Ullswater. Incidentally, it was by the shores of Ullswater that Wordsworth and his sister, Dorothy saw the daffodils that inspired one of his most famous poems.

Among Wordsworth's wide circle of friends were two well-known anglers of the day, Sir Humphry Davy and Professor John Wilson. Davy, a distinguished chemist but with poetic pretensions, helped Wordsworth to edit his *Lyrical Ballads*. He visited the Wordsworths on several occasions and no doubt went fishing with William. In his book, *Salmonia or Days of Fly-Fishing* (1828), Davy praised Wordsworth as a friend of fishing and fishermen. John Wilson, the wealthy son of a Scottish manufacturer, was a great admirer of Wordsworth's poetry, so much so, that he came to live at Windermere to be close to the Wordsworths. Wilson himself loved the outdoor life and was a keen angler and field sportsman. In June 1809, Wordsworth joined Wilson's fishing party on an expedition to Wastwater. The party consisted of thirty-two, ten of whom were servants. Writing in *Blackwood's Magazine* (May 1834), under the pseudonym 'Christopher North', Wilson recalls one day in particular:

Perhaps a better station than any yet mentioned is at Wastdalehead. From the Stye runs one stream, and down Moresdale another - which may be both angled in a day. And in a day - the longest of the year - we once killed in the two twenty-seven dozen (trout) - none of them above a pound.

In 1820, with the aid of a reference from Sir Walter Scott, Wilson was appointed Professor of Moral Philosophy at Edinburgh University. However, even though he spent a large part of the year in Edinburgh, he continued to visit the Lake District and to fish with Wordsworth. Wilson records a rather poignant story concerning Wordsworth and his younger brother, John, shortly before he drowned when the ship he was commanding was wrecked off the south coast:

Wastwater from the south-west. Photograph courtesy of Ericoides (Creative Commons 3.0 license).

Now beneath that mountain (Helvellyn) there is a little tarn (Red Tarn). Two persons were sitting silent and alone beside that tarn, looking stead-fastly on the water, and lost in thought. These were two brothers who dearly loved each other, and had done so from earliest youth to man-hood. The one was enjoying his own thoughts. The other, younger by a few years, and had gone to sea, but had lately returned to see his brother, and resolved to live with him. His brother accompanied him on his way to join his ship for the last time, and here they sat, about to part. They had talked over their future plans of happiness when they were again to meet, and of their simple sports. As their last act, they agreed to lay the foundation stone of a little fishing hut, and this they did with tears.

John Wordsworth died on 5th February, 1805, and not only had Wordsworth lost a much-loved brother, but also an angling com-panion. It is clear from Wilson's account that Wordsworth and his brother fished Red Tarn and one wonders whether they ever caught one of the vendace, which inhabit its chilly depths. Wil-son himself considered the trout of Red Tarn to be of very poor

John Wilson.

quality, 'soft as butter, black as tar, weak as water', unlike the trout described by Wordsworth in a passage from *The Excursion (1814)*, which Wilson greatly admired. In the poem, the Poet, the Recluse and the Pedlar, after their mountain walk, accompany the Rector to his mansion. While they are being entertained, two young anglers enter, one of whom is proudly displaying his catch, laid on a blue slate stone:

Between his hands he holds a smooth blue stone,
On whose capricious surface is outspread
Large store of gleaming crimson-spotted trouts;
Ranged side by side, in regular ascent,
One after one, still lessening by degree
Up to the dwarf that tops the pinnacle.
Upon the Board he lays the sky-blue stone
With its rich spoil; - their number he proclaims;
Tells from what pool the noblest had been dragged;
And where the very monarch of the brook,
After long struggle, had escaped at last -
Stealing alternately at them and us
(As doth his Comrade too) a look of pride.
And, verily the silent Creatures made
A splendid sight together thus exposed;
Dead - but not sullied or deformed by Death,
That seemed to pity what he could not spare.

(THE EXCURSION, BOOK VIII, LINES 556-571)

One of Wilson's last references to Wordsworth occurs in an article in *Blackwood's Magazine* (May 1843). By now Wordsworth was seventy-three years old and preferred to take a more relaxed role:

We must not say that we were a great, but may say that we were once a good angler. You may ask Wordsworth. He will tell you of our killing a creelful in two hours in the beautiful liquid link uniting Grasmere and Rydalmere, one day when Ned Hurd (a local angler) himself could not move a fin. But Ned had no idea of fine tackle - and ours was like the gossamer - invisible but in the sun-glint, and then our flies were so life-like that you thought you heard them hum. The great poet lay on the bank near the bridge, with a placid smile on his noble features, as at every other throw we hooked a golden star, and bid it shine on the sward among the brackens; yet, ever and anon, the fixed dim eyes told that his spirit was in meditation's umbrage, haunted by sights too ethereal for sense to see, and we knew that we passed to and fro before his couch an unregarded shadow. Divine day! And yet but one of a celestial series! - closed now - haply never to be continued.

Like his angling companion, the Reverend Joseph Sympson, Wordsworth lived to a ripe old age. He died, aged eighty, on 23rd, April, 1850 and his body lies at rest in Grasmere churchyard.

Grasmere church.

Modern charr lure on Watson's The English Lake District Fisheries.

Charr bells on the end of traditional rods, Windermere.

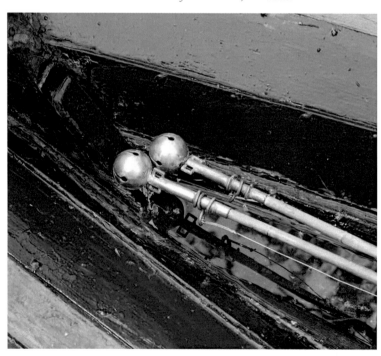

Previous Page: Grasmere from The English Lakes *by E. W. Haslehust.*

Right: Charr fishing on Windermere in 2010.
Photos courtesy of Andrew Herd.

The Waterloo Fly

The dressing for this fly is taken from John Kirkbride's Northern Angler, *published in 1837, and was possibly designed to commemorate the Battle of Waterloo in 1815.*

This version of the fly is taken from a late nineteenth century catalogue of flies by Hutchinson & Son of Kendal. Although it bears the same name as the fly above the dressings are completely different.

Some Hutchinson & Son Lake District Patterns.

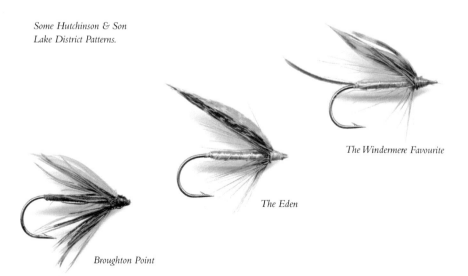

The Windermere Favourite

The Eden

Broughton Point

Left: Boat fishing on Derwentwater. Photo courtesy of Jon Ward-Allen.

The Archdeacon, an Eden salmon fly.
Dressing from John Waller Hills' My Sporting Life.

The Bulldog, a popular salmon fly for the Eden, devised by
Carlisle tackle-dealer, Robert Strong.

Right: Salmon fishing on the Lune in the 1960s.

Two of John Wilson's flies.

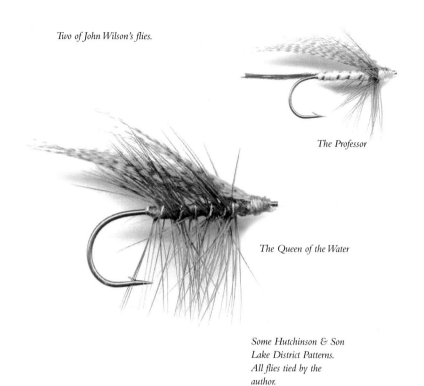

The Professor

The Queen of the Water

*Some Hutchinson & Son
Lake District Patterns.
All flies tied by the
author.*

Two favourite flies of John Beever of Coniston.

The Black Caterpillar

The Bracken Clock

All flies tied by the author.

THIRLMERE, OR WYTHBURN WATER, CUMBERLAND.

10

An Angler's Best Friend
THE STORY OF CHARLES GOUGH

Some time ago I made a pilgrimage to the top of one of England's highest mountains, Helvellyn, in search of an angler or, to be more precise, in search of a monument to an angler. The angler in question was the luckless Charles Gough, whose bones now lie at rest in the Friend's Burial Ground at Tirril, between Pooley Bridge and Penrith.

In his early years Charles Gough was brought up as a Quaker but was later expelled from the Society after joining a volunteer corps, as Quakers abhor violence and refuse to take part in warfare. Charles Gough, who hailed from Manchester, was an aspiring artist and a friend of William Green of Ambleside. Gough was also an angler. One of his favourite angling expeditions was to Wythburn Lake (now Thirlmere), which lies at the foot of Helvellyn on the road between Grasmere and Keswick. Thirlmere was originally two lakes until 1880, when it was dammed to provide a reservoir of drinking water for the people of Manchester. According to John Watson in, *The English Lake District Fisheries* (1899):

The Thirlmere of old contained trout, pike and perch, and for its trout it was justly famous. The peaty holes, known as Wythburn bogs, contained fine yellow trout, and good fish could always be obtained near the mouths of the numerous feeders.

On the 18th of April, 1805, Charles Gough left home, accompanied only by his spaniel bitch, en route for Thirlmere on a fishing expedition. As the day was relatively fine, he stopped off for liquid refreshment at an inn in Patterdale at the head of Ullswater, where he was hoping to find someone to guide him over the hills to his destination. Unfortunately, because of a review taking place that day in Penrith, no one was available to escort him. Undaunted, Charles and his spaniel set off alone.

Anyone familiar with the Lake District will be able to confirm that the weather can be very changeable, particularly around Easter, when it is not unusual to encounter four seasons in one day. Not surprisingly, therefore, within an hour of leaving the inn it began to hail and a thick blanket of fog descended on the hills. Nothing more was heard of Charles and his spaniel for quite some time.

Two months later, on the 20th of June, a solitary shepherd was tending his flock near Red Tarn Crag, not far from Helvellyn, when his attention was drawn to the howling of a dog. It was Charles Gough's spaniel watching over the remains of her master. The shepherd summoned help from some locals who, on reaching the spot, found the body lying at the foot of a steep crag, with the skull detached from the body and lying several feet away. His fishing rod was still at the top of the crag while his small bundle was discovered half way down. Little flesh was left on the body and it seems he may have provided welcome carrion for the foxes and birds of prey that haunt the hilltops.

How the hapless Charles died is not certain but it seems likely that, in the dense fog, he lost his way and fell over the precipice.

In August, 1805, not long after this terrible event, Walter Scott, the famous poet and author visited his good friend William Wordsworth, who was living at Dove Cottage in Grasmere. The

View from the Gough Memorial on Helvellyn. A sketch by the author.

Wordsworths were noted for their plain and simple living and this was not to Scott's tastes. It is said that during his visit, tired of his hosts' monotonous diet, he rose early, climbed out of the window, and went to the local inn for a good meal.

However, while staying with the Wordsworths, he accompanied William and Humphry Davy, author of *Salmonia or Days of Fly Fishing* (1828), on a walk over Helvellyn. Their progress was rather slow since Scott had contracted polio as a child and was lame in his right leg, so Humphry Davy became bored and made his own way back to Grasmere. On the journey they passed near to the spot where poor Charles Gough had come to grief and Wordsworth regaled Scott with the story. Both Scott and Wordsworth were keen anglers themselves and could empathise with the hapless angler. Indeed, Wordsworth himself regularly fished Red Tarn, which nestles beneath Helvellyn and is the highest tarn in the district at a height of 2,356 feet. Scott was so affected by the story that he was moved to write about it in a poem called *Hellvellyn*. It is interesting to note that Scott's spelling, Hellvellyn, contains an extra letter 'l', rather appropriate in the circumstances!

HELLVELLYN

I climb'd the dark brow of the mighty Hellvellyn,
Lakes and mountains beneath me gleamed misty and wide;
All was still, save by fits, when the eagle was yelling,
And starting around me the echoes replied.
On the right, Striden-edge round the Red-Tarn was bending,
And Catchedicam its left verge was defending,
One huge nameless rock in the front was ascending,
When I marked the sad spot where the wanderer had died.

Dark green was that spot mid the brown mountain-heather,
Where the Pilgrim of Nature lay stretched in decay,
Like the corpse of an outcast abandoned to weather,
Till the mountain-winds wasted the tenantless clay.
Not yet quite deserted, though lonely extended,
For, faithful in death, his mute favourite attended,
The much-loved remains of her master defended,
And chased the hill-fox and the raven away.

How long didst thou think his silence was slumber?
When the wind waved his garment, how oft didst thou start?
How many long days and long weeks didst thou number,
Ere he faded before thee, the friend of thy heart?
And, oh, was it meet, that - no requiem read o'er him -
No mother to weep, and no friend to deplore him,
And thou, little guardian, alone stretch'd before him -
Unhonour'd the Pilgrim from life should depart?

When a Prince to the fate of the Peasant has yielded,
The tapestry waves dark round the dim-lighted hall;
With scutcheons of silver the coffin is shielded,
And pages stand mute by the canopied hall:
Through the courts, at deep midnight, the torches are gleaming;
In the proudly-arch'd chapel the banners are beaming,
Far adown the long aisle sacred music is streaming,
Lamenting a Chief of the people should fall.

Sir Walter Scott with his favourite dog, Maida.
From a sketch on stone by J. R. Hamerton.

But meeter for thee, gentle lover of nature,
To lay down thy head like the meek mountain lamb,
When, wilder'd, he drops from some cliff huge in stature,
And draws his last sob by the side of his dam.
And more stately thy couch by this desert lake lying,
Thy obsequies sung by the grey plover flying,
With one faithful friend but to witness thy dying,
In the arms of Hellvellyn and Catchedicam.

Wordsworth, too, independently of Scott, wrote a poem on the
same subject entitled *Fidelity*, and it is interesting to compare
the two.

FIDELITY

A barking sound the Shepherd hears,
A cry as of a Dog or Fox;
He halts and searches with his eyes
Among the scatter'd rocks:
And now at distance can discern
A stirring in a brake of fern;
From which immediately leaps out
A Dog, and yelping runs about.

The Dog is not of mountain breed;
Its motions, too, are wild and shy;
With something, as the Shepherd thinks,
Unusual in its cry:
Nor is there any one in sight
All round, in Hollow or on Height;
Nor shout, nor whistle strikes his ear;
What is the creature doing here?

It was a Cove, a huge Recess,
That keeps, till June, December's snow;
A lofty precipice in front,
A silent tarn below!
Far in the bosom of Helvellyn,
Remote from public road or dwelling,
Pathway, or cultivated land;
From trace of human foot or hand.

There sometimes does a leaping Fish
Send through the Tarn a lonely chear;
The Crags repeat the Raven's croak,
In symphony austere;
Thither the Rainbow comes, the Cloud
And Mists that spread the flying shroud;
And Sun-beams; and the sounding blast,
That, if could, would hurry past;
But that enormous Barrier holds it fast.

Not knowing what to think, a while
The Shepherd stood; then makes his way
Towards the Dog, o'er rocks and stones,
As quickly as he may;
Nor far had gone before he found
A human skeleton on the ground;
Sad sight! The Shepherd with a sigh
Looks round, to learn the history.

From those abrupt and perilous rocks
The Man had fallen, that place of fear!
At length upon the Shepherd's mind
It breaks, and all is clear:
He instantly recall'd the name,
And who he was, and whence he came;
Remember'd, too, the very day
On which the traveller pass'd this way.

But hear a wonder now, for sake
Of which this mournful Tale I tell!
A lasting monument of words
This wonder merits well.
The Dog, which still was hovering nigh,
Repeating the same timid cry,
This Dog, had been through three month's space
A Dweller in that savage place.

Yes, proof was plain that, since that day
On which the Traveller thus had died,
The Dog had watch'd about the spot,
Or by his Master's side:
How nourish'd here through such long time
He knows who gave the love sublime,
And gave that strength of feeling, great
Above all human estimate.

As well as these poetic memorials to Charles Gough, a physical memorial to him was erected at the top of the path from Striding Edge to Helvellyn in 1890. Its inscription reads as follows:

BENEATH THIS SPOT WERE FOUND IN 1805
THE REMAINS OF CHARLES GOUGH
KILLED BY A FALL FROM THE ROCKS
HIS DOG WAS STILL GUARDING HIS SKELETON.
WALTER SCOTT DESCRIBES THE EVENT IN THE POEM
I CLIMBED THE DARK BROW OF THE MIGHTY HELLVELLYN.

WORDSWORTH RECORDS IT IN HIS LINES ON
FIDELITY WHICH CONCLUDES AS FOLLOWS:

THE DOG, WHICH STILL WAS HOVERING NIGH,
REPEATING THE SAME TIMID CRY,
THIS DOG, HAD BEEN THROUGH THREE MONTH'S SPACE
A DWELLER IN THAT SAVAGE PLACE.

YES, PROOF WAS PLAIN THAT, SINCE THE DAY
WHEN THIS ILL-FATED TRAVELLER DIED,
THE DOG HAD WATCHED ABOUT THE SPOT,
OR BY HIS MASTER'S SIDE:
HOW NOURISHED HERE THROUGH SUCH LONG TIME
HE KNOWS, WHO GAVE THAT LOVE SUBLIME,
AND GAVE THAT STRENGTH OF FEELING, GREAT
ABOVE ALL HUMAN ESTIMATE.

Not only did the fate of Charles Gough and his faithful dog inspire Wordsworth and Scott to verse, this tragedy has inspired a number of writers to put pen to paper including Canon Hardwicke Rawnsley and Richard Adams, author of *The Plague Dogs* (1977). A number of artists such as Sir Edwin Landseer,

Above: The memorial to Gough on Helvellyn

Right: Sir Edwin Landseer's painting of the Gough story.

Francis Danby, Richard Westall and Sam Bough, were moved to give their own interpretations. Indeed, so great was the literary and artistic response to this tragedy that in January 2003 the Wordsworth Trust mounted an exhibition at Grasmere, entitled 'The Unfortunate Tourist of Helvellyn and his Faithful Dog'. A book bearing the same title was published to coincide with the exhibition.

As I toiled up Helvellyn in the drizzling rain and stood for a while contemplating the hapless Gough and his memorial, my thoughts turned to the anglers of today and how easy it is to reach their favourite waters. The Hampshire Avon, Rutland Water, the Spey, even distant places like Alaska or the Kola Peninsula are all easily reached by modern transport. How far removed from the days of Charles Gough, when fishing his favourite water involved a solitary hike over one of England's highest peaks, yet, how alike also, in our quest for that ever elusive place that will fulfil our angling dreams!

11

John Wilson
THE FISHING PROFESSOR

In many ways, John Wilson was the forerunner of the many thousands of people who flock to the Lake District each year to enjoy outdoor pursuits. Wilson was a powerful, larger than life character who loved to ride, row, hunt, shoot, fish, walk and even wrestle. He was also blessed with a sharp intellect and was a great admirer of Wordsworth's poetry. He was an accomplished poet himself and, writing under the pseudonym of 'Christopher North', he contributed many articles to the popular *Blackwood's Magazine.*

Although he spent considerable time in the Lake District, Wilson was actually born in Paisley on the 18th of May, 1785, the son of a wealthy gauze manufacturer who died when John was only eleven years old. He was the fourth child, but the eldest son, and had nine brothers and sisters. In her *Memoir* of her father, published in 1862, Mrs Gordon gives us a fascinating glimpse into his childhood and of his early preoccupation with angling:

In his childish years John Wilson was as beautiful and animated a creature as ever played in the sunshine. That passion for sports, and especially angling, in which his strong nature found such characteristic vent in after years, was developed at an age when most little boys are still hardly safe beyond the nurse's apron strings. He was but three years old when he rambled off one day armed with a willow-wand, duly furnished with a thread line and crooked pin, to fish the 'wee burnie', of which he had taken note, away a good mile from home. Unknown to anyone, already appreciating the fascination of an undisturbed and solitary 'cast', the blue-eyed and golden-haired adventurer sallied forth to the waterside to spend a day of unforgotten delight, lashing away at the rippling stream.

In his *Recreations of Christopher North,* published in 1842, Wilson vividly recalls the excitement engendered by his first fish, still fresh in his mind years after its capture. It is a passage that will trigger similar reminiscences from thousands of anglers, as they recall that first step on the road to an all-consuming pastime.

A tug - a tug! With face ten times flushed and pale by turns ere you could count ten, he at last has strength, in the agitation of his fear and joy, to pull away at the monster - and there he lies in his beauty among the gowans and the greensward, for he has whapped him right over his head and far away, a fish a quarter of an ounce in weight, and, at the very least, two inches long! Off he flies, on wings of wind, to his father, mother, and sisters, and brothers, and cousins, and all the neighbourhood, holding the fish aloft in both hands, still fearful of its escape, and, like a genuine child of corruption, his eyes brighten at the first blush of cold blood on his small fumy fingers. He carries about with him, upstairs and downstairs, his prey upon a plate: he will not wash his hands before dinner, for he exults in the silver scales adhering to the thumb-nail that scooped the pin out of the baggy's maw.

Following on from his education at the local school in Paisley, Wilson was sent to the neighbouring parish of Mearns to continue his education under the guidance of the Rev. George

M'Latchie. One of his fellow pupils, Sir John Maxwell Pollok, gives us a fascinating glimpse into Wilson's early angling prowess:

He was above me in the ranks of the school, in stature, and mental acquirements. I may mention as an illustration of the energy, activity, and vivacity of his character, that one morning, I having been permitted to go and fish in the burn near the kirk, and having caught a fine trout, was so pleased, that I repaired to the minister's study to exhibit my prize to Dr. M'Latchie, who was then reading Greek with him. He, seeing my trout, started up and addressing his reverend teacher said, 'I must go now to fish.' Leave was granted, and I willingly resigned to him my rod and line; and before dinner he reappeared with a large dish of fish, on which he and his companions feasted, not without that admiration of his achievement which youth delights to express and always feels.

(*Memoir of Christopher North* BY MRS GORDON, 1862)

One further incident from his childhood years is worth recalling since it gives further insight into the character and stamina of the young John Wilson. One morning, at sunrise, he went off to a distant loch to check on a night-line he had baited and look at a trap he had set for a glede (a kite). As he was making his way home, carrying over his shoulder an eel as long as himself, he was overtaken by a moorland mist in which he lost his way. The mist turned into a storm, complete with thunder and lightning. Several hours later, when the sun had returned, a couple of servants from the manse, who had been sent out to find his dead body, found him very much alive but soaked to the skin. After a hot whisky-toddy with brown sugar, he was bundled off to bed by way of punishment!

At the early age of twelve he entered Glasgow University, where he studied under the renowned George Jardine, professor of Greek and Logic. He remained at Glasgow for six years, during which time he lived with the professor and his family. During his time at Glasgow, he met and fell in love with a young woman, Margaret Fletcher. In 1803, he went up to Magdalen College, Oxford, where he was not only a brilliant student but also excelled at sports. One of his most remarkable feats at Oxford was to leap across the river Cherwell, for which he won a wager of one hundred sovereigns (an enormous sum of money in those days). Wilson was also renowned for his pugilistic skills, as the following incident from his daughter's *Memoir* records:

Meeting one day with a rough and unruly wayfarer, who showed inclination to pick a quarrel, concerning right of passage across a certain bridge, the fellow obstructed the way, and making himself decidedly obnoxious, Wilson lost all patience, and offered to fight him. The man made no objection to the proposal, but replied that he had better not fight with him, as he was so and so, mentioning the name of a (then not unknown) pugilist. This statement had, as may be supposed, no effect in damping the belligerent intentions of the Oxonian; he knew his own strength, and his skill too. In one moment off went his coat, and he set upon his antagonist in splendid style. The astonished and punished rival, on recovering from his blows and surprise, accosted him thus: "You can only be one of the two; you are either Jack Wilson or the Devil." This encounter, no doubt, led, for a short time, to fraternity and equality over a pot of porter.

Although he graduated from Oxford with a first-class degree and was the first to receive the Newdigate Prize for Poetry, his time there was not altogether a happy one since his sweetheart Margaret had eloped to New York with his younger brother, Charles.

In 1807, at the age of twenty-two, Wilson concluded his university career and bought an estate overlooking Windermere at Elleray on the slopes of Orrest Head, where he soon set about enlarging the cottage. (When his father had died in 1796, Wilson had inherited a large fortune amounting to £50,000.) It was during the same year that Wilson first met the poet Wordsworth, who at that time was living at Allan Bank in Grasmere, and the two of them soon struck up a lasting friendship. Life at Elleray proved idyllic and Wilson was able to indulge his passion for poetry and outdoor recreations, as well as cultivating the society of the Lakes Poets: Wordsworth, Southey and Coleridge.

The cottage at Elleray.

In the summer of 1809, Wilson organised a week-long angling excursion for his friends among the mountains and tarns of Lakeland, which he later recalled in a poem entitled, *The Angler's Tent*, published in 1825. Among the gentlemen of the party was Wilson himself, Wordsworth, De Quincey, Alexander Blair and several others. The whole party consisted of thirty-two, ten of whom were servants brought along to look after the tents and baggage necessary for a week's sojourn in the mountains. The tent with its furniture was carried by twelve ponies. After passing through Eskdale, they headed on to Wastwater, setting up camp at Wasdale Head. During the days that followed the various members of the party pursued their sport in the neighbouring becks and lakes, meeting up again in the evening.

Wastwater.

On the first Sunday (a day of rest from angling), while encamped at Wasdale Head, some of the local inhabitants, together with people from neighbouring valleys, came to visit the strangers in their tent. It was a beautiful evening and a wonderful time was had by all. At a late hour the guests departed with much mirth and singing as they made their way up the surrounding mountains under the light of a refulgent moon. The images and feelings of those few happy days and especially that delightful evening, Wilson has preserved for posterity in his poem, *The Angler's Tent*.

The poem itself is far too long to quote in full and, unfortunately, contains little of angling interest. However, it does convey the sense of joy and pleasure at spending a whole week under canvas amidst the remote lakes and mountains:

> *Seven lovely days had like a happy dream*
> *Died in our spirits silently away,*
> *Since Grasmere, walking to the morning ray,*
> *Met our last lingering look with farewell gleam.*
> *I may not tell what joy our being filled,*
> *Wand'ring like shadows over plain and steep.*
> *What beauteous visions lonely souls can build*
> *When 'mid the mountain solitude they sleep.*

A little later in the poem he gives us a glimpse inside the tent, which he refers to as a 'bower', strewn with the anglers' equipment:

> *Within that bower are strewn in careless guise,*
> *Idle one day, the angler's simple gear;*
> *Lines that, as fine as floating gossamer,*
> *Dropt softly on the stream the silken flies;*
> *The limber rod that shook its trembling length,*
> *Almost as airy as the line it threw,*
> *Yet often bending in an arch of strength*
> *When the tired salmon rose at last to view.*

Nowadays, a tent or two at Wasdale Head would scarcely raise an eyebrow, but in the early nineteenth century it must have presented an unusual sight and news of it soon spread among the country-folk:

Then did we learn that our stranger tent,
Seen by the lake-side gleaming like a sail,
Had quickly spread o'er mountain and o'er vale,
A gentle shock of pleased astonishment.

Within a short space of time the tent was surrounded by a merry band of curious locals, dressed in their Sunday finery:

And thus our tent a joyous scene became,
Where loving hearts from distant vales did meet
As at some rural festival, and greet
Each other with glad voice and kindly name.

Wilson and his party welcomed the visitors with open arms and regaled them with stories:

Happy were we among such happy hearts!
And to inspire with kindliness and love
Our simple guests, ambitiously we strove,
With novel converse and endearing arts!
We talk'd to them, and much they loved to hear,
Of those sweet vales from which we late had come;

For though these vales are to each other near,
Seldom do dalesmen leave their own dear home:
Then would we speak of many a wondrous sight
Seen in great cities, - temple, tower, and spire,
And winding streets at night-fall blazing bright
With many a star-like lamp of glimmering fire.

Not only did Wilson and his friends regale them with their stories, they were generous with their wine, too. The children of the party were fascinated by the angling equipment lying around the tent, the like of which they had never seen before. One child, bolder than the rest and despite the protestations of his parents, dared to touch some of the 'tempting treasures'. As a result, the kindly anglers gave the children a few of their flies 'to use with caution'.

All good things come to an end and, all too soon, it was time for the guests to depart back to their remote hamlets and farmsteads, which they did with many a backward glance:

Backward they gazed, as slowly they withdrew,
With step reluctant, from the water-side;
And oft, with waving hand, at distance tried
Through the dim light to send a last adieu!

Following his extravagant angling excursion, Wilson returned to Elleray and continued to live the life of a country squire. Not only did he enjoy angling, he also kept a small fleet of boats on Windermere, which kept several boatmen employed. His favourite boatman was a man called Billy Balmer, with whom Wilson had several adventures, one of which nearly resulted in the loss of their lives. One stormy December night, with the snow falling fast, Wilson was tempted to venture out on Windermere. Setting off with Billy from Miller-ground, they steered a course for Bowness. Soon, darkness enveloped them and they lost their way completely. Eventually, they managed to find a landing place and, half-frozen, spent the night by a blazing fire in

After angling, cock-fighting was a favourite pastime of John Wilson. Print by Henry Thomas Alken.

the cottage of the toll keeper on the Ambleside road. In addition to boating, Wilson was passionate about cock-fighting, an interest he had cultivated at Oxford and at Elleray he bred game-cocks. According to his daughter, he took great care over the breeding and training of his fighting cocks, to such an extent that his birds gained a formidable reputation throughout the district, his favoured bird being 'Lord Derby'.

About the same time that Wilson settled at Elleray, a family by the name of Penny, who had made their fortune in the slave trade, took up their abode at Gale House, Ambleside and it was not long before Wilson became acquainted with one of the daughters, Miss Jane Penny. The romance blossomed and they were married in May 1811.

The couple lived happily at Elleray for four years until calamity overtook them. Most of his fortune was lost by the dishonest speculation of an uncle, in whose hands Wilson had placed it, and he was compelled to seek gainful employment. Although he did not give up Elleray, he went to live with his mother in Edinburgh, where he trained as an advocate, being elected to the Faculty of Advocates in 1815. He did not, however, find the law to his taste and soon took up writing, becoming the principal writer for *Blackwood's Magazine*, as well as publishing volumes of poetry.

Towards the end of 1819, Wilson with his wife and, by now, five children, left his mother's house and set up home in Ann Street. The following year, with the help of a glowing testimonial from Sir Walter Scott, he was elected to the chair of Moral Philosophy at the University of Edinburgh. He proved to be an excellent choice for the post and was much revered by his students. For the last thirty years or so of his life he divided his time between Edinburgh and Elleray.

Not long after his appointment as a professor, he devised a fly for lake and sea trout, which became known as The Professor. An interesting story is told concerning his invention of this fly. One day, while Wilson was fishing a loch on which the trout were rising freely, he ran out of flies. Having just a few hooks and some silk with him, he devised a fly with buttercups for the body and leaves and bits of dried grass for the wings and hackle. Much to his amazement he caught fish with this improvised pattern and, on returning home, he tied the fly again in a more durable form. In its final form the fly consisted of a tail of red ibis, a body of yellow silk, light brown mallard wings and a natural red cock's hackle. The tail is sometimes omitted. In addition to the Professor, Wilson and his brother James are credited with the creation of another fly, the Queen of the Water. This fly is similar to the Professor except for the body, which is orange and a palmered red hackle. Both of these flies proved popular in America as well as the United Kingdom.

Apart from *The Angler's Tent*, much of what we know of his fishing in the Lake District comes from a review he wrote, published in *Blackwood's Magazine* in May, 1834 of Stephen Oliver's, *Scenes and Recollections of Fly-Fishing in Northumberland, Cumberland and Westmorland* (see Chapter 12).

He modestly claims that he was not a great angler and he was certainly no fly-fishing purist. He considers the river Eamont around Dalemain to be one of the most beautiful streams in the world but it never fulfilled his expectations, except once, when he killed a creelful of herring-sized trout with salmon roe as bait. However, he is full of praise for Ullswater:

Ullswater.

But of all the lakes there is none comparable to Ullswater - we mean to the angler - and perhaps we may add, to the painter. Some dozen years ago, an annual party of gentlemen from Manchester - and eke from Liverpool - used to make bloody work with the May-fly - with the green and the grey drakes. That was, of course, pretty early in the season; but we have slain our scores all the summer through, on all sorts of days, with all sorts of flies - sometimes from the shore - up to the arm-pits - for there is beautiful wading - sometimes in a boat, with mine host himself at the oars - and skilfully did he let us drift by deep and shallow. Did ever a man so corpulent handle a landing-net with such nicety and precision? Ah! what is become of that broad brown face with its beaming smile, to which we have known a shy trout rise, supposing it to be the sun coming out of a cloud!

In all of the North he claims there is no better beck for worm fishing than the Deeble:

. . . but you must use a stiffish rod, and a short stout line, for you have to lift the pounders and the half-pounders perpendicularly out of pools that go plumb-down into a darksome depth - over your head alder or

birch-trees, and you often crash your way through the hazels, starting from her nest the soon-returning linnet.

We learn that Hayeswater is the favourite tarn of his friends from Ambleside and that its trout are the size of herrings, but far more delicious than herrings. He even recalls them sizzling in the pan, as the landlady of an inn at the foot of Kirkstone, turns them lightly over with her knife in the buttered meal. However, all anglers have their off days when the fish refuse to cooperate and such was the case when he fished Haweswater and the river Lowther with his friend, William Garnet. On their return to the inn in which they were staying, they happened to look over a bridge and spied a large trout below sucking in insects. Temptation got the better of them:

. . . putting a snood over his head, we whisked him into the upper air like winking, and then 'we popped un in a bag, ma boys - and yoited off to town'.

From the river Cocker between its source and Buttermere he claims to have taken fine trout after a flood but at other times no sport worth the name is to be found there. Between Buttermere and Crummock Water he has taken some noble 'Crummockers' with minnow and worm. Between Crummock Water and the village of Lorton the angling is good but difficult. Of the trout in Red Tarn he is rather scathing:

. . . the trouts in Red Tarn are curiosities - soft as butter, black as tar, weak as water, and apparently, in spite of their names, descended from an original cross - mules in this instance breeding - between an eel and a frog.

Ennerdale is one of the quietest and least frequented lakes and, according to Wilson, afforded some prime angling. He recommended hiring a boat from the man who lived in a cottage halfway down the lake, who was also an excellent guide. The lake still provides good trout fishing for today's angler. He is full of praise for the trout of Devoke Water – 'you may kill but few, perhaps none, but then those few!' Windermere fishes well in the May-fly season and its trout are magnificent. The pike of Rydal Water are like sharks but you require permission to fish from the Lady of the Hall and the boat in the boat-house is chained to the stone by an inexorable lock!

Although he spent a great deal of time fishing in the Lake District, Wilson, being a Scotsman by birth, felt that the fishing did not bear comparison with that to be found north of the border:

The truth is, that there is what we, Christopher [his pseudonym] *and a Scotchman, call first-rate angling in few, if any, of the dear English lakes. But a first-rate angler may have a first-rate day's amusement in almost any one of them, if chance, fortune, fate, and all the elements happen, at some felicitous conjuncture, all to favour him.*

Buttermere.

Despite his reservations concerning the quality of its angling, John Wilson continued to visit the Lakes until his death in Edinburgh on the 3rd of April, 1854, and even as he lay dying, his thoughts turned to angling and the mountain streams he so loved. Propped up with pillows, he surrounded himself with his fishing tackle and carefully picked out flies from his pocket-book while recounting to those assembled by his bed stories of his bygone angling adventures. A statue to his memory was erected in Princes Street Gardens, Edinburgh, in 1865.

12

Stephen Oliver
AN ANGLING TOUR OF THE LAKELAND HILLS

Although tourism in the Lake District started to develop in the second half of the eighteenth century, it wasn't until 1847, when the railway line to Windermere was opened, that the Lake District became accessible to the wider public. Originally, it was planned to extend the line to Ambleside, at the head of the lake, but the plan was dropped since it was felt there would not be enough demand to meet the expenditure. A railway line to Lakeside was opened in 1869, which was linked to two steamers on the lake, giving the tourist access to other parts of Windermere.

However, even before the coming of the railway, a little book entitled *Scenes and Recollections of Fly-Fishing in Northumberland, Cumberland and Westmorland,* was published in 1834 with the express purpose of giving advice to the angler wishing to visit the Lake District. The book, written under the pseudonym of 'Stephen Oliver', takes the reader on an angling tour of the Lake District hills. This is an important book since it is the first work to deal extensively with fishing in the Lake District.

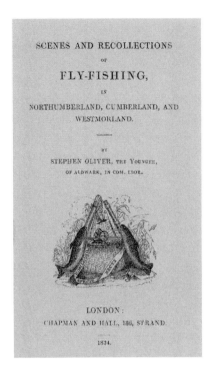

The author's real name was William Andrew Chatto, who was born on 17th April, 1799, in Newcastle. The author's father was a merchant and, after education at the local grammar school, William followed in his father's footsteps and became a merchant. Around 1830, he acquired the business of his cousin, a wholesale tea-dealer, in Eastcheap, London. Four years later, he relinquished his business interests and embarked on a writing career. *Scenes and Recollections* was his first book to be published, followed a year later by *Rambles in Northumberland, and on the Scottish Borders*. In 1836, writing under the pseudonym of 'P. Fisher', he wrote *The Angler's Souvenir*. All three books are now very much sought after by angling book collectors. From 1839 to 1841 he edited the *New Sporting Magazine*. Also in 1839 he was elected an honorary member of the Antiquarian Society of Newcastle-on-Tyne. He died in the Charterhouse, London, on 28th February, 1864, and was buried in Highgate cemetery.

Stephen Oliver (I shall use his pseudonym) was a keen fly fisher and, although not a purist, was scornful of coarse fishing. One of the characters in *Scenes and Recollections* states that, if he had the misfortune to live in London, he would give up angling altogether! He recommends that, in the height of summer, the South-country angler should make an angling tour of the hills of Cumberland and Westmorland. Before embarking on his tour he recommends that the angler should make his way to York, either by the mail, post-coach, or in his own carriage. From York the tour is to be made in stages, the first stage being to Kendal.

Stage One - York to Kendal

At York he advises the angler to dismiss his retinue and to forward his travelling trunk to Kendal. The trunk should contain a few extra shirts and Wordsworth's poems, except for the volume he is currently reading. With regard to the angler's attire he recommends a plain brown or dark green coat, in the style of a shooting jacket, trousers of a colour that will not show up stains of mud or clay, lamb's wool stockings, short gaiters and a pair of stout walking shoes. He should carry an extra shirt and pair of stockings in his creel. The angler's coat and trousers should be made of cloth that is not too thick or heavy, since they will dry sooner when wet. He warns against velveteens, fustians and moleskin since, if the angler needs to swim a mile or two, they would prove too heavy when wet. It seems that Oliver was accustomed to swim across Ullswater or Bassenthwaite to avoid a long journey by road! The angler might also consider wearing a cork jacket (such as life-boat men used to wear) to access any part of a lake to enjoy his sport. It seems that float-tubing is not a new idea!

With regards to fishing tackle, lines and flies should be stowed in the creel. The rod should be jointed and equipped with a strap for slinging over the shoulder. A good stick, which can be fitted with a screw-in gaff, completes the outfit.

From York the angler is advised to make his way to Masham, where he might take a grayling in the Ure. After visiting the ruins of Jervaulx Abbey he should proceed to Sedbergh via Askrigg, making a detour to Aysgarth Falls. From there he recommends fishing down Garsdale en route to Sedbergh. The river Lune, which flows about a mile west of the town, formed the boundary between Yorkshire and Westmorland. Oliver regards it as an excellent trout stream and suggests that the angler fishes down it to Kirkby Lonsdale.

For fly fishing in the Lake District Oliver recommends that the angler should fish fine, with a cast consisting of a single stout hair (presumably horse hair) at the end. Where larger fish might

Fishing on the Ure at Aysgarth.

be expected he suggests using gut in preference to hair. The angler should never use more than two flies on his cast, with the dropper being two and a half to three feet from the point fly. His favourite flies include: a small yellow mayfly, the grey-drake, a wren's tail and a grouse hackle fly. If the fish are rather sullen and not rising to the fly a gentle (maggot) on the point of the hook might produce some sport. After a shower, when the water starts to fine down, fishing with a small worm at the tail of a pool will often tempt a fish or two. However, should the angler start catching eels on the worm, he should move immediately since he will not catch trout where eels are present as they drive the former away.

After exercising his skill on the Lune, he recommends the angler to walk over to Kendal for a change of clothes and forward his trunk to Keswick.

Stage Two - Kendal to Keswick

From Kendal the angler should take the Carlisle coach as far as Shap, sixteen miles north. However, before leaving he ought to stock up with brandlings and gentles from one of the numerous tan-yards in the town. After visiting the ruins of Shap Abbey the angler will find good sport on the Lowther, which should be fished down to Askham. From Askham it is only a short journey to Pooley Bridge, at the foot of Ullswater, where the angler will find a good inn. Oliver regarded Ullswater as exceeding both Windermere and Derwentwater in the lonely grandeur of its scenery and he recalls how he was once on the lake when a thunderstorm arose. Should that happen to the angler, he has this advice:

Let him directly lay in his oars, that nothing may divert his mind from the contemplation of the scene; composing himself in the stern-sheets of the boat, with his eye bent on the dark thunder-cloud which hides the peak of Helvellyn, let him, amidst the conflict of the elements, wonder and adore . . .

Stramongate Bridge at Kendal.

Oliver mentions in passing that Ullswater contains a species of trout which very much resembles a charr and that they are potted and sold as charr. In fact, in Oliver's day in the early part of the nineteenth century, Ullswater *did* contain charr. John Watson, writing in 1899, claims that:

A century ago charr were common in Ulswater. At some time subsequent to this they steadily declined; until about twenty years ago they became practically extinct. There is little doubt but that this result was principally brought about by pollution from the Greenside lead mines.

With regards to the river Eamont, which flows out of Ullswater, Oliver states that its trout are not generally large, but it is possible to take around a score of fish between Pooley Bridge and Tirril, weighing from ten to twelve ounces, when the water is rather high. Interred in the Friends' Burial Ground at Tirril are the remains of Charles Gough, the hapless angler who perished in the hills on the way to fish Wythburn (see Chapter 10). After fishing the Eamont the angler should make his way to Keswick, situated just north of Derwentwater, and a short distance from

Fishing on Ullswater.

Bassenthwaite Lake. Although Derwentwater contained pike, trout and perch, Oliver considered it too much fished to afford much amusement to the angler. In those days the lake was infested by scoundrels who fished with laths and otter-boards.

Although he was a great admirer of Wordsworth, Oliver was less enamoured of the poetry of Southey, as the following tale of an evening spent at a friend's house in Keswick makes clear:

The writer was sitting in a friend's garden one evening, when he heard a strange discordant noise at the foot of the lake, which he mistook for the evening tattoo of a bittern, till he was informed that it proceeded from Mr. Southey, who was thus exercising his vocal powers, at a somewhat loud pitch, for the benefit of his health . . .

According to Oliver the best fishing around Keswick is on the river Derwent before it enters the lake of the same name and, after passing through Bassenthwaite, contains large trout weighing from two to five pounds, which require stronger tackle. After a few days sojourn in Keswick, presumably to change shirt and stockings, the angler is recommended to dispatch his trunk to Ambleside or Bowness.

Stage Three - Keswick to Bowness and Ambleside

From Keswick the angler should proceed up Borrowdale and over the hills to Buttermere, which Oliver regards as one of the best fishing stations in the Lake District. As well as Buttermere and Crummock Water, which both contain trout, charr, pike and perch he recommends the angler to fish the river Cocker, which issues out of Crummock Water and flows through the Lorton Vale before joining the Derwent at Cockermouth. Should the angler wish to fish for salmon or salmon-trout (sea trout) he suggests fishing the Derwent below Cockermouth to Workington, where it enters the sea. However, he is rather dismissive of salmon fishing:

*Though perhaps as many salmon and salmon-trouts are taken in the
Derwent by the rod and fly as in most rivers in England, yet salmon fishing in this river is but a dull recreation after all; and he ought to be
endowed with an extraordinary portion of patience who professes it exclusively. When fishing in a river frequented by salmon, it may be well
enough to try a salmon fly now and then; but it seems scarcely worth
the while of an amateur fisher to try a whole day for a single bite, and
sometimes not that, and at the end of a month's diligent angling to be
only able to give an account of half a dozen fish which in strictness are
entitled to the name of salmon.*

I must admit to sharing some empathy with Oliver's views of
salmon fishing. Although I caught my largest salmon to date, a
fish of 16½lb, on the Derwent, I have also flogged away for days
on end on the same river for not even a pull! Oliver complains
of gangs of poachers both on the Derwent and on the Eden who
kill salmon at the back end of the year for the sake of the roe,
which they sell for bait to 'pseudo-anglers' for five to eight
shillings a pound. He claims that roe from poached Derwent
salmon is employed as bait in the Annan, the Tweed, the Wharfe,
and Driffield Beck.

Oliver cannot leave Buttermere without recounting the story
of Mary Robinson, the maid of Buttermere:

*In the autumn of 1802, Keswick and the peaceful vale of Buttermere
were visited by a plausible swindler of the name of Hatfield, who assumed
the name of the Honourable Col. Hope, then member of Parliament for
Dumfriesshire, and in that character married an interesting girl, - afterwards so much spoken of as Mary of Buttermere, - the daughter of the
person who kept the inn there (The Fish Inn). After figuring in the above
character for two or three months, though not without suspicion of his
being an impostor, the fraud was detected and exposed by a gentleman
of the name of Hardinge, to whom Col. Hope was personally known. On
this discovery Hatfield made his escape, but was soon afterwards taken
and sent to Carlisle, where he was convicted of forgery, and hung,
pursuant to his sentence, on 3rd September, 1803.*

The coach from Keswick to Bowness. Photograph by Alfred Pettitt.

It transpires that Hatfield was not only a forger but also a bigamist. He even claimed to be an angler who boasted of his fishing exploits in the Scottish Highlands. However, it appears that in the vale of Buttermere he used a rod 'like an arrant bungler', which led the curate of Buttermere to suspect that he might be an impostor long before the truth came out.

From Buttermere Oliver advises the angler to hire a guide and head off over the hills to Wastwater, 'one of the most retired and seldom-visited of all the lakes'. Wastwater and the river Irt, which issues from it, contain trout. Nowadays, it would not be possible for the angler to follow in Oliver's footsteps and fish in England's deepest lake since Wastwater is owned by the National Trust and fishing is no longer permitted. Should the angler wish to spend a few days fishing the Mite and the Esk, both of which afford good fishing, he will find a good country inn at Ravenglass.

After fishing in the vicinity of Ravenglass, the angler should make his way to Broughton and thence via Seathwaite to Coniston, fishing the Duddon along the way. The scenery of the Duddon Valley above Seathwaite sends the author into raptures:

*Above Seathwaite, in the solitude of grey crags and russet hills, where no
sound is heard save the fall of the river, and where no wealthy trader's
fantastic mansion mars the simplicity and grandeur of the scene, Nature
speaks with a sweetly solemn voice to the heart and to the imagination
of her children.*

With regards to Coniston, much loved by that other Lakeland
angler, Arthur Ransome, the author is rather dismissive. He
admits that it contains excellent charr but affords only indiffer-
ent angling. From Coniston he advises the angler to proceed by
way of Hawkshead to Esthwaite, which contains pike, perch and
trout, and 'affords better sport to the angler than either of the
larger lakes in the vicinity' (Coniston and Windermere). This
statement still rings true today. Esthwaite is now run as a commercial trout fishery and is stocked with hard-fighting rainbow
trout, which in turn provide a ready meal for the resident pike,
which grow exceedingly large. The road from Esthwaite takes
the angler to Far Sawrey, where he can take the ferry across Windermere to Bowness. Oliver recommends spending a few days at
Bowness, occasionally trying for a pike, before taking a boat to
Low Wood and walking to Ambleside to fish the Brathay. One
final duty is required of the angler before he commences his
homeward journey - a visit to the poet Wordsworth at Grasmere!

The Windermere ferry.

Final Stage - Ambleside to Kendal And York

Farewell lovely lakes and sparkling streams! Your purity is unsullied by no drains from a crowded factory, where man weaves the web of his own misery and degradation, and where the bud of childhood is blighted ere it be blown . . .

With that fond lament, the angler boards the coach for Kendal, from where he may continue his route to York by way of Settle and Malham Cove, thus completing his angling tour.

13

John Beever
A VERY PRACTICAL ANGLER

In 1849, a slim little volume was published, entitled *Practical Fly-Fishing: Founded on Nature*. Its author, who wrote under the pseudonym 'Arundo' (meaning a 'reed' in Latin), was John Beever of Coniston. The book gives instructions for dressing the most useful flies for trout and grayling, together with instructions for making fly-rods. The book's sub-title claims that the information contained within was based on the author's forty years' experience of fishing in various parts of the United Kingdom.

John Beever was born in 1795, the son of William Beever, a Manchester cotton merchant. On his father's retirement from business the family moved to Birdsgrove, near Ashbourne in Derbyshire, where the young John spent his formative years. From an early age he developed an interest in natural history and became an ardent sportsman and fisherman. Around 1810 he was taken under the wing of Frank Ogden, a Matlock chaise driver, who taught him the finer points of fly fishing. Ogden was an excellent fly dresser who taught his young ward to obey nature's laws and to observe closely the real flies upon which the fish were feeding and to imitate them. Beever describes their first encounter at Cromford Bridge on the river Derwent:

Let no learner despair, or think to himself, I shall never be a fly-fisher; I shall never return home with a basket full of fish. Depend upon it, you will. Industry, neatness, and perseverance, will do anything.

I was standing on the margin of the broad and beautiful pool, below the bridge at Cromford; the flies were on the water; the fish were rising; but I could take nothing.

A brisk and cheerful little man jumped over the wall, and came to me in his shirt sleeves, with a fly-rod in his hand. It was Frank, the chaise-driver of Matlock, one of the nicest and best fishers in England - always true to his colours. And what was better, one of Nature's gentlemen. I showed him the fish I had been throwing at, and he took them. Then he showed me his flies, and kindly told me what they were, and pointed out their resemblance to those which I had seen upon the water.

I followed him for some time, to watch him fish, and to ask from him such information as occurrences suggested, which he kindly gave me; and I have never desponded since.

Cromford Bridge on the river Derwent.

The youthful Beever proved to be an excellent pupil and carried out his master's principles for over forty years in frequent visits to Scotland, Wales and even France, as well as the Lakes and Derbyshire. Not only did Frank Ogden pass on his skills to the young John Beever but also to his own son, James Ogden, a pioneer of the dry fly and friend of Alfred Ronalds, who set up as a fishing tackle maker in Cheltenham. James Ogden was also an accomplished fly dresser who wrote *Ogden on Fly Tying* (1879), an influential work, now highly collectable.

In 1827, the Beever family moved to Thwaite House at Coniston, a beautiful property overlooking Waterhead at the northern end of the lake and halfway between Coniston village and Brantwood, the home of John Ruskin. Four years later, in 1831, William Beever died. Following his father's death, John remained at Coniston with his elder sister, Anne, and three younger sisters, Mary, Margaret and Susanna. Their mother had died when the children were quite young. Their brother, Henry, became a solicitor in Manchester, but died in 1840. At Thwaite House they lived a simple country life and, while his sisters pursued their interests in the botany of the area, John became increasingly interested in ichthyology and built a pond at the back of the house where he could study the growth and habits of fish. This pond, which was formed by damming a rill flowing down from Guards Wood, was stocked with various species of fish. Once a year he would catch the fish and examine their growth.

The pond not only enabled Beever to study the habits of fish, it also served as a reservoir for a water-wheel, which drove a lathe in the loft of the coach-house. He put the lathe to good use by turning all sorts of useful items, including the fishing rod described in his book. With the help of William Bell, a young local joiner, he built a printing press on which he printed the little books written by his sister, Susanna. In addition, he printed texts and tickets for the local Sunday school.

His *Practical Fly-Fishing* proved to be his only literary venture. W. G. Collingwood, the assistant of John Ruskin and author of *The Lake Counties* (1902), described the book as 'the results of a ripe experience noted down without affectation or ambition of style or system'. In his book Beever stresses the importance of observing the flies on the water and imitating them as closely as possible. All too often fly fishers lack confidence in their obser-vation of the fly life, especially on a water they have never fished before, and are sucked into buying flies from a local supplier:

The great majority of fishers have no confidence in their own flies, when off their usual beat. Perhaps they travel four or five hundred miles to a river, and see upon the water half a dozen kinds of flies, the very coun-terparts of those seen near home at the same time of year. Instead of beginning to fish with confidence, how do they act? They send for some tailor, cobbler, or superannuated keeper, who tells them that they have not in their whole stock a fly worth a bawbee.

What are they to do? - He can sell them some which will kill. The fisher generally falls into this trap.

The majority of the book is taken up with a list of thirty artifi-cial flies, together with their dressings and advice on when to use them. The list is the mainstay of Derbyshire and Lake District patterns, many of which date back to the beginning of the nineteenth century or even earlier. Not surprisingly, perhaps, many of the flies listed appear in W. Aldam's, *A Quaint Treatise on 'Flees and the Art a' Artyficiall Flee Making'*, which, although it was published in 1876, is derived from a manuscript dating to the early years of the nineteenth century, written by an old man who fished the Derbyshire streams. Beever singles out a number of flies of particular interest to the Lake District fisherman. These include: the Black Caterpillar, the Bracken Clock and the Black Ant.

He recommends that the Black Caterpillar be dressed in two sizes, small and large. The smaller fly he recommends for stream fishing, especially in the middle of May when the hawthorn fly (*Bibio marci*) appears on the bushes. The large Black Caterpillar is described as an excellent fly for lake and tarn fishing. He also tells of an interesting sighting of a similar fly near Coniston:

A few years ago, a large flight of insects came out in the neighbourhood of Coniston, of a kind which I have never noticed before or since. They were in every respect but one, quite similar in size and appearance to the Black caterpillar. The whole of their legs and thighs were a deep claret colour, whilst in the caterpillar they resemble black sealing-wax. In the time of their appearance also there was a difference, as this flight came in September. It was difficult to walk in the lanes without treading upon some of them: they were all over the lake, and upon the hedges, fields, and fells; in fact, they appeared to be everywhere, and remained about a fortnight.

The Bracken Clock is an old Lake District favourite, the word 'clock' being an old North Country word for beetle. Beever describes it as follows;

The Bracken Clock is a beetle, bred in light sandy ground, with a south or west aspect. It is very common in Cumberland and Westmoreland, where it is generally called 'The Clock'. It is first seen about the middle of May, and generally lasts about a month . . . When this fly is numerous, there is no good fly-fishing for a month after it is fully out. The fish glut themselves with it, and it soon makes them soft and out of condition.

The Black Ant fly is added in a postscript to the main text and is described as making its appearance in August or September:

This fly is an inhabitant of woods and coppices, and is very abundant in the neighbourhood of the English Lakes. The nest is often of enormous size, sometimes containing more than a cart-load of sticks and small twigs. The Vale of Duddon swarms with Wood Ants, and is the only place in which I have seen the Wryneck, which is said to feed principally on these insects.

He recommends that the fly dresser uses hooks made by Mr Philip Hutchinson, late partner of, and successor to, the famous Adlington of Kendal. As well as giving the dressings and instructions for use of artificial flies, Beever also gives detailed instructions on rod-making. After a discussion of the suitability of various woods for use in rod-making he gives us a description of his ideal fly-rod, together with detailed measurements and tapers.

This rod consists of three pieces: - The butt is of yellow-pine, and is five feet long; the middle is of logwood, four feet long; the top, also of logwood, is three feet three inches and a half.

Apparently, the rod described in the book was the result of a long experiment and was made about 1837. To help build his rod Beever enlisted the help of William Bell, a young joiner of Hawes Bank, Coniston.

John Beever outlived the first edition of his book by just ten years and ten days, dying on 10th January, 1859, aged sixty-four. The last seven years of his life were clouded in illness as a result of an unsuccessful operation, which affected his brain. He was buried in the Beever's family tomb in the grounds of St Michael and All Angels Church, Hawkshead.

Forty-four years after the publication of *Practical Fly-Fishing*, a second edition was brought out in 1893, under the author's own name. This edition contained a memoir of the author, written by W. G. Collingwood, and appendices on artificial flies, fly-rods, landing-nets and charr fishing by Arthur Severn and Agnew Ruskin Severn of Brantwood, described as experts with the rod. In his memoir of the author, Collingwood tells of the need for a second edition:

This little book has long been a favourite with those who happen to own copies, somewhat rare, of the original edition. They say there is nothing like it; and now that the prospects of anglers in the Lake District are improving, Practical Fly-Fishing, ought to be within the reach of every amateur.

During the forty years or so since the first edition the fishing on Coniston had deteriorated owing to the poisonous matter washed into the lake by the copper mines. However, by the 1890s the copper mines had almost ceased operating and water quality was improving. A local angling association had been formed and Coniston and neighbouring tarns were being re-stocked with trout and charr imported from Windermere or bred in a pond near Coniston Hall. However, such is the enduring popularity of this little book that a facsimile of the first edition was printed in 1970, making it available to new generations of Lake District anglers and a fitting tribute to its author.

14

Dr John Davy
ANGLER AND SURGEON

Sir Humphry Davy (1778-1829) was one of the leading chemists of his generation, best known today for his invention of the 'Davy' lamp, which helped to save the lives of thousands of miners. He was also an angler and a poet, of whom Coleridge declared, 'had he not been the first chemist, he would have been the first poet of his age'. He was a friend of Wordsworth, whom he visited on a number of occasions and it is possible that he even fished with him. In 1828, the year before he died, he wrote a book on angling, *Salmonia or Days of Fly Fishing*, which proved very popular and ran to five editions and was also published in the USA in 1832. The book is modelled on Izaac Walton's *Compleat Angler* and takes the form of a dialogue between Halieus (an angler), Ornither (a lover of field sports), Poietes (a lover of nature) and Physicus (a lover of natural history). Unfortunately, it contains little of interest to the Lakeland angler, except for some discussion of the natural history of the charr.

Less well-known, though in many ways no less distinguished, was John Davy, Sir Humphry's younger brother. Like his older brother, John Davy was born a long way from the Lake District, in Penzance on the 24th of May, 1790. He studied medicine at the University of Edinburgh, qualifying as a doctor in 1814. Following his graduation he joined the British Army Medical Department as a surgeon and spent a number of years in service abroad. In 1821, he was appointed Inspector General of Hospitals and he used his position to travel to a number of British colonies, including India, Ceylon and Barbados. Between 1827 and 1829, he attended on his brother during his convalescence in Ravenna and was present at his death. In 1830, he married Margaret Fletcher and two years later was elected a Fellow of the Royal Society. From 1836 to 1840 he produced nine volumes of the collected works of his brother. Finally, after a brief spell living in the West Indies, he returned to England in 1854 and retired to Lesketh How, Ambleside. Like his brother, John Davy was a keen angler and wrote two books on angling. The first, published in 1855, was *The Angler and his Friend*, which takes the form of a conversation between Piscator (an angler) and Amicus (his friend). The book, divided into colloquies (conversations) rather than chapters, is mainly concerned with his fishing exploits in Ireland. However, one colloquy is devoted to trout and charr fishing on Haweswater in the Lake District.

The angler and his friend, who has just travelled up from London, make their headquarters at the village inn at Bampton Grange, a couple of miles from Haweswater. The friend is a little disconcerted at the thought of staying at the village inn but the angler reassures him and states that he has brought with him some 'creature-comforts' to make their stay more bearable. These include good bread, butter, milk, eggs and a pigeon pie, which 'will make us tolerably independent of the casual supplies of the place'. After securing the services of a local keeper, they venture out on to the lake in search of trout and charr. The angler recommends a cast of three flies: a Broughton Point (invented around 1830 by a Penrith shoemaker, after whom it was named),

Woodcock and Hare's Ear and a Hawthorn Fly. According to Davy, the charr of Haweswater were much freer risers than elsewhere:

. . . the charr of Haweswater often rises freely at the fly, as I trust we shall find. I have heard of two anglers in one day killing here, fairly fishing with the fly, nine dozen of charr, and what is remarkable, without taking a single trout.

The fish are obviously feeding and within a short time they have taken a dozen trout and six charr. The angler hands over his rod to the keeper while he proceeds to discuss the natural history of the charr with his friend. The keeper, too, soon makes a surprising capture:

I have a fish which is neither a trout nor a charr. Surely it must be a schelly. The landing-net, if you please, sir. It is a schelly, and it is the first I have ever taken with the fly, and the third or fourth only that has been so taken within the memory of man.

After their success on the lake, they proceed to fish the beck, which issues from the lake before returning to the inn to feast on the fruits of their day's sport.

Following the publication of *The Angler and his Friend*, Davy wrote another fishing book, *The Angler in the Lake District*, published in 1857. This book followed the same format as the previous one and comprises a series of colloquies or conversations between Piscator (an angler) and Amicus (his friend) as they fish their way round the Lake District. Although it purports to be an angling book, it also contains much on the history, customs and natural history of the area.

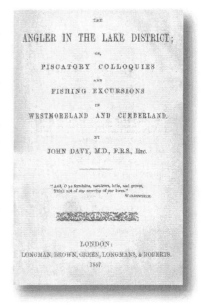

THE

ANGLER IN THE LAKE DISTRICT;

OR,

PISCATORY COLLOQUIES

AND

FISHING EXCURSIONS

IN

WESTMORELAND AND CUMBERLAND.

BY

JOHN DAVY, M.D., F.R.S., Etc.

"And, O ye fountains, meadows, hills, and groves,
Think not of any severing of our loves."
WORDSWORTH.

LONDON:
LONGMAN, BROWN, GREEN, LONGMANS, & ROBERTS.
1857.

In the first colloquy, the angler's friend is impressed by the dish of potted charr he has just been served:

How good are these potted fish which I have been enjoying along with your eulogy of the district! Are they the famed charr of your lake, or trout? One pleasant property belonging to them is their freedom from bones. Is this in consequence of solution in the process of cooking, or one of the felicities specially belonging to a fish of your favoured country?

After reassuring his friend that he has been eating charr and not trout, the angler relates that a lot of the so-called 'potted charr' sold in Lake District inns is in fact potted trout:

Know that a large proportion of the so-called potted charr is trout; the distinction is difficult; and if the trout be of good quality, it is not, when thus prepared, inferior to charr. As to your second question, if you carefully examine the fish you are eating, you will find that it retains its bones; but that, instead of being hard and resisting, as they originally were, they are now soft and yielding. This change is the effect of the cooking.

After giving him a neighbour's recipe for potted charr the angler and his friend set off for a day's fishing among the mountain tarns above the village of Grasmere. Their first port of call was Codale Tarn (which he refers to as Coodle Tarn), where the angler recommends a cast of brown flies. They met with little success, the friend taking an ill-fed trout of about half a pound. From there they descend to Easedale Tarn, where they fare a little better and take nine herring-sized trout between them. While fishing the tarn the angler (presumably Davy himself) mentions that he has stocked the tarn with charr, hatched at his own house. Unfortunately, the stocking does not appear to have been successful – I have fished Easedale Tarn a number of times and have taken a number of small hard-fighting trout on the fly and a number of perch on worm but never a charr. On their way down to Grasmere they make a cast or two in Sour-Milk

Gill, which issues from the tarn, and the friend manages to catch a rather poor specimen with a large head, dark, lank body, and shattered tail fin.

Their next excursion is to Santon Bridge where they obtain permission from the owner of Irton Hall to fish the river Irt, which flows out of Wastwater and into the sea at Ravenglass. During the nineteenth century the Irt was famous for the extremely rare black pearls that grew in its fresh-water mussels. Poaching of the pearls is thought to have led to the mussels becoming extinct in the river. Although Davy makes no mention of poaching pearls he does mention another type of poaching employing 'hods'. While they are walking its banks, the angler's friend happens to notice some small platforms projecting into the river and is given the following explanation:

They are here called 'hods', and are made of wicker-work, sticks thrust into the overhanging bank, and crossed with others, and covered with turf. Their intent is to produce deep shade, a tempting resting place during the day for the larger fish, which, as I before mentioned, when speaking of the evening angling, shun the garish light. There is, I know, one close by. Ha! I see the landlord is going to the garden with a lister, that three-pronged spear in his hand. Let us follow him; I dare say he is about to look into his hod, with the hope of getting a fish in part for his supper fare and in part for our dinner . . . See, he removes some dried ferns, and now through the opening he has made, he looks into the water. Now he clutches his spear, and carefully introduces it without raising his head. Be sure there is a fish there. He strikes, and with effect! Behold the prize, 'a mort', (a local name for a sea trout) of at least three pounds, - a fresh-run fish, and in excellent condition.

After dining on the fish at the inn, the angler and his friend go off to fish the river where the angler catches two morts, a 'spod' (a small sea trout) of about ten ounces and a few small brown trout. His friend hooked and lost a fine mort and caught a dozen small trout, hardly worth taking.

From the Irt they move on to Wasdale Head and, after taking

up residence in a local farmhouse, they hire a boat to fish Wastwater, where they hope to catch trout, charr and possibly a 'botling'. The angler confesses that he has never caught a 'botling' himself nor even seen one:

I can speak of the Botling only from what I have heard concerning it, for I have never seen it. I owe all I know of it chiefly to one of the states-men of the place, himself an angler, and whose house is the chief resort of tourists . . . According to him, the Botling is always a male; he describes it as a powerful fish, differing chiefly from the common trout in its greater size, greater thickness, and the marked manner in which its under jaw is turned up and hooked. It varies in weight from four pounds to twelve pounds; one of the latter weight, which he killed with the lister, he found, on measuring, so thick, that its girth exceeded its length by four inches. In colouring and marking, he said, it also resembled the ordinary lake trout, the brown spots on its back being only proportionally larger.

From Davy's description it appears that the 'botling' is, in fact, a ferox trout, a large piscivorous trout, which inhabits deep lakes and feeds largely on a diet of Arctic charr. In the hope of catch-ing such a monster, the angler decides to troll with a brass minnow while his friend opts to troll with a cast of three flies: a Coch-y-bonddu, a Broughton Point and a red hackle fly. Unfor-tunately, the ferox fails to make an appearance and they end the day with a few small trout.

The Angler's Inn on the shore of Ennerdale Water is their next port of call. Sadly, the Angler's Inn no longer exists. In 1960, it was planned to raise the level of the lake by 4½ feet to supply an extra six million gallons of water a day to West Cumbria. In anticipation of the scheme going ahead the inn was demolished - needlessly, as it turns out since the scheme never went ahead. Now, just the rem-nants of its jetty and discarded Victorian beer bottles can be seen at time of serious drought. However, a brochure dating to the late 1950s gives some idea of its former glory.

Ennerdale Water is the most westerly lake in the Lake District National Park and is less frequented by anglers than many of the

other lakes. The lake water is crystal clear and a good ripple is needed for fly fishing to be effective. The lake holds stocks of trout and charr, although the latter have been struggling of late and are now protected. In Davy's day, however, good catches of trout could be made and he mentions one angler who caught fourteen dozen in one day, many of a pound in weight. He also records a trout of six pounds taken by an angler whilst trolling. Unfortunately, the angler and his companion are less successful, taking less than a dozen, 'not one of them a respectable size'.

From Ennerdale they go on to fish the Esk and the Duddon without a great deal of success. While returning from an excursion to St John's Vale, the angler's friend asks why they have by-passed Rydal Water, Grasmere and Thirlmere. The angler replies:

Simply because I could not promise you sport in them. In each of them there are pike as well as trout; and that may be one and probably is the chief cause that angling is bad in them. Rydal Lake and Thirlmere are both tolerably preserved; and as the trout in them are of excellent quality, it seems more than probable that were it not for the pike - that most voracious of fishes - they would soon be plentiful. Another cause, in addition, operates in Grasmere - it is over fished, and another, that the lath or otter is used in it, as it is also, though in a lesser degree, in the others.

It is clear from this that Davy himself was no great lover of pike or pike fishing. After fishing the rivers Greta and Derwent with only a modicum of success, they turn their attention to Derwentwater, where the angler manages to land a decent-sized trout without the aid of a landing-net:

AMICUS. Ah, you have a fish, and he fights bravely. Where is the landing net?

PISCATOR. Forgotten, the boatman says, in our haste. Never mind. My pannier is at hand; it will serve the purpose for want of a better. Immerse it well. There is our fish summarily secured, and safe in the basket by one act. It is a beautiful fish, well fed, over a pound, short and thick, silvery below, of a rich olive brown above; a good specimen of the Derwentwater trout, and I am sure it will cut red and be well flavoured when dressed.

While making their way to fish Crummock Water, the angler and his friend discuss the weather, which leads the angler to relate a tragic story of two men and a boy from Kentmere who went from there to fish some of the mountain tarns. It is reminiscent of the story of Charles Gough (see Chapter 10):

I will relate to you one instance, a well authenticated one, which occurred only a few years ago in the persons of two men and a boy belonging to Kentmere, who went thence to fish in some of the mountain tarns. The time was towards the fall, early in November. Not returning, their friends

GRASMERE.

became alarmed, and a search was made for them, the people of the coun-
try all round joining in it, according to custom. When hope of finding
them was nearly given up, they were discovered all three together under
the shelter of a rock; the bodies of the men resting in a sitting posture,
that of the boy on the knee of one of the men, with a bit of bread in his
hand - all three wet and cold, and stark dead, without any appearance
of bodily hurt. They were considered storm-stricken; overtaken, as it was
known they had been, by a violent gale accompanied by heaven rain.

The Lake District weather is prone to violent mood changes and
Davy's story sends out a potent message to all who fish in the
area, especially those seeking the solitude of the remote high
tarns. After taking eight fish on Crummock Water, the largest of
which scarcely exceeding half a pound, the angler and his friend
make their final excursion to Windermere. After setting off in a
boat from Waterhead they manage to take a couple of fine trout
on the fly. To end the day, the boatman sets up his lath-tackle,
baited with minnows, in the hope of taking a charr or two. The
line controlling the lath-tackle is attached to a pole standing erect
in the stern of the boat. A bite is signalled by the vibration of the

pole tip. Unfortunately, they meet with no success and the boat-man drops them off near the ruins of the Roman fort at Ambleside, from where it is a short walk to the angler's home at Lesketh How.

And so the angling excursions come to an end. In many ways the title of Davy's book, *The Angler in the Lake District*, is misleading. Although the angler and his friend do go on several angling excursions throughout the district, each excursion provides a springboard for Davy to discuss the natural history, archaeology and customs of the area rather than a detailed account of the fishing itself. However, it does make for interesting reading and gives a valuable insight into the state of the fishing during the mid-nineteenth century

15

George Foster Braithwaite
THE ANGLING MAYOR OF KENDAL

George Foster Braithwaite was a very busy man. Not only was he a woollen manufacturer, Mayor of Kendal on six occasions, a JP, and a County Alderman, he was also father to thirteen children, the author of the *Salmonidae of Westmorland* (1884) and a keen angler. He was born in Kendal on 16th August, 1813, the fourth son of Isaac Braithwaite, a drysalter (a dealer in a range of salt and chemicals for preserving food) in the town. Both his parents were prominent members of the Society of Friends, although their son did not long continue his adherence to that communion. After completing his education at the age of sixteen he was sent to Liverpool where he was apprenticed in the office of a firm of West India merchants. It was here that he developed a considerable acumen for business.

After four years in Liverpool he returned to his native town where he joined with his brother, Charles, in the purchase of a woollen manufacturing business. The business soon prospered and they extended their operations and branched into the tweed trade, for which Kendal became famous.

In 1844, at the age of thirty-one, Braithwaite was baptised in St John's Church, Hackney in London. It is thought that he was baptised in order to marry and two years later, on 23rd June, 1846, he married Mary Savory of Stamford Hill, London. After their marriage they settled in Highgate, Kendal. Whilst living in Highgate a terrible storm occurred one night, which resulted in the blowing down of a chimney. Unfortunately, the chimney crashed through the roof of the adjoining house killing a hapless lady who was asleep in bed. During the 1860s, Braithwaite built Hawesmead in Kendal, where he resided until his death.

As a woollen manufacturer he travelled throughout the Lake District in search of suitable Herdwick wool for his business and became intimately acquainted with the Lakeland topography. In April, 1856, he met with a serious accident while driving home from a Bible Meeting at Grayrigg. He was driving a pony gig, when a dog ran out and startled the pony. The pony swerved to avoid the dog and Braithwaite was thrown out and suffered concussion of the brain and remained insensible for three days afterwards. The after-effects of the accident remained with him for many years.

Three years prior to his accident he was elected Town Councillor, a position he was to retain for thirty-five years. In 1865, he was elected Mayor of Kendal for the first time. He eventually held the mayoralty six times, the last time being in 1879. He was very much involved with Kendal Parish Church and filled the office of Churchwarden for many years. Following his death, his family paid for a new clock to be installed in the church tower in his memory and a commemorative plaque in his honour can still be seen at the back of the church today.

In 1884, four years before his death he published a book on angling with a rather long title, *The Salmonidae of Westmorland, Angling Reminiscences and Leaves from an Angler's Note Book*. Many of the chapters in the book had originally appeared as articles in the *Westmorland Gazette*. The writer of Braithwaite's obituary in the *Kendal Mercury and Times* (24th February, 1888) was fulsome in its praises:

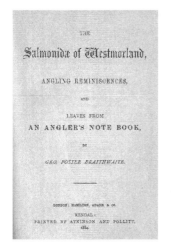

It is not too much to say that in years to come Kendalians will be proud of Mr. Braithwaite's little book, and sorry that he did not write more; for his descriptions are careful and happy, his humour always abundant, and his enjoyment in cottage homes and wayside hotels, where he met hospitable and interesting characters on his fishing excursions, is pencilled with a grace and accuracy which lend a charm to his little book not often surpassed by the best of writers.

Indeed, it is from this little book that we learn about Braithwaite the angler. A third of his book is devoted to the fish of the Lake District and the methods of their capture, both by angling and by less sporting means. He gives a particularly interesting insight into lath or otter board fishing, which was widely practised in the Lake District and on Scottish lochs until it was made illegal in 1884. This method of fishing is still practised in Scandinavia on large lakes, and I have seen otter boards or laths for sale in Norwegian tackle shops. The lath or otter was basically a wooden board, which was weighted to float on its edge in the water. A line was attached to one side in such a position that when the lath was towed through the water, it angled away from the shore and out into the lake. The line which towed the lath was armed with a number of flies on droppers. If lath fishing was undertaken from a boat, the line was attached to a pole in the boat and two laths could be employed simultaneously, one from each side of the boat.

It appears that Braithwaite was, in his younger days before the lath was banned, fond of this method of fishing and he is almost moved to poetry in describing its practice:

Embarking in his boat at Bowness, a gentle breeze ruffling the surface of the lake, the lath or otter with its ten flies was launched, and the line looped to the mast. *The oars, hitherto managed by the attendant, are given up to the angler, who guides his course so that the line runs over the banks and shallows. Now he sees some large boulders in the water, and by a skilful movement causes the lath to run close round them, keeping his main line well up, the flies dancing on the waves. Up jumps a fish taking the line down with it, and making the boat quiver. Presently it gives a high leap and reveals a lovely trout, of two pounds weight at least. The line is skilfully handled, and, finally, after many attempts of the fish to escape, during which time the hopes and fears of the angler alternate, the prize is secured, and the line again extended for a fresh capture. To what beautiful scenery did this mode of fishing introduce us as the boat glided slowly into the lovely bays and skirted the various islands, some clad with luxuriant foliage, under which was a carpet of primroses and wild hyacinths; others rocky and picturesque in form; or, on rounding a headland, to behold the magnificent background formed by the Langdale Pikes, Loughrigg, Fairfield, Nab Scar, and other well-known mountains, leaving pictures on the imagination which are lasting sources of pleasure.*

Like William Wordsworth (see Chapter 9), Braithwaite seems to have enjoyed fishing for pike with trimmers. At the Museum of Lakeland Life at Abbot Hall, Kendal there is a box of mixed tackle belonging to Braithwaite, which in addition to his rather motheaten fly wallet, contained a number of trimmers marked with Braithwaite's initials GFB. Unfortunately, in his book he has little to say about the use of this method of fishing in the Lake District, but he was clearly aware of it and relates a fascinating story concerning the capture of a pike on a trimmer in the Avon:

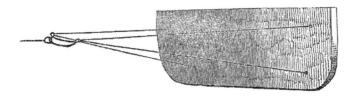

A lath or otter board.

Lath fishing.

A trimmer was set in the Avon over night. In the morning a heavy pike was caught. Proceeding to extract the hooks, the gentleman was obliged to open the fish, when he found another pike of considerable size inside the first, and in whose mouth his hooks were fast. This second fish was opened to get at the hooks, when a third pike of ¾ lbs. weight, which had taken the original bait, was found partially digested.

Trimmer fishing seems to have been a popular pastime with young boys and it was much practised on Windermere and the larger lakes, which contained a good head of pike. Trimmers were mainly fished in the weedy bays where pike like to lay in wait for their unsuspecting prey. Small perch were invariably used as bait and a fisherman might employ as many as twenty trimmers at once. It appears that trimmers were often marked with numbers or with the fisherman's initials, just like Braithwaite's, and bets were sometimes placed on which trimmer would catch the biggest pike.

With regard to more conventional methods of angling, we learn that Braithwaite threw his first piece of string into a stream in April 1821, at the tender age of eight. He was staying at the home of Daniel Weaver, a family friend who lived near Ings. After watching a local angler catch several trout out of the river Gawen he decided he would like to have a go himself:

Mr. Weaver dressed me a fly on a real hook; it was not a crooked pin, and then, with a line made of noggywife thread and a small hazel stick, I walked off, prouder of my tackle than in after years I felt with the best London made fly-rod, to fish in a small stream which ran by the road-side. After patiently casting my fly for ten minutes my efforts were rewarded by a sharp twitch at the hook, which caused the rod to bend. I held on expecting to see a silvery trout struggling for its liberty, but it was either too large for my unpractised hands, or else it got into the swift run of the swollen stream and then under a wall, where I lost both it and my fly.

A trimmer once belonging to Braithwaite, from a collection of his tackle donated to the Museum of Lakeland Life in Kendal.

Few anglers forget their first clumsy attempts at trying to catch a fish and Braithwaite was no different, but from that moment onwards he was an angler. His first real success came in the spring of 1828. After making himself a rod out of red pine and logwood, he set off early one May morning to Scarfoot Mill on the river Mint where he caught his first trout, a fish of four ounces. He rushed home with his prize catch, arriving at seven-thirty, just in time for breakfast. As we have already seen, at the age of sixteen he was sent to Liverpool, where we learn that he occasionally angled for dace. However, his desire to be a fly fisher never left him and during his holidays he regularly fished the Mint with his youngest brother.

On returning to Kendal after serving his apprenticeship he began to fish the Lune in the neighbourhood of Borrow Bridge. One memorable day in June, 1836, he managed to take a fine basket of trout. The Lune had been very low for several weeks due to a lack of rain. However, in the first week of June it rained continuously for three days and the river was once again in fine fettle. Braithwaite and his friend, Thomas Rigge, set off for the river early:

Oh it was a grand morning; all nature seemed to rejoice; the fields, hitherto almost brown with drought, were clothed with an emerald hue; the air was delicious with the perfume of primroses and wild hyacinths, and our spirits were elated with the prospect of good sport. Our host and hostess, Mr. and Mrs. Noble, encouraged us with hope, and provided as usual a plentiful breakfast - Mrs. Noble's ham and eggs were always excellent. The Lune was bank full and a splendid colour. Every throw brought a rise, and had we been experienced anglers we should have filled our panniers. At Carlingill we saw our friend, the late W. G. Best, who had fished up the 'fair mile' to meet us. How he did pull them out! We all met at Borrow Bridge. W. Best had ten pounds of grand trout. I had four pound. I forget the number in Mr. Rigge's pannier, but we were pleased with the excursion.

We learn from his book that, in forty-eight years of fishing the Lune, Braithwaite never caught a trout over one pound in weight. He also claims that two of his close angling companions, Richard Herd and William Best, both experienced Lune anglers, also failed to catch a trout over that magical figure. Ironically, however, one July day he lent his fishing rod to the grandson of the Rev. John Sedgwick, vicar of Howgill. The young man was no angler but returned after a short time minus rod but clutching a trout which weighed one and a half pounds. When asked how he had managed to land such a fish, the young man replied, "I pulled till it came to the side when I drew it on the stones." The trout had apparently succumbed to a small dotterel fly. Nowadays, due to increased stocking by angling clubs, trout above a pound in weight are not uncommon on the Lune and the author himself has caught a number of trout above that weight in the river.

Although Braithwaite preferred fly fishing, he was no purist and enjoyed trolling with live minnow on Ullswater, as the following account of a few days trolling in 1836 with his friend, Thomas Rigge, shows:

We had fair sport, catching from 10lbs. to 14lbs. each day, principally trout, with a few good-sized perch. The largest trout did not exceed 1lb.; the largest perch 1½ lbs., a very fine fish. We usually fished up to Lyulph's Tower, and calling at Howtown on our return reached Pooley Bridge about seven in the evening.

While they were fishing Ullswater on that occasion, a gentleman from Penrith, by the name of Kirkbride, caught a splendid 8lb trout on fly while fishing in the middle of the lake. Braithwaite believed it to be a ferox trout. As well as trolling on Ullswater, Braithwaite and his friend fished a deep hole in the river Eamont, where they caught a number of chub using cheese curd as a bait.

Not surprisingly, since he lived in Kendal, Braithwaite often fished on Windermere, either with the fly or trolling a live minnow. In May 1839, he spent a few days with his friend, John Crosfield of Rothay Bank, who acted as gillie:

Ullswater, from Braithwaite's book.

The weather was beautiful, and the first morning he said if I liked to go in his boat he would be glad to row, which acceptable offer was immediately fallen in with and away we went, and as soon as the boat was fairly out of the shallow water at the mouth of the river, I ran out for the first time on Windermere two trolling lines with minnows. Presently a good tug, and very soon a lovely Windermere trout about 14oz. was in the boat. This was encouraging, and it was not long before the line was again fishing. Just as we were passing a most tempting spot for a trout Mr. Crosfield, resting on his oars, called my attention to a beautiful view and proceeded to expiate thereon.

Unfortunately, Mr Crosfield appears to have expiated too long and Braithwaite was forced to forego his fishing! However, that same afternoon he engaged the services of a professional boat-man and had some good sport with the fly.

On another occasion, in 1842, while staying with the Cros-fields, not only did he fish the Rothay and Windermere, he also had a rather tetchy encounter with the poet Wordsworth. It was the day of the Ambleside Rushbearing Festival, which celebrated the ancient custom of annually replacing the rushes on the earth floors of churches. It is a festival that still continues to this day. After fishing in the morning Braithwaite attended the festival, held in a local field, in the afternoon:

Underneath a large oak tree lay Wordsworth, waving a stick, which like some of his ideas could only have a charm to him from its simplicity and to others from being in his possession. He appeared well, and when I offered to assist him to rise, he jumped up exclaiming, "I have not lost all my youth yet."

In addition to the rivers and lakes of the area Braithwaite occasionally wet a line on one of the many mountain tarns. On one occasion, while fishing Sty Head Tarn, his sport was ruined by a peal of thunder:

Next morning we proceeded by the Strands to Wastdale Head. Anxious to try Sty Head Tarn I hurried up the pass, and thought success would crown my efforts, for the fish rose beautifully, when all on a sudden a peal of thunder dispersed my pleasing anticipations. The fish gave over rising, and I made the best of my way to Seathwaite, where carriages were in waiting to take us to Lodore Hotel, from whence we took a boat to Keswick.

Until its prohibition in 1861, Braithwaite occasionally fished with salmon roe as bait. He appears to have learnt this method of fishing from a skilled exponent of the craft, Thomas Hartley of Egremont, otherwise known as 'Shear Tom', from his profession of knife grinder. One evening, while walking over Pelter Bridge on the Rothay, he spied 'Shear Tom' at work. Using a size 5 hook and small lead bullet, he allowed the bullet to drop to the bottom and left the roe to wave about with the current:

Now few fish would remain long except under cover in such rough water, but the quiet pool below being well stocked with trout, they becoming aware of the close proximity of a delicious morsel by the smell carried down with the stream, traced the scent until they found the roe which eagerly seizing they were caught.

After witnessing 'Shear Tom's success, Braithwaite begged him to have a go and promptly extracted several more trout from the swim.

George Foster Braithwaite's angling career was brought to an end on 20th February, 1888. He had gone to London to conduct some business on behalf of Kendal Corporation. After lunching with his brother, Isaac, he proceeded to the home of Miss Savory, his sister-in-law, with whom he had been staying. As he was taking off his overcoat, he began to feel unwell and went directly upstairs to rest. Shortly afterwards he became unconscious and in less than five minutes he had ceased to breathe. The cause of his death was believed to have been sudden heart failure consequent on a chill.

The whole of Kendal was in mourning for his loss and the flags at the Town Hall and Parish Church were flown at half-mast in his honour. A most fitting tribute was paid to him by the obituarist of the *Kendal Mercury and Times* (24th February, 1888), who, amongst many other things, wrote:

He was a fisher by nature, by education, and by all the tastes that a love of poetry and the beautiful afford - and it is hard to say whether the love of angling, his passion for it, or the devotion to public life and the interests of his native town most absorbed his thoughts.

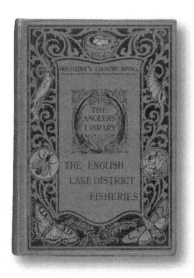

16

John Watson & the Guide Writers

Without doubt the most useful book to have been published on fishing in the Lake District in the last couple of hundred years is John Watson's, *The English Lake District Fisheries*, first published in 1899. Such was its popularity that it was reprinted in 1905 with a revised and updated edition coming out in 1925. The first edition was written at the request of Sir Herbert Maxwell, editor of *The Angler's Library*, of which Watson's volume forms a part. Watson himself was clearly an angler and in his Preface to the book he tells us that he visited and fished almost every lake and river of the district, including the almost innumerable mountain tarns. The result is a wonderful volume, which gives us a fascinating insight into the state of the Lake District fisheries at the start of the twentieth century and although some of his material is now outdated there is still a great deal of interest to the Lakeland angler of today.

The opening words of Watson's obituary, published in the *Westmorland Gazette* on the 6th of October, 1928, effectively sum up the nature of the man:

Photo by A. Pettitt.

WINDERMERE.

[To face p. 67.

One who loved the wild creatures of the countryside and admired the flowery mantle of nature passed away peacefully in his sleep on Saturday in the person of Mr. John Watson, Eden Mount, Kendal, at the age of 69.

John Watson was born in Kendal in 1859, the son of William Watson, a master tailor. We learn from his obituary that from boyhood he loved the countryside and studied the habits of birds, animals and fishes. He spent long summer holidays in the Sleddale valley, where he cultivated these interests and while still in his teens he became a regular contributor to the *Westmorland Gazette*. Later, he became a contributor to the *Cornhill* magazine, *The Field*, and *The Westminster Saturday Gazette*, as well as other national papers and magazines. He trained as a teacher and in the 1881 census he is recorded as being a school teacher residing at the Manchester School for the Deaf and Dumb. However, he appears not to have been suited to the teaching profession and by 1885 he was living back in Kendal and was secretary of the Kent Angling Association.

The year 1888 proved a momentous one for the twenty-nine-year-old Watson, since not only did he get married to a Miss Emily Farrer of Kendal, he also founded the Northern Newspaper Syndicate. The Syndicate prospered under his guidance and the business grew until an established connection was gained with newspapers in this country, the colonies and the United States. Eventually, he became the proprietor of the *Kendal Mercury and Times*, which he took over from Edward Gill.

In 1889 he was elected a member of Westmorland County Council, being elevated to alderman in 1910. His main interests on the County Council lay in the prevention of river pollution and the protection of wild birds. For fifteen years he served as chairman of the Pollution of Rivers Committee. In 1914 he was made a magistrate for Westmorland County. For several years he served as president of the Kent Angling Association and was a member of the Kent, Lune, and Eden boards of conservators.

Opposite: Windermere, from The English Lake District Fisheries.

Outside his journalistic and business interests, Watson was a keen angler and ornithologist, as well as being an enthusiastic breeder of old English game birds. He had an extensive knowledge of natural history, as his obituary writer relates:

Mr. Watson was a true field naturalist, a delightful companion on a country walk. He would draw attention to the beauties of flower and foliage, the flight and song of various birds, adding charming little anecdotes of his first-hand observance of wild life. In particular he possessed an almost uncanny knowledge of bird calls, and knew the twittering of our rarer birds as well as the ordinary rambler knows the song of the thrush.

His love of natural history led to the publication of his first book, *A Year in the Fields*, in 1888. Other books soon followed, including: *Sylvan Folk, Sketches of Bird and Animal Life in Britain* (1889), and *Nature and Woodcraft* (1890). Of special interest to anglers, apart from *The English Lake District Fisheries* (1899 and 1925), are his *Sketches of British Sporting Fishes* (1890), *The Confessions of a Poacher* (1890) and *Poachers and Poaching - Knowledge Never Learned in Schools* (1891).

The last two titles are interesting and the knowledge of poaching contained within them appears to have come from a boyhood acquaintance of Watson's, whom he refers to as 'old Phil'. It is clear that Watson learned a great deal of the ways of animals, birds and fishes from this character, as the editorial note from *The Confessions of a Poacher* tells us:

I never met any man who was in closer sympathy with the wild creatures about him; and never dog or child came within his influence but was permanently attracted by his personality. Although eighty years of age there is still some of the old erectness in his carriage; some of the old fire in his eyes . . . In my boyhood he was the hero whom I worshipped, and I hardly know that I have gone back on my loyalty.

From these *Confessions* we can learn a great deal about the poaching of game, especially fish, in nineteenth century Lakeland. One of the poachers' most effective methods of taking salmon and trout was by netting a pool in the river and they were careful to survey the intended pool in the daytime before netting it at night. Cunning water-bailiffs often 'thorned' a good salmon pool (i.e. placed thorn bushes in a pool anchored down by stones) to entangle the poachers' nets, as the following passage relates:

During summer, when the water is low, the fish congregate in deep 'dubs' [pools]. This they do for protection, and here, if overhung by trees, there is always abundance of food. Whenever it was our intention to net a dub, we carefully examined every inch of its bottom beforehand. If it had been 'thorned', every thorn was carefully removed - small thorn bushes with stones attached, and thrown in by the watchers to entangle nets. Of course fish-poaching can never be tackled single-handed. In 'long-netting' the net is dragged by a man on each side, a third wading after to lift it over the stakes, and to prevent the fish from escaping. When the end of the pool is reached the salmon and trout are simply drawn out upon the pebbles.

We learn that the nets used to capture salmon and trout were rarely kept at home but were secreted in stone heaps or among bushes close to where they were going to be used. If, for some reason, the nets had to be kept at home, then it was only for a short period since they did not want the police coming with a search warrant. The police occasionally found nets hidden in a chimney, under a mattress, or, in one case, wound about the portly person of a poacher's wife!

Other methods employed by Lakeland poachers included spearing or leistering salmon on their spawning redds, although such fish brought little money as 'the flesh of spawning fish is loose and watery, insipid and tasteless'. Another common method of extracting salmon and trout from their spawning redds was by the use of 'click' hooks. These were large salmon hooks with lead added to balance them and add weight, which were attached to a long cord.

When a salmon is seen the hooks are simply thrown beyond it, then gently dragged until they come immediately beneath; when a sharp click sends them into the soft under parts of the fish, which is then dragged out.

We learn that some poachers even resorted to shooting salmon with a gun, a method that had the advantage of quickness, and in skilled hands a gun could be used without injuring the fleshy part of the fish. However, there seemed to have been a certain code of honour among poachers and poisoning a pool with chloride of lime was frowned upon by the majority of poachers who regarded it as a cowardly method, which killed everything, great and small, for miles downstream. Most poachers even had a great deal of respect for their adversaries, the water-bailiffs, as the following extract makes clear:

Mention of the water-bailiffs reminds me that I must say a word of them too. Their profession is a hard one - harder by far than the poacher's. They work at night, and require to be most alert during rough and wet weather; especially in winter when fish are spawning. Sometimes they must remain still for hours in freezing clothes; and even in summer not unfrequently lie all night in dank and wet herbage.

So much for Lakeland poachers, but what can we learn of Watson the angler? Most of what we know of his angling career is gleaned from his book, *The English Lake District Fisheries*. We learn a little of his philosophy of angling from his introduction. He had no time for angling books that resembled tackle manufacturers' catalogues. He also believed that the angler who prided himself on the quantity and glory of his outfit was not the angler who generally caught the most fish, as the following makes clear:

To the writer, it is almost a truism that the angler who gets the biggest baskets is he of little tackle - who ties his own flies, and can dress a killing imitation by the waterside.

As secretary, and later, president of the Kent Angling Association, Watson fished a great deal for the sea trout in the river running through his native town and the very first chapter of his book is devoted to fishing that river. It is clear that he was not a fly fishing purist, although he does give advice on suitable flies for sea trout. When the water was clearing after a spate he recommends the quill minnow (invented by James Garnett of Kendal in 1873), and worm fishing with Pennell tackle when the river was slightly discoloured. For sea trout fishing he used a 12½-foot three-piece greenheart rod, made by Farlows of London. He turned to this rod after a locally-made rod (perhaps made by Hutchinson of Kendal) proved too heavy and cumbersome. Although he wrote a couple of books on poachers and poaching he was clearly aware of the damage they could do to a river. He states that twenty years ago (i.e. the 1870s), the Kent was one of the best trout streams in the country but had been ruined by a

ON THE KENT.

Photo by J. H. Hogg.

combination of poaching, pollution, land drainage and removal of cover and habitat. Throughout his life he fought tirelessly for the improvement of rivers and served on several conservancy boards. With regard to salmon fishing on the Kent, he was witness to one of the largest salmon taken on the river, a fish of 30lb, killed at the Waiste by a Mr R. Garnett on a Silver Doctor salmon fly. The fish took three hours to land.

From his descriptions of other rivers in the Lake District, it is clear that he was well-acquainted with those in the southern area but less so with those in the north and he leaves the description of the Eden and the Derwent to J. B. Slater and G. E. Lowthian respectively. Not surprisingly, perhaps, considering he lived in Kendal, he fished Windermere and was captivated by its beauty in all the seasons of the year. He was particularly fond of trout fishing through a summer night:

Its ordinary aspects are known to thousands of people; fewer know the great charm of trout fishing through a summer night; and fewer still, perhaps, the almost inexpressible beauty of being abroad on the lake just at the dawn of a new day in May or early June.
These are things which must be experienced -
they leave impressions which can
never be translated.

He was a devotee of trolling for trout, employing two rods, one equipped with a natural bait, the other with an artificial. He claims that the biggest trout are caught in this way and refers to fish of 7 and 8lb taken by trolling. His own captures, however, were a little more modest but one evening he caught three trout, weighing 1½lb, 2lb, and 2½lb, and he claims to have rarely taken a fish of less than 1lb, using this method. Not surprisingly, perhaps, for every fish caught on an artificial bait he caught two on a natural one. As well as trout he enjoyed trolling for pike, as the following passage illustrates:

Opposite: On the Kent, from The English Lake District Fisheries.

Coniston Water.

[To face p. 97.

The shallow water from Belle Isle to Rawlinson's Nab is good pike ground, and better still is the Parsonage Bay; while, further down the lake, Grass Holme is a favourite spot. At the first named place I have more than once had a pike on each rod at the same time, and upon one occasion almost succeeded in landing three fish with two baits - a bigger fish having seized a smaller one as it was being pulled in.

In addition to Windermere, Watson fished other lakes in the district and early in the season of 1898 he recorded a red-letter day on Haweswater. It was one of those Lake District days when it rained, blew, hailed and snowed, occasionally all at once. Watson, however, persevered with big flies sporting plenty of tinsel and managed to catch forty trout and two charr. Coniston was another lake frequently fished by Watson and he claimed to have taken the largest and best fish he had ever caught in the district while fishing the rocky ledges of one of the lake's two islands. In Watson's day Coniston abounded with small fish and he felt the lake would benefit from systematic netting:

I have closely examined and fished Coniston in varying conditions, and have come to the conclusion that what the lake lacks is (for a time at least) systematic netting conducted under some authoritative governing body. It contains far too many fish.

On one of his best days on Coniston he landed nine brace of trout and the flies he recommends for the lake are: March Brown, Woodcock and a nondescript chestnut-brown fly with tinsel body; later in the season, March Brown, Green-Drake, and Zulu. I suspect that these flies would be just as successful today.

Watson fished most of the tarns in the Lake District, even camping for ten days at a time by the side of Red Tarn, which lies immediately beneath Helvellyn. He recommended that the angler who wished to indulge in tarn fishing should burden himself as little as possible - good advice that still holds true today. For tarn fishing he used a light 10-foot or 10½-foot greenheart rod, made by Farlows:

Opposite: Coniston Water, from The English Lake District Fisheries.

*With one of these the writer has fished most of the tarns in the Lake
District, and nothing could be more useful or appropriate. They will kill
any fish the angler is likely to come across, and for lightness and effec-
tiveness nothing could be better.*

One of his most killing methods of tarn fishing was with the
natural bracken clock; however, with regard to artificials, he recommends small, dark hackled flies. On one occasion he caught
thirty trout from Small Water, while on another occasion he had
a magnificent bag of rudd from Whinfell Tarn:

*Probably Whinfell Tarn is the only sheet of water in the district which
contains rudd. Common in southern waters, it is always a rare fish in the
north. The writer has taken rudd here with roach tackle and baits, but on
one occasion took upwards of a hundred fish in a comparatively short
time, which weighed nearly a hundredweight. This was at the close of a
hot day in July, when it was observed that shoals of large rudd were
swimming about on the surface of the tarn taking small flies. Happening to have a cast of trout flies on gut, these were put on, and a fish was
taken at almost every throw. The cast became so abraded that it smashed,
and hauling in the big rudd was at an end. The catch, with the crimson
sun on their golden scales, was an exceedingly handsome one.*

After a long and distinguished career, Watson died on 29th
September, 1928, at his home in Eden Mount, Kendal, following a long illness, which prevented him from taking part in the
activities he loved so much. Since 1925, when the second
edition of his *English Lake District Fisheries* was published, a number of other angling guides to the Lakes have appeared but, in my
opinion, none to compare with Watson's.

The more recent guide books, which I have found most help-
ful in my pursuit of Lakeland fish, include *An Anglers' Guide to
the Lake District*, by Geoff Parkinson and James Holgate, first published by Castabout Publications in 1984, with a revised and
enlarged edition published by the *Westmorland Gazette* coming
out in 1987. Geoff Parkinson is a devoted pike angler with many

big fish falling to his rod. He was editor of *Pikelines*, the journal of the Pike Anglers' Club from 1985 to 1987 and has fished extensively in the Lake District. James Holgate, who sadly passed away in June 2009 at the young age of fifty-one, was also a very keen pike angler with an extensive knowledge of Lake District waters. Like Parkinson, Holgate also served as editor of *Pikelines* during the mid-1980s. He wrote a number of books on pike angling and was editor of both *Pike and Predators* and *Coarse Angling Today* magazines. In addition to the *Anglers' Guide to the Lake District* Holgate also wrote a book on the fish of the Lake District entitled *Reflections Upon Lakeland Angling,* published in 1989 by Cast Publications. For those interested in the fish of the Lake District this book is well worth seeking out.

In 1996, Chris Sodo, another very experienced Lakeland angler and president of Windermere, Ambleside & District Angling Association, brought out a very useful guide to angling in South Lakeland, entitled *The Fisherman's Guide to South Lakeland.* I have found this beautifully illustrated book particularly useful since it contains colourful maps of the various waters showing some of the fishing hotspots, which can save the visiting angler a great deal of time and trouble in locating the fish. This book, too, is well worth seeking out.

The most recent, and certainly the most comprehensive of the modern guides, is Laurence Tetley's *The Lake District Angler's Guide*, published by Cicerone Press of Milnthorpe in 1999. The guide lists the fishing opportunities on forty-seven rivers and streams, over a hundred still waters and includes a section listing twenty-seven fishing tackle outlets in the area.

The problem with most angling guide books, however, is that they soon become outdated. Fisheries change hands, day ticket prices increase, contact details change and new fishing rules and regulations are introduced. It is highly likely, therefore, that in the future we will not see again the likes of Watson's *English Lake District Fisheries*. Most of the information required by the angler venturing into the Lake District can now be found online on sites like *lakedistrictfishing.net*, the website compiled and maintained by Windermere, Ambleside & District Angling Association.

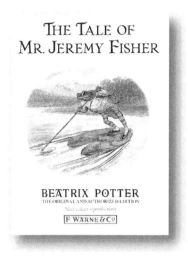

17

Beatrix Potter
IN SEARCH OF MR JEREMY FISHER

The film, *Miss Potter*, starring Renée Zellweger and Ewan McGregor, sparked a renewed interest in the life and work of Beatrix Potter. After watching the film I was transported back to my childhood and I remembered my mother reading the tales of Beatrix Potter to me when I was very young. My favourite story at that time was *The Tale of Mr Jeremy Fisher*. The story concerns a frog, Mr Jeremy Fisher, who lived in a damp house at the edge of a pond. One day he decided to go fishing for some minnows. He hoped to catch enough to invite his friends, Mr Alderman Ptolemy Tortoise and Sir Isaac Newton, to dinner. After digging some worms and donning a mackintosh and a pair of goloshes, he embarked on his boat (a lily-leaf) to the middle of the pond. Equipped with a wicker creel, a stalk of grass for a rod, a horse-hair line and red float, he began fishing. The fishing proved to be slow but, after partaking of a butterfly sandwich for lunch, he recommenced with renewed vigour. A bite soon followed and the red float bobbed in the water. He struck and hooked not a minnow but a three-spined stickleback which, after being landed, promptly jumped back into the water. Then a terrible thing happened. A huge trout leapt out of the water and grabbed Jeremy Fisher and pulled him down to the bottom of the pond. Fortunately for Jeremy, the trout did not like the taste of his mackintosh, and promptly spat him out to live another day. Instead of minnows for dinner, Jeremy and his guests dined on roasted grasshopper with ladybird sauce.

The story itself, first published in 1906, is beautifully illustrated with Beatrix Potter's watercolours. These small paintings have been favourably compared to Thomas Bewick's vignettes because of their minute attention to detail. Jeremy Fisher's creel, his float and even the fish themselves are meticulously drawn and based on close observation. It leaves the reader in no doubt that Miss Potter herself was familiar with fish and fishing.

The Tale of Mr Jeremy Fisher is probably the first fishing story that thousands of children will have read and I wonder how many of them, either consciously or subconsciously, have been inspired to take up angling as a result? I remember even now being fascinated as a child by the red float bobbing on the water as the stickleback nibbled the worm. But where did the inspiration for this story come from? How did Beatrix Potter acquire her knowledge of angling? To find the answers we need to look at her life.

Helen Beatrix Potter was born in 1866 in London to a wealthy Victorian family. Her parents, Rupert and Helen, both hailed from families that had made their fortunes in the Lancashire cotton industry. Her father, although trained as a barrister, rarely practised and spent most of his days at gentlemen's clubs. Beatrix herself was a lonely child and was educated at home by a succession of governesses. She had little opportunity to mix with other children and even her younger brother, Bertram, was sent away to boarding school. However, Beatrix was very fond of animals and she had a succession of pets to keep her company: mice, rabbits, hedgehogs and frogs. Indeed, she seems to have created her own little world around these animals and they provided a substitute for human company. As well as keeping pets, she soon discovered that she had a talent for drawing and painting and spent a lot of time drawing her pets.

For eleven summers from 1871 to 1881 Beatrix and her family spent three months at Dalguise House near Dunkeld in Perthshire, which her father rented. From 1882 onwards, following a large increase in the rental of Dalguise, they spent a number of summers in the Lake District, first at Wray Castle and then at Lingholm and Fawe Park by Derwentwater. These places had an enormous influence on the young Beatrix Potter. Her father and grandfather were keen fishermen and Dalguise House, situated on the west bank of the Tay proved an ideal location.

Below: Dalguise House in Perthshire and (right) Wray Castle, where the Potter family spent many summers.

Her father spent a lot of his holiday fishing and shooting and invited a number of his friends to join him, including the Quaker, John Bright and the Pre-Raphaelite artist, Sir John Millais, a keen angler and inventor of the Millais salmon fly. No doubt it was here, and later in the Lake District, that Beatrix gained her knowledge of fish and fishing. Indeed, a surviving photograph from this period shows the young Beatrix sitting in the garden at Dalguise with her father and mother together with a brace of salmon, caught by her father, on the lawn in front of her. Another photograph shows Beatrix and her brother Bertram sitting in the back of a rowing boat about to embark on a fishing party on the Tay. Over dinner at Dalguise, fishing was a common topic of conversation and Beatrix recalls her father's friend, Sir William Brown annoying the butler by manoeuvring the cutlery around the table to illustrate his fight with a giant salmon. It was at Dalguise that Beatrix developed a passionate love of nature and, together with her brother spent hours roaming the hills and fields, sketching what she saw.

As she grew older, she became particularly interested in fungi and lichen and she struck up a friendship with Charlie Mackintosh, the postman at Dalguise and keen amateur naturalist. During the winter months, when she was back in London, Mackintosh would send her specimens of fungi to draw. Indeed, Beatrix became something of an expert on fungi and she even wrote a scientific paper on the subject, which was presented to the Linnaean Society. However, she was not allowed to read her paper in person since women were barred from attending meetings. Many of her scientific paintings of fungi can now be viewed at the Armitt Museum and Library at Ambleside.

In the Lake District the family spent their summer vacations at a number of locations including Wray Castle on the shores of Windermere, and Fawe Park and Lingholm near Derwentwater. Fishing and boating on the lakes was a favourite pastime. It was at Wray that she first met the Reverend Hardwicke Rawnsley, vicar of Wray, who encouraged her writing and painting and instilled in her a great love of the Lake District and its conservation.

Beatrix Potter's first venture into publishing occurred when she was twenty-four. For Christmas 1889 she had designed and painted a series of Christmas cards and place-cards. Her uncle, Sir Henry Roscoe, was impressed by these and suggested she submit them to a publisher. Subsequently, she designed six cards using her pet rabbit, Bounce, as her model. Her brother, Bertram, delivered them personally to the firm of Hildesheimer and Faulkner. The following day she received a cheque for £6 and a request for more drawings. The company produced cards of some of her drawings, the rest they used to illustrate a booklet of verses by Frederic E. Weatherly, entitled *A Happy Pair*.

In 1892 and 1893 the family returned to Scotland for their annual vacation. In 1893, they rented a house in Dunkeld called Eastwood, situated on the banks of the Tay. It was from here, on 4th September, that she wrote an illustrated letter to Noel Moore, the son of a former governess who had fallen ill:

My dear Noel,
I don't know what to write to you, so I shall tell you a story about four little rabbits, whose names were Flopsy, Mopsy, Cottontail and Peter.
They lived with their mother in a sand bank under the root of a big fir tree.

Here, in essence was the *Tale of Peter Rabbit*, which Beatrix herself published privately in 1901 in an edition of 250 copies. A year later it was published by Frederick Warne with coloured illustrations.

The Tale of Peter Rabbit was an immediate success and within a year it had sold over 55,000 copies. Not surprisingly, her publishers were eager for more and in 1903 two more of her stories were published, *The Tailor of Gloucester* and *The Tale of Squirrel Nutkin*. The latter story was set on the shores of Derwentwater where the Potters spent a number of their summer holidays. One of the illustrations features the squirrels fishing for minnows to take as a gift to Mr Brown (an owl) who lived on Owl Island (St Herbert's Island). They managed to catch seven fat minnows, which they presented to Mr Brown in return for permission to gather nuts on the island.

Over the next couple of years more of Beatrix Potter's tales were published, which resulted in a close relationship developing between Beatrix and Norman Warne, her publisher. Eventually they fell in love and in the summer of 1905 Norman proposed to her. Much to her parents' dismay Beatrix accepted his proposal. Her parents felt that she was marrying beneath her social status. However, her engagement to Norman was short-lived since later that summer he fell ill and died of leukaemia at the end of August. It was during the same summer that Beatrix learnt that Hill Top Farm at Near Sawrey was up for sale. She knew the village well having spent many summer holidays in the area. With the help of royalties from her books and a small inheritance she had received, she concluded the purchase of Hill Top in November.

The Tale of Mr Jeremy Fisher was one of the last stories she had discussed with Norman Warne before his death. She had originally proposed doing a story about a frog in a letter to Norman in November 1902 and in February 1905 she sent him the text of *Jeremy Fisher*. Like *The Tale of Peter Rabbit* the story began life in September 1893 as an illustrated letter to Noel Moore's brother, Eric, written from Eastwood House the day after the letter to Noel. The character, Jeremy Fisher, was almost certainly based upon the frogs that Beatrix had kept as pets. In the letter, Jeremy's home was a little house on the banks of the Tay where he spent his time fishing. A year later, in 1894, she produced a series of pen and ink sketches for the firm of Ernest Nister entitled 'A Frog he would a-fishing go'. Eventually the drawings appeared in two of Nister's children's annuals. Following the publication of *Peter Rabbit* in 1902 she bought back the frog drawings from Nister so that there would be no question of copyright ownership when she revised the story for Warne's.

During the winter of 1905 and spring of 1906 Beatrix spent as much time as she could at Hill Top where she produced many sketches of Esthwaite Water and Moss Eccles Tarn. When *The*

Above: Moss Eccles Tarn and (left) Hill Top Farm, home of Beatrix Potter.

Tale of Mr Jeremy Fisher was published in July 1906 the setting for the story was changed from the banks of the Tay to a pond covered in water-lilies, believed to be modelled on Moss Eccles Tarn situated above the village of Near Sawrey. Another source of inspiration for the story was the work of the popular children's illustrator, Randolph Caldecott, who had written and illustrated a story entitled *A Frog He Would A-Wooing Go.* Beatrix's father admired Caldecott's work and had bought two of his frog drawings. Jeremy's elegant Regency attire is almost certainly based on Caldecott's frog.

Over the next few years Beatrix spent as much of her time as possible at Hill Top and began to increase her land holdings by buying up adjacent fields when they became available. In May 1909, she bought Castle Farm, a farm opposite Hill Top and above the Kendal Road. The purchase of this farm brought her into contact with the local solicitor, William Heelis, whose offices

were in nearby Hawkshead. Heelis was well placed to know in
advance when land was coming up for sale and he kept Beatrix
informed as she endeavoured to increase her land holdings.
Gradually the pair fell in love and they were married in October 1913, when she was forty-seven and he was forty-two.
The marriage proved a very happy one. William was a keen
angler and field sportsman and shortly after they married
Beatrix purchased some land above Near Sawrey, which included
Moss Eccles Tarn. The tarn had been artificially created around
1900 following the damming of a stream. Beatrix set about
planting trees around the tarn and stocked it with trout for
William. They spent many a happy evening together fishing on
the tarn as the following letter of June 1924 to her friend Louie
Choyce illustrates:

*Yesterday evening was the first really warm night. William and I fished
(at least I rowed) till darkness; coming down the lane about eleven. It was
lovely on the tarn, not a breath of wind and no midges. The fish were
'taking short', running at the fly without getting hooked, but he caught
4 which was plenty. We put back the smallest, the other 3 weighed over
4lbs together, the biggest was 1 lb 10 ozs. They were exciting to catch as
they fought and made rushes to get under the boat.*

Throughout the remaining years of her life Beatrix became
increasingly interested in farming and was an expert on the
breeding of the native Herdwick sheep, winning many prizes at
local agricultural shows. She was also passionate about the preservation of the Lake District and was actively involved in the
National Trust. When she died in 1943 she bequeathed over
4,000 acres of land to the National Trust, together with her farms,
cottages and flock of Herdwick sheep. In addition, she left the
enduring legacy of twenty-three books, which continue to
delight succeeding generations of children.

HERE AND THERE
AN ANGLER'S MEMORIES
BY
TINDALL HARRIS.

A chatty little volume of Reminiscences
of Fishing in Cumberland, Scotland,
Ireland and New Zealand.

Cloth, 134 pp.   Illus.   Price 3/6 net; by post 3/10.
BOOK DEPARTMENT,
The Fishing Gazette, Ltd., 19, Adam Street, Strand, London.

18

Here and There with Tindall Harris

Tindall Harris was not a native of the Lake District, although he lived near Derwentwater for a number of years in the early part of the twentieth century. In 1924, aged sixty-two, he wrote a book of angling reminiscences entitled *Here and There, An Angler's Memories*, the first chapter of which deals with his fishing experiences in Cumberland.

Tindall Harris was born in Leighton Buzzard, Bedfordshire on 28th June, 1862. His unusual forename was taken from his paternal grandmother, Isabella Tindall. His father was Theodore Harris, a banker, who came from Middlesex, while his mother, Ann Fletcher, hailed from Cumberland. Thus he had Cumbrian blood in his veins. He was educated at Oliver's Mount, Scarborough, from where he proceeded to Gonville and Caius College, Cambridge, in the autumn of 1880. After graduating in 1884, he followed in his father's footsteps and became a banker. In November 1897, he set off on a trip round the world on the P&O ship *Himalaya*, arriving at Adelaide on Christmas Day. On Christmas night he had a wonderful dinner on board ship and the captain's health was drunk with great enthusiasm. From Adelaide he went on to Melbourne and from there to New Zealand. The crossing from Melbourne to New Zealand was a little rough, as the following amusing incident makes clear:

One Sunday, somewhere between Hobart and New Zealand, we were sitting at lunch in the saloon, and the ship was rolling rather heavily. I was at a narrow table seating eight, three on each side and one at each end, placed athwart the vessel. At one end, and with her back to the starboard side of the ship, sat a middle-aged lady neatly attired in black silk and making one think of 'Charley's Aunt'. We were taking our soup - or trying to - and we had the 'fiddles' on as a safeguard, when suddenly a much bigger roll than usual occurred. The 'Charley's Aunt' end of the table sank prodigiously and all our plates of soup were at once shot, in spite of fiddles, into the poor lady's lap.

On arrival in the South Island of New Zealand he fished the river Rangitata, where he caught a number of fine trout including a specimen of 8lb. The fish were caught on a Whitebait Phantom, a light minnow made to imitate the whitebait on which the trout feed. A little later he fished the river Rakaia, where he killed a few fish. On moving to the North Island he caught some good trout up to 2 or 3lb, with natural grasshopper. But first, he had to catch the grasshopper!

One crawled about on hands and knees with an empty matchbox until a sufficient supply was obtained, then impaled a hopper on the hook, and cast it like a fly, but very gingerly or it would come off.

However, it was not only trout he caught in New Zealand. While staying with the family of a friend who owned a sheep station on the Canterbury plains, he met and fell in love with another guest from England, Emily Naylor. They married in Melbourne, before returning home via the Pacific, San Francisco and New York, arriving in Liverpool on 15th October, 1898. The 1901 census records Harris and his wife living at Portinscale, near

DERWENTWATER.

Keswick, where he is described as being a colliery owner. His mother's family were clearly well-to-do and his uncles, Isaac and William Fletcher, were successively MPs for Cockermouth. Not surprisingly, since he lived near Keswick, he fished a great deal on Derwentwater.

In his book, *Here and There* (1924) we learn that he fished Derwentwater more than any other Cumberland lake and he is full of praise for the lake and its trout:

The Derwentwater trout, when you get him, takes a lot of beating. Two years ago I had the opportunity of comparing with, within a day or two, the edible qualities of the inhabitants of Loch Leven and Derwentwater respectively and the Derwentwaters I really think 'had it'. The trouble with our Derwentwater friends, or foes, seems to be that, owing to a very generous larder on the lake bottom (sometimes when caught their mouths being full of water snails), they are not quite so keen as they might be on artificial flies, but Derwentwater, being one of the most beautiful lakes in the world, has power to soothe in part even the unsuccessful angler. The western shore of the lake on a fine morning in early June, with the fresh green of the oaks overhanging the rocky shore, is surely almost matchless.

Harris often fished Derwentwater with Harrison Dixon, another resident of Portinscale. Dixon was a very keen angler who might be seen on the lake on any favourable spring day. When the trout season was over he would turn his attention to the lake's resident population of pike and perch. Harris' largest trout from Derwentwater involved Dixon and another friend who was awarded the CMG during the First World War. (The CMG, meaning a Companion of the Order of St Michael and St George, was awarded to individuals for important non-military service in a foreign country.)

A friend who was fond of fishing, used to come with his wife and stay with us for a week or two about Mayfly time. He afterwards, by the way, received the CMG for war service in the Ypres Salient and elsewhere. One morning, the wind being East, he and I were drifting across from the Cass towards Nichol End landing. We were perhaps 100 yards off the latter when a fish took my fly. As it was evidently a big one my friend wound up his own line and took the oars. Enter (as they say on the stage) Harrison, making gently down the lake for home, and negligently trailing a cast of flies behind his boat. Somehow or other his line mounted the bows of our boat, and his tail fly got firmly embedded in the exact centre of the back of my friend's coat, who was engaged at the moment in keeping us off the reeds. It was almost like a proposition in Euclid. I was attached to the fish, the future CMG was attached to the oars and could not leave them, and was also himself being 'played' by Harrison at a distance of some 40 yards! Somehow, we got that fly out, or cut the gut, I forget which, and were able to carry on. The trout when netted weighed 3lbs, and was the biggest I have ever killed on Derwentwater.

Another familiar figure on Derwentwater was Tom Hudspith (shown opposite), a keeper employed by Mr Reginald Marshall. Hudspith could always be recognised on the water because of his unique style of fishing. His flies only remained on the water for a few seconds before being recovered for a fresh cast. Harris tells a rather tall story concerning old Tom Hudspith:

Well, old Tom was out duck-shooting one day, but the ducks were not accommodating, so he started trolling for pike. He soon caught a large fish - I think 37lbs was mentioned - and, as it lay gasping in the boat a couple of ducks flew out of its mouth. Picking up his gun Tom got them both with a right and left.

Harris was concerned at the quality of trout fishing on Derwentwater and felt that it could be improved by reducing the number of pike in the lake. He refers to an experiment twenty years previously (around 1900) when the lake was netted and a good number of pike were removed. One of the pike caught was found to have no less than three undigested trout inside its stomach. Harris himself had the head of one of these pike, a 22-pounder, set up. He also felt that the fishing rights on Derwentwater should be vested in a responsible committee or trust, which would control the fishery in the interests of local people and visitors alike.

His best day's trout fishing on Derwentwater occurred at Whitsuntide, 1922, when the trout were well on the mayfly. On that memorable day he took nine fish, ranging in size from ½lb to 2lb. Harris believed there were two distinct populations of trout in Derwentwater:

There is an extraordinary difference in the fish one gets on Derwent-water. I got two yesterday (May 26th, 1924) with Mayfly of just over 1lb apiece and within about 100 yards of the same spot. One was bright and silvery, like a Loch Leven, the other brown and yellow bellied; both were pink-fleshed and equally good eating. These lake fish never seem to be much out of condition, even when caught in March.

He thinks the difference in colour of the trout could be attributed to some fish put in the lake some years previously, which had not inter-bred with the others. Nowadays, Derwentwater is perhaps more noted for its pike fishing than trout fishing and, although Harris mainly fished for trout, he occasionally fished for perch and pike. His largest pike from Derwentwater weighed in at 14lb and was caught trolling.

As well as fishing Derwentwater, Harris fished a number of other lakes in the area. As a youngster he recalls fishing for perch with his brothers on Bassenthwaite. On one memorable day they caught sixty good fish. On another occasion he recalls trout fishing on Bassenthwaite when he caught five trout, which all weighed exactly 1¼lb each. In addition, he fished Loweswater, Crummock Water and Buttermere. He tells an amusing story of a day's fishing on Buttermere with Harrison Dixon:

I occasionally had a day with Harrison, and I remember fishing Buttermere with him on one occasion. We had had a long day, and although we worked hard had only managed to secure half a dozen fish. Before starting home we went into the hotel for some tea, and I stupidly left the fish in a net on a seat outside. A marauding cat took advantage of our absence to tear a hole in the net and clear off with several of our fish. When I came out I was annoyed, and said so, but Harrison's good-natured face showed not a flicker of irritation, and all he said was, "Oh, it doesn't matter."

In addition to the lakes, he fished some of his local rivers, including the Eden and Derwent. At the beginning of his book he recalls a fortnight's salmon fishing on the Eden at Wetheral towards the end of March. He was clearly no fly-fishing purist, as the following account indicates:

I well remember that last day of that fortnight; it was towards the end of March. My wife had to return home by the morning train; I said I would follow in the afternoon and have one more try before lunch. Well, I fished all morning blank, and about mid-day found myself on a very good pool.

I fished it first with a fly, then with angel minnow, and finally, as a last resort, with prawn. Just as I was winding the prawn in, preparatory to giving up, I got a heavy pull. It felt like a good fish, and in about a quarter of an hour I had a beautiful fresh-run twenty-pounder on the bank. This was certainly luck, occurring as it did at the penultimate moment. The fortnight produced three fish, but the other two were smaller.

He only fished the Derwent occasionally and once hooked a salmon at the railway bridge near Brigham Station, below Cockermouth, which he lost after playing it for twenty minutes. He relates an amusing story concerning the Quaker and Liberal statesman, John Bright, salmon fishing on the Derwent;

The late Mr John Bright made his initial attempt at salmon fishing on the Cumberland Derwent, somewhere below Ouse Bridge. To make quite sure, he gave his line, just above the reel, a turn round his forefinger. A fish shortly after took his fly, with fortunate results to itself, but rather otherwise to the great man's digit. Being a Quaker he would be limited to what one would call plain language! He afterwards became a very keen salmon fisher.

John Bright.

As well as fishing in New Zealand and the Lake District, Harris fished extensively in Scotland and Ireland. During the First World War he served as a Red Cross ambulance driver in France, where he had a number of escapades. On one occasion, as he was hammering a nail into his hut wall, he managed to dislodge a fire extinguisher, which fired itself off and promptly drenched a number of the hut's occupants who were trying to get some sleep!

In his later years Harris moved to Scarborough, where his wife seems to have hailed from. He died in March 1955, at the ripe old age of ninety-two in Salisbury. Harris was one of the early motoring pioneers and as well as recording his angling memories in *Here and There*, he also wrote a book on his motoring experiences entitled *Motoring Experiences in Peace and War* (1928). Both books are written in a fluent, chatty style and are full of amusing anecdotes concerning his angling and motoring experiences. They are well worth seeking out.

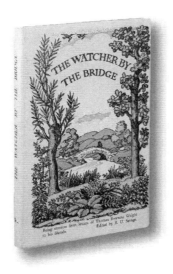

19

Thomas Bowness Wright
THE WATCHER BY THE BRIDGE

Few fishermen can walk over a bridge over a river without paus-
ing for a moment and peering into the watery depths below. I
certainly can't! Not long ago, I recall walking over a bridge span-
ning the river Calder in Lancashire and leaning over the parapet
to gaze into the water below. My attention was immediately
caught by a pair of barbel spawning in the shallows by the bridge
abutment. Every movement of the larger of the pair, a fish of
around five or six pounds and presumably the female, was being
shadowed by the male, a fish of around three or four pounds,
ready to fertilise her eggs. I must have stood there for fully fifteen minutes, totally absorbed by the spectacle. I was similarly
entranced by the sight of salmon excavating their redds as I
peered over a bridge on the river Nith. At the bridge over
the river Ribble at Paythorne in Lancashire, it was a tradition
for locals to gather on the third Sunday of November, known
as 'Salmon Sunday', to watch salmon spawning in the shallows
below.

Thomas Bowness Wright, an inhabitant of the tiny hamlet of Gaisgill near Tebay and schoolmaster of Longdale School, was not only an angler but an habitual watcher from the local bridge over the river Lune. His observations of the local flora and fauna, much of it observed from the bridge, was conveyed in a series of letters to his friends, especially the Reverend E. U. Savage, vicar of Ings, and writer of a natural history column in the *Westmorland Gazette*. From 1921 onwards, many of his letters were addressed to Arthur Astley, Savages's successor as natural history columnist, who wrote under the nom-de-plume 'Alpha'. Not long after Wright's death in 1935, these letters were edited by Savage and published by Titus Wilson of Kendal in 1936, in a book entitled *The Watcher by the Bridge*. These charming letters, dating from 1917 through till December 1934, contain much of interest to the angler and naturalist and give a wonderful insight into the state of the natural environment almost a century ago.

Thomas Bowness Wright was born on 15th December, 1865, at Old Hutton, Westmorland. His father and grandfather were both blacksmiths and it was almost certainly from them that he inherited his considerable practical skills. It appears that the family moved to Kendal while Thomas was still a child. In the 1881 census he is recorded as being a pupil teacher, residing at Strickland Gate, Kendal. Pupil teachers completed a five-year apprenticeship in teaching and learning within a school context before qualifying as an assistant teacher. By the age of twenty-five he was working as a schoolmaster in Kendal. In October 1907, at the age of forty-one, he married Agnes Taylor and not long afterwards they moved to Gaisgill where he became master of Longdale School. They had two sons, Henry and Edgar. He remained at Longdale School until his retirement at the end of September 1930.

While living at Gaisgill, it appears that Wright was in the habit of going to the bridge over the Lune after supper to smoke his pipe. It seems that he spent considerable time there talking to passers-by and observing the wildlife around him. He would often return home quite late and then begin writing up his observations until the early hours of the morning. In his letters he frequently records sightings of otters:

17th June, 1918.

About two hours ago I went to The Bridge to smoke an after-supper pipe and see what was to be seen - if anything. Really it was the otter I went to look for and took the glasses, they gather the light somewhat, even after dusk. It is a long time since I saw an otter until last week. On the 12th I saw one come up, and on the 15th one passed through the pool going down, I only saw the waves.

COMMON OTTER.

18th June, 1921.

Now to those otters. I'm one of the luckiest fellows alive. I've been privileged to see a few of the antics of the wild creatures, but last night was, I think, the night of my life. I'd been to Tebay and got back a few minutes before 10. I locked my bicycle up and as I put the keys away spake thus to the wife of my chest, "I think I'll have a walk to The Bridge." I fancy I've made the remark more than once before. The hedge on this side, below The Bridge, is now laid and there is a view of the river before you reach The Bridge. Sometimes the creatures are disturbed if you look over The Bridge. So last night I peeped over the wall before I got there. What! The pool was agitated in a way that told its own story. There he went into the drinking gap. Now under the ash tree root. Out again into the stream and a plop up. He was making up under The Bridge so I crossed the road and waited. Waves! He's coming! Two! Two otters about 10 lbs apiece. Twins, so far as appearances went. Sometimes slopping along under the overhanging bank, sometimes diving like two grey fish.

Up they went by the usual route, but not in the usual way. They seemed to be hungry and were diligently searching for food: it took them quite a long time to work the stretch between The Bridge and the bend.

But when they reached the bend, what a commotion! Wild ducks raising Cain! Water flying, dark objects splashing, ditto rolling and tumbling and running about in the water and on the cobble bed. Which was duck and which was otter I couldn't make out and I had no glasses...

There are several other references to sightings of otters and their antics, and one report in December 1931 of the tragic death of an otter, attacked by two sheep dogs. Although otters are now making something of a comeback following years of persecution and pollution, it is clear they were far more numerous in Wright's day. Elsewhere in his letters he records sighting of hares, rabbits and even a stoat swimming across the river. One evening in 1921, while the family were seated at dinner with the door wide open, a bird appeared on the flags at the door and looked in. It turned out to be a corncrake. In another letter dated 25th June, 1929, he mentions that there has been a corncrake about. Nowadays, due to changes in agricultural practices, you would be unlikely to find a corncrake in the Lake District. They are now mainly confined to the Hebrides and Western Isles of Scotland and the only time I have seen a corncrake was at the Balranald RSPB reserve on North Uist.

Wright encouraged his pupils to take an interest in natural history and on several occasions they brought unusual creatures to school for their master to identify, as the following letter records:

25th June, 1929.
A boy brought some newts to School a short time ago and we kept them during the morning in a bucket with some good sized stones and water . . . I let the children see me handle them and showed them how harmless the pretty creatures are.

Throughout the letters there are numerous references to angling and it is clear that Wright was mainly a fly fisherman for the trout, sea trout and salmon of the Lune. Occasionally, however, he does refer to other freshwater fish and in a letter dated 11th May, 1920, he recalls a day many years before when he fished Whinfell Tarn with G. A. Hutchinson, a member of the famous hook-making family of Kendal (see Chapter 8):

Although I look back, through many years, to a famous day he (Hutchinson) and I had among the rudd at Whinfell Tarn. I caught the first fish - a nice rudd - which Addie (Adlington) carefully killed and packed away in weed and afterwards stuffed. It found a resting place in Carlisle Museum and may be there yet.

Wright was clearly not a fan of eels. In a letter of 18th February, 1919, he quotes angling author Carter Platts on eels, 'the eel is composed of slime, immortality and cussedness'. Elsewhere in the same letter he recalls an accidental capture of an eel:

Did you ever get an eel fishing at night? I once foul-hooked one with fly off the tail end of the Island. Ugh! If you are ever in a similar plight perhaps you will agree with Carter Platts.

On the upper Lune before the Second World War, fishing for trout with the natural stone fly was commonly practised, although Wright himself did not care for the method and preferred to use the artificial fly. In a letter of June 1918, he complains that the river is dead low and the only successful anglers are those employing the stone fly. The following June he voices a similar complaint. However, he did have some success with the trout, as the following letter to E. U. Savage shows:

14th October, 1919.
I trust the fishing has been better with you than with us. I got one two lbs two ozs at Tebay on 27 September with fly: became momentarily attached to one as good, or better, on 30th: landed one 14 ozs on 3 October.

In a letter of 15th March, 1921, he writes that he went fishing after tea and managed four fish, which his wife served with chips for supper! May 1922 proved to be a good month and in the space of three days he caught twenty-five fish. The year 1924 was apparently a poor season for fly fishing although the worm fishers were making some fine catches. However, in a letter dated 13th June of that year he does mention that he had had a good day, taking six fish.

As well as trout, he also enjoyed sea trout fishing, and the following letter vividly captures the excitement of latching on to one of these splendid fish:

8th June, 1920.
I took the rod and went to the New Bridge where you [E. U. Savage] had pointed out to me a good fish. I stood in the road and made a cast or two. By and by up came his nibs - a roll over and then he shot like a bullet nearly out of the low end of the pool. Back again right up under the bridge. Back and forward he went pulling and tearing about like a good one: it was the best fight I ever had, I think, at that place. I was quite sure it was foul-hooked and comforted myself that a foul-hold, in a fish, is generally a good one. When I finally did get my own way I ran him out and annexed No. 1 - and it was not foul-hooked, but a nice sea

A summer scene on the river Lune by Reginald Aspinwall, 1904.

trout 10 ounces. That was about 9.30. I went on to Longdale Beck foot and brought a small one out. A cast or two and I was into another good one, which put up a similar splendid fight to No. 1 and turned out to be another sea trout of 10 ounces. I put the flies over them again and finished by taking four in all from the pool. I came away about 10 with five nice fish.

As well as fishing, Wright was a very practical man, and not only did he dress his own flies, he also made much of his own tackle. One of his favourite flies was a black fly with wings made from the shining feather of a rook. He believed the fish mistook it for a beetle and he reported that he had good sport with it in the autumn of 1920, fishing at night when the moon was big. In addition to dressing flies, he boiled his own wax for fly tying. He even made his own rods and reels and devised a circular saw for splitting cane, geared up by an old Eagle cream separator, which he had bought for a shilling. His lathe, too, was made up of oddments but, on it, he managed to turn plates for two trout reels and was hoping to develop a salmon reel. Such was his skill that he was commissioned by a local angler to make a landing-net. His crowning glory must surely be the 17-foot salmon rod that he made in 1919. The rod had a solid cane butt, a reed cane middle and a built cane top. It wasn't long before he put his new rod to use complete with a Thunder and Lightning salmon fly - Gaisgill pattern - tied by his own hands. He records the capture of a number of salmon in his letters but his biggest fish is dramatically described in a letter dated 12th December, 1934, just a few months before his death, and refers to a fish caught in October of that year.

The last three days of the month were passable and I came to the con-clusion I must either risk it or miss the season. So off I went and tried likely - as I thought - places here and there without result until I got to the Banker Dub. There was a nice run through and just where the stream began to break 'R-r-r' I could feel there was a bit of weight. Then the fight began - and it was a fight. I think it was about as stubborn a fish as I've ever handled - boring and boring and then a spell of sulking. I wanted it out of the Dub because I thought I'd make more of it if I had it in the long, streamy, shallower stretch below. And another thing - my great dread - I knew there was a big slab sticking out of the bank and resting on another with its end projecting vertically above the gravel. I didn't want it to thread this needle and I dare not try to skull-drag it for I had my strong rod, and only a medium cast and a small fly - about an eight. Happily we kept clear. Before we left the Dub it made some violent efforts to free itself - came out on the top and shook itself and lashed and rolled; but the climax in the drama came when it stood almost perpen-dicular on its head and gave a grand lash with its tail hoping, I expect, that it might break the line. But it didn't. I think, perhaps, the next stunt was a sulk on the far side. I could see the line which appeared to go into the gravel but could not see the fish and I couldn't understand being 'hung-up' on gravel. So I began to wade out and investigate. Yes, it was there all right and I think it didn't go up the Dub after that - not far if it did. Then down stream for about, perhaps, 250 or 300 yards - but not all at once! It was a slow game and I seemed to be gaining little ground in the way of killing it - the weight was there. But by and by I got it into the side at a place where I thought I might be able to get a hold. It was close to the bank and well up in the water. Here goes! I quietly approached, quietly laid my left hand on its back with fingers well over, found the 'handle' and - grab! Up! Out it came! Ugh! It's slipping! I dropped my rod and eased its head up, looked where my line was and found the fly had dropped out. All clear! Forward! I dropped it and went for a 'rock' to finish it. Near shave wasn't it? I think the hook had been in the thin skin inside the lower jaw: it is very thin there and the bone very hard. Forty minutes I'd been at it and my right arm ached intensely.

The salmon weighed 17lb 6oz. Sadly, a few months later, on 18th May, 1935, Thomas Bowness Wright passed away in Westmorland County Hospital, Kendal, following a brief illness. He left his estate, valued at a little over fifteen hundred pounds, to his widow. However, before he died he passed on his love of fishing and the natural world not only to his own two sons Henry and Edgar, but also to the Rev. Savage's son, Peter. In a letter dated 8th May, 1922 he wrote:

Catching fish is only a part of the greater life of the quiet nature-loving angler.

I totally agree with Wright's sentiment. There is far more to fishing than simply catching fish - *piscator non solum piscatur* - as the motto of the Flyfishers' Club elegantly states.

Not long ago I visited Gaisgill, where I learnt from a local that Wright's house had been demolished several years ago. However, Longdale School (now a private house) and the bridge over the Lune, where he spent many happy hours watching the river and its wildlife, still remain.

20

William Nelson
A FISHER IN EDEN

Every young angler needs a mentor, someone who will teach him or her the rudiments of angling - how to tie on a hook, what type of float to use, how to shot it, how to cast a fly and what fly to use at certain times of year. I was lucky. My mentor was my best friend's father who lived across the road from my house. His name was John and, along with my best friend, he took me on his fishing expeditions to local lakes and canals and, occasionally, even further afield to the Lancaster Canal and Glasson Dock. It was from him that I learnt the rudiments of angling and I am eternally grateful. Angling has been an important part of my life for over fifty years and long may it continue.

William Nelson, author of *Fishing in Eden* (1922), one of the classic angling books of the twentieth century, also had a mentor, whom he refers to as 'Bob'. As a result of research carried out by the angling historian, John Austin, it appears that Bob's real name was Tom Harrison, a stonemason living in Bongate, Appleby. William Nelson, too, was born and spent his formative years at Paradise Cottage in Bongate. In fact, Nelson was born on 16th June, 1862, the son of Joseph Nelson, a yeoman farmer, whose family had lived near Appleby for several generations. Nelson attended the local school in Appleby and was much impressed by the teaching methods of its master, who often took the children out into the local area on field trips.

Nelson seems to have had an idyllic childhood, helping out on the family farm and at the local mill where, together with the miller's sons, he helped to turn the oats on the drying-kiln. During the summer time, Nelson and his friends could often be found by the Eden or its tributaries in search of trout, but not with rod and line:

There was no Board of Conservators on the Eden then, and one could do pretty much as one liked. In summer time one of our great pleasures was to organise trout-grappling expeditions up the tributary becks of the Eden. We knew every 'hold' under sod and stone where good trout lurked, watching through their little doorways for the fish food that came float-ing down. Stripped to the waist, or with our shirt sleeves rolled up, we jumped from bank to bank and stone to stone, and tried every 'hold'. There was not much of what is known in modern language as 'trout-tickling' in our method of work. If we touched a fish in its little house we always took good care to block up the doorway with our hands, and, seizing it by the gills, soon had it bouncing out far back on the bank. There was great competition and racing for the well-known good 'holds', which were always the abiding places of sizeable trout. They were like particular runs of the main river, which the experienced fisher-man knows carry good fish. Take one out to-day and there is another of pretty much the same size in its place to-morrow.

In this way the young Nelson developed an intimate acquain-tance with the river and its tributaries and an instinct for good reaches of water.

During the winter time, when the river and becks were frozen, Nelson and his friends enjoyed tracking otters and other wild animals in the snow. There were few boys in his circle of friends

Appleby Castle by Thomas Hearne.

who could not set snares for rabbits or night lines for trout. Indeed, it was the setting of night lines that inspired the young Nelson to take up fishing with rod and line. Eventually, he managed to make his own rod with a larch butt and lancewood top, equipped with rings and holders bought from the local ironmonger's. A local farm provided the material for a line:

It was necessary to go off again foraging for material, and at a neighbouring farm where there were, and are still, white horses, I managed to get sufficient hair to set about spinning a line. If Hardy's existed at that time, I had not heard of it, or that such simple things as lines could be bought for money, even had I possessed it.

He acquired a reel and hooks by saving up his pocket money and managed to obtain permission from the Steward at Appleby Castle to fish its waters. Like most youngsters, his first attempt at fishing was not as successful as he might have hoped. Fishing in a spate, he managed to hook a fish, but struck so hard that he snapped the larch butt of his rod just below the splice. Many years later, history almost repeated itself when he was teaching his youngest son to fish:

There is evidently something in heredity, for the first time I took my youngest boy out to fish I tackled him up, put him into a deep hole, and sat down behind him to put on a minnow myself. Just as I was in the act of tying I was astonished to get a hard knock on the top of the head, and found it to be a half-pound trout he had thrown over his own, without any thought of waiting for a net. He was as proud as Lucifer, and, in spite of all I said, would set off home, a distance of a mile and a half, to show the monster to his sister. He did not snap his rod, but he forgot to take it home with him.

It was the sudden death of his father in 1875, when the young Nelson was only thirteen that brought him into closer contact with Bob, the angling mentor who was to have such an influence on his life. As we have already seen, Bob was a local stonemason and a keen angler. He was also a good singer who was popular at local concerts for his tenor solos. Around the time of his father's death, Nelson's voice began to break and, as a result, he lost his place in the local choir. Bob was anxious that some of the young men should learn bass and not be lost to the choir. Therefore, he organised singing practice for them at his home, more particularly, in his kitchen, which according to Nelson was the most attractive place he had ever been in.

There were cases of stuffed birds and animals on the walls: a shot gun hung to the big ceiling-beam, and by the side of the mantelpiece an old yeomanry sword.

Not surprisingly, the talk often turned to fishing and the boys would sit enthralled as they watched Bob tying the delicate North-country flies, much used on the Eden.

It was our custom to gather round his kitchen fire on winter evenings, when the wild helm blew across the snow-clad Pennines, and watch him tie his flies, and make up his casts for the coming season.
He was always looking forward to each new spring time of his sport with an infectious kind of boyish enthusiasm; an enthusiasm which appealed to us, and made us ever his willing and devoted disciples.

As well as fly dressing, Bob instructed his disciples on the making and repairing of fishing rods, oiling reels and patching waders. During the summer he taught them to cast a fly on the Eden below Appleby Castle.

In *Fishing in Eden* (1922), Nelson affectionately recalls his first fishing expedition with Bob on that river. After tying on a cast of three flies, a Light Snipe at the tail, a Blue Hawk on the middle dropper and a Partridge and Orange on the top dropper, Bob gave his young acolyte the following advice:

"Ye mun use a short line, fish up and across towards t' far bank, and mind ye keep raisen t' point o' yer rod efter t'flees are on t' watter, but doan't click back as ther fawen. Ye'll freeten t' fish if they see a row o' flees trailen ower their heeds. Yer cast mun come doon wi' t' watter, and when it's gitten a yard or twea below ya and beginnin' to trail throw again."

Taking heed of Bob's advice, the young Nelson managed to catch a few trout but lost a number of fish through striking too heavily. At the end of the day, Bob walked home with a pannier full of fish while Nelson returned with his pannier half full but with a head filled with the valuable lessons of his mentor.

Following that first outing, Nelson fished many times with Bob and gradually, under the watchful eye of his mentor, became an accomplished angler. The time comes, however, when every young man has to earn a living and in the census of 1881, William, who was now eighteen, was recorded as being a joiner and cabinet maker with the firm of Slinger and Gowling of Appleby. Not long afterwards, he decided to better himself by attending Elmfield College in York and then King's College, London, where he studied to be a teacher. After graduating with a Master of Arts degree, he gained employment as superintendent of the London County Council's School for the Deaf. He had a particular interest in the Sloyd system of education (developed in Finland), which was based on handicrafts, no doubt inspired by his carpentry skills. By 1891, he was back in the north and senior master at the Royal Residential School for the Deaf in Manchester. A year later, he married Annie Read, the daughter of a London doctor and took up a post as Organiser of Manual Instruction for the Manchester School Board. During the same decade he published a book on woodwork education entitled, *Woodwork Course for Boys* (1893).

The start of the twentieth century saw him back at the Royal School for the Deaf, this time as headmaster, a position he was to hold for the next twenty-five years. During the Great War he assisted the Ministry of Pensions by assessing soldiers made deaf by the noise of battle, for which he was awarded the OBE in June, 1918. However, two years earlier, one of his sons, Joseph Lawrie, a Second Lieutenant in the Manchester Regiment, was tragically killed by the accidental discharge of a rifle.

Throughout his time in Manchester, Nelson never forgot his roots in Appleby and returned frequently to fish the Eden. As well as fishing, he enjoyed golf and was a founder member of the Appleby Golf Club, established in 1894, and treasurer of Manchester Golf Club from 1906 to 1909. Over the years he wrote a number of articles on angling for *The Penrith Observer*

Opposite: Flies from Fishing in Eden.

and the *Fishing Gazette*. His greatest contribution to angling literature, however, was *Fishing in Eden*, published in 1922 and now a classic of its genre. As well as dealing with his angling apprenticeship under Bob, the book describes his various methods of fishing for trout and grayling in the Eden and its tributaries, as well as examining aspects of the trout's biology and the insects on which it feeds.

Like many anglers of his era, Nelson was no fly-fishing purist and would resort to the natural creeper and stone fly, worm or minnow, as conditions dictated. Fishing the natural creeper (the nymph of the stone fly) and the stone fly, is a form of angling rarely practised nowadays. Nelson himself realised that this was bait fishing and was aware that some anglers despised bait fishing. As its name implies, the stone fly is mainly found in stony rivers in the north of England, Scotland and Ireland. Creeper fishing is normally at its best from the beginning of May, and lasts until the nymph has left the water. Nelson preferred to fish it when the water was low and the weather bright. He comments that the creeper is tougher than the stone fly and requires less careful casting.

Stone Fly   Creeper

The creeper is fished in strong streams, and the rougher the streams are the better. The rapid runs under banks, by the sides of gravel beds, are always very deadly places. If the water happens to be fairly full when the creeper is on its precarious, and often slow, way to dry land, the edges of the river are the places to fish.

To obtain a supply of creepers, Nelson would wade into a suitable stream, holding a net firmly on the bottom. Then, he would shuffle his feet on the bottom to dislodge the stones, resulting in the creepers being washed into his net. For fishing the creeper, Nelson used a two-hook rig, with lower hook inserted at the top, thick end of the tail and the top hook inserted through the tough skin of the thorax. In his book, Nelson describes a successful day's creeper fishing on the Eamont.

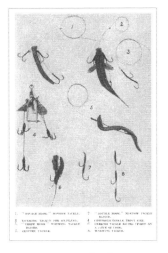

After fishing up about a mile and a half I came across two men in the middle of the water, also using creeper. On being asked how they were getting on, one of them said, "Very badly," and the other that, "the water was too high for any sport at all with the creeper." They did not inquire what I had done, but my basket was quite heavy. I passed on behind them, throwing straight up with a very short line, and dropping the bait no more than a foot from the edge. By the time I had reached Brougham I had a full load of beautiful trout!

Nelson liked fishing the natural stone fly, as opposed to the creeper, and he would cast to rising fish. He considered the best places for this method of fishing to be the quiet runs below banks, around stones and roots, and in eddies over the main stream. His tackle consisted of a ten-foot-six fly rod with a three yard tapered cast at the business end. When he first started employing this method, he found that the fish, in rising to the large fly, frequently missed it. Acting on Bob's advice, he started to clip off half of the fly's wings, and from that day onwards few fish were missed.

Clear water worm fishing, when the river is low, is another branch of angling rarely encountered nowadays. It was the long dry summer of 1887 that first tempted Nelson to try this method. With Bob's assistance, he made a long, light double-

The lower Eamont facing Cross Fell.

handed rod and, following directions in Stewart's, *Practical Angler* (1871), soon tied up suitable three-hook tackles. He soon found that smaller worms of an inch and a half were more effective than larger ones and that the worm should not be allowed to curl up but should be fished on the hook fairly straight. His best day using this method occurred in 1889, when he was asked by the proprietor of a local hotel to acquire some trout for the sheriff who was paying a visit.

I set off, therefore, with the strong desire to requite him. The trout were in a taking mood, and all the conditions ideal. The long, two-handed rod had been discarded for a less clumsy and much more enjoyable Hardy 'Pennell'. I found things waiting for me almost as though the trout had known the sheriff could not sit down to dinner without fish.

By soon after twelve o'clock the strap was biting into my shoulder, and I was glad to turn out the contents of my pannier into a butter bowl at a farm, to be called for later on. Between three and four it was getting heavy again, and the great day came to a glorious end with the capture of a three-and-a-half pounder - the bonniest fish I have ever caught, before or since.

On getting home I emptied the take of nineteen and a half pounds into a favourite old butter basket of my mother's, and sent them down to my friend in good time for his evening guests.

Nelson rarely fished the minnow outside the months of August and September and, when he did fish it, it was in water not usually fished with the fly. After catching his minnows in a wire minnow trap (he believed minnows from Windermere to be the best), he preferred to preserve them in an old tobacco tin in layers of salt. He believed that minnows preserved in this way were more effective than those preserved in formalin. In fishing the minnow, he often used a Malloch reel 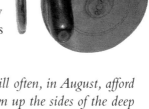 combined with a short greenheart spinning rod. In coloured water, he liked to mount the minnow on 'crocodile' tackle, while in clearer water he preferred to use 'double hook' minnow tackle (see illustration on page 227). As well as fishing the minnow on the main river, he would sometimes employ it on becks:

Beck fishing with minnow and a long rod will often, in August, afford a delightful day's sport. The minnow is thrown up the sides of the deep pools and streams, and dragged past the lairs under the banks. Very few beck fish can resist a bait of this kind as it spins past their peep holes.

As well as being an accomplished trout fisherman Nelson was also a very good grayling angler and Arthur Ransome, in his obituary of Nelson, records that he had been asked to write a book on grayling fishing but refused as he did not want people to believe he was trying to supersede Pritt's classic. The grayling is not indigenous to the Lake District and was, in fact, first introduced into the Eden system by Nelson's uncle, George Alderson (1819-1892). Alderson farmed at Great Musgrave and was married to Frances Nelson, the sister of William's father. One night in 1880, acting on the instructions of Christopher Thompson, a keen grayling angler, Alderson tipped a tank of grayling fry over the church wall and into the Eden. The fish soon settled down in the deeper water around Ormside and Appleby and by 1890 had gained a footing as far as Kirkby Thore, and three years later anglers were catching odd ones at Temple Sowerby. Nowadays, grayling are not only found in the main river but in several tributaries, including the Lyvennet, Crowdundale and Marton Beck. One of the most poetic passages in Nelson's book concerns autumn grayling fishing on the Eden:

If a choice has to be made of time, there can be no doubt that fly fishing in the autumn stands pre-eminent. October in Westmorland is often a delightful month, and I at least like to tramp my way to the fishing through the woods of crackling, fallen leaves, to see the beeches and the bracken ablaze in sunlit brown, and, here and there, to pick off the bushes a ripe hazel nut.

The peewits and golden plover are at this time of the year gathered together in noisy circling crowds, and the gay tailed pheasants disappear under the bushes.

If the beginning of a trout fisherman's content is in the spring it may well be said that it has a glorious and protracted ending in the autumn for the man who loves to throw a fly over both grayling and trout.

The last chapter of Nelson's book (Chapter XIII) contains extracts from the diary of an anonymous wet fly fisher, who is described as 'a good friend of my boyhood days, as good a fisherman as 'Bob', but more dour and solitary in his habits.' However, through the careful researches of John Austin, it now appears that this anonymous angler was Tommy Howe (1872-1955), one of the all-time fly fishing greats on the Upper Eden. As a young man Howe had fought at the Relief of Mafeking (1900) but by trade was a watch repairer. He was a dedicated fly fisherman who had an intense dislike of spinning with a fixed-spool reel. He was also critical of anglers who tipped their flies with maggots when fishing at dusk. He was a skilful fly dresser who tied his flies in hand without the aid of a vice. In his book, Nelson records extracts from Howe's diary between 9th March and 30th May. These extracts record the number of fish caught and the flies on which they were caught. It was not unusual for Howe to catch in excess of a dozen fish in a day and, on 9th May he caught fifty trout on a team of flies, which included a Light Woodcock, Dark Snipe and Water-hen and Red. His most killing flies include: the Light Snipe, Orange Partridge, Blue Hawk, Light Woodcock, Dark Snipe and Light Starling. All of these flies are illustrated in the frontispiece of Nelson's book and are just as effective today as they were almost a hundred years ago.

In 1925, after almost twenty-five years as a headmaster, Nelson was renovating Paradise Cottage in Appleby, in preparation for his retirement. He had recently made the acquaintance of Arthur Ransome, with whom he fished on a number of occasions. He was due to retire in April, 1926 and was looking forward to returning to the old family home and to fishing and playing golf. Unfortunately, fate took a hand and on Tuesday, 29th December, 1925, Nelson succumbed to pneumonia and by Friday, 1st January, 1926, he was dead.

Arthur Ransome paid a fitting tribute to him in his angling column in the *Manchester Guardian*, which later appeared in his book, *Rod and Line* (1929).

Few who fish the length of the Eden between Wild Boar Fell and Armathwaite will come to their river this year (1926) without a feeling that Eden will never be the same again. The river has lost a great fisherman who will be remembered long after all of us have laid rod and creel away for the last time. William Nelson was a schoolmaster and a golfer. I knew him as neither, though I believe he drove a straight ball and, teaching the deaf and dumb, did noble work in his profession. But it was fishing that he cared for most and he knew the Eden as few men knew it.

21

John Waller Hills
POLITICIAN & ANGLER

John Waller Hills is a name not readily associated with angling in the Lake District. Nowadays, Hills is chiefly remembered as a politician and for his book *A Summer on the Test*, first published in 1924 and running to several editions. It is regarded as a masterpiece of angling literature and evokes a period when the Test was at its best and not spoiled by commercial interests. Hills also wrote a fascinating biography of William James Lunn, keeper of the water on the Test belonging to the Houghton Club. However, although Hills was predominantly a dry-fly angler who fished the chalkstreams of southern England, he was brought up in Cumberland and had learned his fishing with wet fly on the Eden. In his autobiographical book, *My Sporting Life*, published in 1936, he tells us that he fished in Cumberland, off and on, for nearly fifty years and almost a third of his book is devoted to his angling experiences in that most beautiful part of the world.

John Waller Hills was born in London on 2nd January, 1867, the second son of Herbert Augustus Hills (1837-1909) and his wife, Anna. He was educated at Eton and Balliol College, Oxford where he read Classics and rowed for the college. In 1897 he qualified as a solicitor and became a partner in the firm Hills and Halsey. In April that year he married Stella Duckworth who tragically died of peritonitis three months later. In 1906 he was elected as Conservative MP for Durham City and not long afterwards gave up legal practice. At the outbreak of the First World War Hills, now aged forty-seven, volunteered and became a captain in the Durham Light Infantry. A year later he was promoted to the rank of major and during the Somme offensive of July 1916 he was made acting lieutenant colonel. In September he was badly wounded and mentioned in dispatches. That was the end of his war.

In 1918 he resumed his political career and four years later he was promoted to a ministerial post as financial secretary to the Treasury. Later that year he lost his seat at the general election and did not return to parliament until December 1925 when he won a by-election at Ripon. He retained his seat in 1929 and in the general elections of 1931 and 1935 but he never held office again. Such is a brief outline of Hills' legal and political career. But what of Hills the angler? Most of what we know of his angling career comes from his sporting reminiscences in *My Sporting Life*, published in 1936, two years before his death.

His reminiscences of angling in Cumberland begin in 1889 when his father took the lease of Corby Castle, renowned for its salmon coops (see Chapter 6)

Ripon Division
Parliamentary By-Election,
1925.

Major Hills comes to the Ripon Division having previously represented the City of Durham in Parliament. This will bring back to many electors memories of Mr. John Lloyd Wharton, who was member for this Division for 20 years, and who also came to us from Durham City.

MAJOR JOHN WALLER HILLS

Vote for HILLS
The CONSERVATIVE CANDIDATE.

Polling Day, Saturday, Dec. 5th.

from Mr Philip Howard. The lease included six miles of the river Eden, from Mill Beck to the Otter's Stone just below Warwick Bridge and it was on the Eden that Hills learned to fly fish for trout and salmon. Although in later life he was known as a dry-fly fisherman, in those early days on the Eden he fished for trout upstream with a team of three wet flies. However, he was not dogmatic in his approach and he claims to have caught many fine baskets of trout by fishing downstream when conditions dictated. His father leased Corby Castle from 1889 until 1902 and in those days the Eden teemed with trout, as Hills himself records:

Trout fishing was good in those early days, better than now. And fishing private water I was not tied down to a limit. I do not believe in limits: I do not think you can overfish big rivers. Most clubs impose them, some going further and restricting not only numbers of trout you may catch in one day, but the number you may catch in a season, or even the number of days on which you may fish, which is to treat the angler as a malefactor, allowed out only on ticket-of-leave. There were more trout in the Eden in those limitless days than now when clubs and associations fetter us with these ridiculous barriers. Many more. If you saw a hatch of March Brown, there seemed to be a trout in every square foot.

Hills also recalled a local Carlisle fisherman, Dickie Routledge (shown right), taking ninety fish from the Eden in one day. When the colonel who owned the beat remonstrated with him for taking so many fish, Routledge replied: "I'll tell ye what, colonel; if ye'll give me leave tomorrow, I'll back myself to kill a hundred in the same water, whatever the sort of day may be." The same Dickie Routledge, when told by

his doctor that he had not six months to live, replied: "Not six months to live! Then I'll spend them fishing." The outdoor life cured him and he lived to a ripe old age, even opening a tackle shop in Carlisle, later carried on by the Strong brothers.

Hills recorded the sort of baskets a good angler on the Eden might expect to take in a typical season by varying his approach:

For a good rod who knew the river, fishing the fly on a good day in March or April, a stone weight, about forty trout, was a good bag. It could often be got, with no harm to the water. At the end of April and during three weeks of May, the creeper, larva of the big stone fly, produced heavy baskets. In May or June fish could always be taken with fly in day-time, but not many, except in slightly coloured water, and then especially if there was a hatch of light olives. Evening fishing from mid-May to the end of July or later was excellent, twenty trout or more being no unusual bag. In July there came in a special sort of angling with the bustard, really a sedge, when you started at midnight and fished till dawn. The trout were then found cruising about in still shallow water over flat rocks. A basket of two dozen could often be made. In August the fly in the day-time and evening killed well, and in September, until fish got out of condition. All through the season from April onwards the clear-water worm was used. But the Eden is not a clear-water river, not a patch on its tributary, the Irthing. And all through the season, spring, summer or autumn, the fly killed in a coloured water. Such was the Fisherman's Year, half a century ago. Throughout it the great bulk of trout were got on fly.

For trout fishing on the Eden, Hills liked to use an 11-foot rod with a flexible top joint, his favourite being a rod made by Walbran of Leeds. The rod accounted for many fish until his brother dropped it into the river and failed to retrieve it! His angling apprenticeship on the Eden was served under two excellent masters, Mr J. Bedwell Slater, secretary to the Fishery Board and John Tuddenham, the keeper on the Corby water. The Eden trout in Hills' time ran about three to the pound and on his best day he accounted for forty-two trout, weighing in at 15lb. On many occasions he caught between twenty and thirty fish. Although he enjoyed trout fishing, Hills was not a fan of the grayling and felt that their introduction into the Eden system was responsible for a decline in the numbers of trout. He also cursed the day when grayling were introduced into the Test from the Avon and fervently hoped that 'these barbarians' would not invade the upper reaches of the Driffield Beck.

As well as fly fishing, Hills enjoyed nothing better than a day's creeper fishing and even when he was elected an MP he always reserved his Whitsuntide holiday for a few days' creeper fishing. In his *Sporting Life* he recalls a day's creeper fishing in May 1900 and gives the reader some idea of the delights of this form of angling:

The first cast with the creeper is like the first shot at driven grouse: you must hit. In fact it is more, for it tells you what sort of day you will have, since there are some places where you are perfectly certain of a chance, if trout are on the creeper. If you draw three or four such spots blank, you can go home; you will get nothing. I had a twelve-foot rod, a nine-foot cast of fine gut, and, of course, no shot. I waded out to where the stream rippled sharply over large shingle, pulled off rather more reel line than the length of my rod, baited, and threw upstream and slightly across to where a trout must be, if they were there at all. I held the point low for a sec-ond or so to let line and creeper sink, my eyes glued to the line. I was just lifting to pick up slack when the line wavered and steadied a second in its race downstream. I struck, and once more experienced that event of magic, the pull of a trout which you did not see take. Is there anything quite like it in all angling? You see nothing, feel nothing, strike against nothing, and yet there is that piece of moving solidity, a trout. And, oddly enough, he was the best of the day: not a pound - pounders are very rare - but three-quarters.

Although the Eden is notable for its trout fishing it is even more noted for its salmon fishing and, in the very first year of his father's lease on the water (1889), Hills was determined to catch a salmon. Equipped with a 17-foot bamboo and lancewood rod, bought for the princely sum of £1 from Strong's of Carlisle, he set out for the Oaktree pool shortly after breakfast on 28th October, 1889.

Fish lay all over, chiefly about one-third of the way down. The day was cloudy with clear patches, wind light from the west, water slightly coloured. I hooked and caught my first salmon, a bright hen fish of 19¼lb. My fly was a grey turkey with a body of violet silk, the Archdeacon, in fact, size No. 1.

Before the season ended on November 19th, Hills had accounted for three more salmon. Although he preferred fly fishing for salmon, he would resort to spinning when the fly failed, as the following entry from his diary records:

April 15th, 1914 - Eden at Corby. Cowies Nab with Tuddenham (the keeper). Sun fly first. Then Oak Tree with brown turkey wing, mixed wool body 2/0. Had pull from small new fish, but didn't hook him. Then at noon killed one 22lb. Cowies Nab on brass angel.

Then to Quarry. Nothing with fly, except a pull on same fly: but hooked beauty on brass angel, but lost him when ready for net through my spinning line breaking. Tested it two days before and could not break it. Now quite rotten.

Then to Island Foot: nothing on fly, but about 5.30 killed in quick succession two, 10lb and 16lb brass angel. Hot, cloudless day, with nice cool N. wind ruffling the water. Water 2 inches over Quarry Cobble and clear.

Hills was friendly with the Scotsman and alumnus of Balliol College, Andrew Lang. As well as being a poet and novelist, Lang was also an angler who wrote *Angling Sketches*, published in 1895 and dedicated to Mrs Herbert Hills, the mother of John Waller, in memory of pleasant days at Corby. Lang was a frequent visitor to Corby Castle and fished with Hills on a number of occasions although he appears not have been the most proficient of anglers and Hills recalls that 'he usually lost his flies one by one

Andrew Lang.

in trees or in trout'. On one occasion, however, Lang excelled himself by catching a salmon of 27lb, aided by Hills:

So after tea [on 6th October, 1892] *I took Andrew Lang out in the boat to the top of the Boat pool. I had my eye on a patch of easy water on the Wetheral bank where running fish often rested. Yes, I said to myself, we ought to get one there. I put him on a large dun turkey with a mixed wool body, 3/0 or 4/0, and sure enough at once he hooked a big one. Now at that time I had not gaffed many salmon, though I thought I knew all about it, and I had only brought a short telescopic gaff. I made a mess of it, touching the fish with the gaff point, an unpardonable clumsiness. Of course he whisked round for midstream like a flash, but in doing so he drove the small of his tail hard on to my gaff, and I whipped him out instantly. It looked like a magnificent shot. I said nothing. He weighed 27lb.*

As well as being an accomplished salmon angler, Hills also taught himself to dress salmon flies with the aid of Captain Hale's *How to tie Salmon Flies*, which he purchased on its publication in

1892. He set himself up in a small room overlooking the river and started by tying the old simple Eden patterns with wings made out of various natural turkey feathers. Eventually he moved on to tying more elaborate flies with married wings such as the Bulldog, a gaudy fly invented by Robert Strong of Carlisle in 1883. The Bulldog became an immensely popular fly on the Eden and, during the thirteen years that the Hills family leased the Corby water, it accounted for 30% of all the salmon they caught on fly. Although he enjoyed dressing salmon flies he admits that he never took to dressing trout flies.

In 1902, following the expiration of the lease on Corby Castle, Hills' father bought Highhead Castle, which stands on a precipitous rock, bounded on three sides by the river Ive. Sadly, the house is now a ruin following a disastrous fire in 1956. The Ive is little more than a beck and belongs to the Eden system. It flows into the Roe, which in turn flows into the Caldew, a tributary of the Eden. The Ive and the Roe became Hills' new playground and he considered the Ive the best of all the small streams in Cumberland. The river was deep, with good holding pools and a good hatch of flies, which included olives, sedges and mayfly. Hills claimed the river contained an inexhaustible head of trout and the more he fished it, the more trout it produced. When the Hills family took over the fishing on the

Highhead Castle.

Ive they found that the stream was heavily overgrown and poaching was rampant. However, after some judicious work by Tuddenham the keeper, the river improved and poaching was controlled. When fishing the Ive, Hills preferred to use two flies rather than the usual three, and to cast upstream. His best recorded catch occurred on 22nd June, 1908, between six and ten at night, when he caught twenty-six trout. The river produced the occasional big fish and Hills' brother claimed to have been broken twice by trout in excess of three pounds. Hills' own best fish from the Ive weighed 1lb 6oz and he claimed that pounders were relatively common.

As well as fly fishing, Hills occasionally fished these small streams with maggot and even claimed that practice with the maggot makes the angler a better performer with the fly.

It gives you an inner knowledge of your water and your trout which fly-fishing never affords. It is like opening a new book, the pursuit is at once simplified, and calls for a higher art. It should only be used when streams have shrunk and shrunk till they are nearly dry. Put on two maggots if the trout will take them, if not one. Cast straight upstream. Use a small single hook and 4X gut, never, of course, any shot. The outstanding difficulty is to know when a fish takes. In sharp water this is easy. You see the line stop or hover for a fraction of a second, but you get better sport in the stiller pools. Here comes your difficulty, for your maggot sinks. Never pull it. I tried oiling all but the last three links of my gut so as to make it into a float, but gave it up, for I caught more without. After a time, your sixth sense is born, and that tells you when a fish takes. It is a delicate art, and difficult.

One of his best days with the maggot was on the Roe in June, 1914, when he caught twenty-three fish. However, he was not always so successful and during the 1912 season he claimed the fish would not look at the maggot. On the whole, he caught far more fish on the Ive and Roe with the fly. While living at Highhead, Hills occasionally fished the Eamont and on one momentous occasion he hooked a salmon while creeper fishing.

The fish made a mighty rush upstream before the hook pulled out.

After the end of the First World War, Hills' father let out the Highhead Castle estate and Hills himself increasingly turned his attention to fishing the chalkstreams. During the last twenty years of his life his parliamentary career began to flourish and in 1929 he was made a member of the Privy Council. Two years later, on 13th June, 1931, he married his second wife, Mary Grace Ashton with whom he had a son. Hills died at his home in Bayswater on 24th December, 1938. He was to have been nominated to a baronetcy in the New Year's honours list of 1939; instead the baronetcy was created in favour of his son, Andrew Ashton Waller Hills (1933-1955). Throughout his life Hills retained a love of the Cumberland countryside and in *My Sporting Life* he wrote:

If my unquiet spirit ever revisits the glimpses of the moon there are three places it will haunt - Ramsbury, Highhead and the Island of Jura.

22

Richard Clapham
A SPORTSMAN ON FELL, BECK & TARN

Although not a native of the Lake District by birth, Richard Clapham spent the majority of his life in Troutbeck, and was a true all-round field sportsman who enjoyed hunting, shooting and fishing by fell, beck and tarn. Richard Clapham came from a well-to-do family and was born at Austwick, near Settle in the Yorkshire Dales in 1878. His father, Thomas Richard Clapham (1837-1910), was the owner of Austwick Hall, a beautiful manor house, originally built as a pele tower in the twelfth century, and now an exclusive country hotel. The hall came into the possession of the Clapham family in 1829, following the bankruptcy of its previous owner, William King. Richard's father, a keen amateur astronomer, built an observatory in the grounds (now demolished) and added a new wing to the rear of the hall.

Richard himself, the eldest of three children, was educated at Giggleswick School, a well-known public school not far from Austwick. After completing his education in 1893, he went to work for a firm of architects in Leeds. However, on finding office work rather tedious, he emigrated to New Zealand in 1900. Three years later, he upped sticks again and moved to Canada, where he met Constance Ellen Du Pre, his future wife. They returned to England in 1910, following the death of his father, and to take up his inheritance. After marrying in Kendal, he moved to Troutbeck, where he lived for the next forty years, first at Rose Cottage and then at Lane Head House. In the 1911 census his occupation is described as journalist. It was whilst living at Troutbeck that he hunted fox, shot grouse and blackcock on Wansfell, and stalked deer in Troutbeck Park. In addition, he hunted hare with beagles, otters with hounds, fished for salmon and sea trout in the Leven, and for brown trout in becks and tarns.

During the First World War he served with distinction in the army, was wounded, but returned to front line duty after several months. He was demobbed in 1919. Clapham was a prolific author and journalist, writing thirteen books, including several novels, and contributing hundreds of articles to sporting journals. In later life, after being struck down with ill-health, he returned to his native Dales and bought a house at Feizor, not far from the place of his birth. He died on 18th July, 1954, and is buried in Austwick cemetery.

Of the numerous sporting books that he wrote, *Fishing for Sea Trout in Tidal Water* (1950) is the most important as far as angling is concerned. As an angler his primary focus was the sea trout of the river Leven, which issues from Lake Windermere and enters Morecambe Bay below the village of Greenodd. During an angling career of over fifty years some of his happiest days were spent fishing for sea trout in the tidal reaches of the Leven and his book is the product of his vast experience with these wily fish. His enthusiasm for the sea trout of the Leven is obvious from the very first chapter:

A daylight run of sea trout and salmon in tidal waters is a sight to be long remembered. Many a time have I sat on the banks of the Leven on a bright, sunny autumn day with a good breeze, and watched the

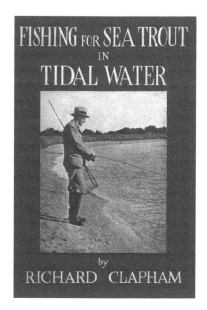

FISHING FOR SEA TROUT
IN
TIDAL WATER

by
RICHARD CLAPHAM

migratory fish flash into the air like bars of silver as they worked their way upstream on the tide. Here a fish would curve back in a neat header, while there another would fall back with a smacking splash that raised a shower of gleaming drops, on these occasions the river seemed to be alive with fish, the sight of which made me eager to try conclusions with them.

Clapham was no fly-fishing purist, nor, unlike many sea trout anglers of today, was he an advocate of night fishing.

Night fishing for me is a real 'Chuck and chance it' business, and in my experience is not to be compared with fishing by day. There are times, of course, when the river is dead low, that you can kill fish by night when they are unapproachable by day. Rather than tackle them by night, however, I much prefer to wait for a rise of water.

Clapham was a pioneer and champion of the fixed-spool reel and his favourite method of fishing for Leven sea trout was spinning a natural minnow. His preferred reel was a trout-size Illingworth with a finger pick-up, combined with a line of 6lb breaking strain. With regard to rods his preference was for one made out of split bamboo, eight to ten feet long. Although he claims to have killed a number of fish using artificial baits, especially Devon minnows, he much preferred to use natural minnows, encased in a Scarab mount.

I have killed plenty of migratory fish with both types of Devon (plain or reflex), but in my experience a natural minnow is a better killer. While the majority of natural bait tackles enable you to spin a minnow

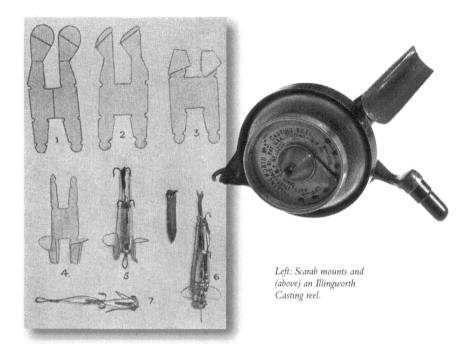

Left: Scarab mounts and (above) an Illingworth Casting reel.

properly, they afford no protection to the bait, and you may have to renew it after killing a fish. In my experience the greatest refinement for holding natural baits is the Scarab, or celluloid envelope. The bait can be seen as the celluloid is transparent, and at the same time is securely held and protected. Very often I have fished for several days with two Scarabs of reverse spin. The Scarab is by far the best tackle for spinning with a natural bait. Another good point about it is that the lead lies in the minnow itself, which makes for greater accuracy if you are casting to a particular spot. . . When wiring a natural minnow into a Scarab, I have for years made a practice of laying a narrow strip of silver paper along one side of the bait. This gives flash when spinning, and it is this flash which attracts predatory fish to their prey.

For trapping his minnows he used a clear glass wine bottle with a hole knocked in the bottom, baited with bread-crumbs. His normal practice was to trap enough minnows for a whole season and then to preserve them in formalin for use when required. As a child, I vividly remember trapping minnows from a local stream in such a bottle, and using them to catch pike in a local lake. Nowadays, it is rare to see anglers using the natural minnow and I cannot remember the last time I saw a Scarab mount in use! However, equipped with such tackle and bait, Clapham was not only successful in luring the wily sea trout of the Leven but also pike and brown trout in lakes and tarns.

On his fishing expeditions to the Leven, Clapham was often accompanied by his wife, Constance, herself an accomplished angler who sometimes out-fished him, as the following extract shows:

Turning the pages of my fishing diary brings back many memories of both good and bad days on the Leven. On one occasion in the middle of October, my wife and I had a day's spinning when the river was running a nice minnow water. As usual there was a good channel above the upper railway bridge which is my wife's favourite stretch. Wild horses could not drag her away from it when conditions are favourable. I left here there and went downstream to another channel about a quarter of a mile away. After spinning carefully for nearly two hours, I at last hooked a sea trout that pulled the scale to 2½lb. Shortly after that my wife came down to see how I was faring, and told me that she had killed a grilse. I asked her to take my place, but she decided to go and try for another. At lunch time I walked up to the bridge, and there I saw two fish lying on the grass. She had done it again.

Although his favourite method of catching Leven sea trout was by spinning, he also fly fished when conditions were right. He believed that the flash of a spinning bait was a great attraction to migratory fish and that sea trout flies, too, should incorporate coloured feathers and tinsel which flash when the light strikes them. His favourite sea trout flies included: Black and Orange; Black and Silver; Mallard and Claret; Connemara Black; Francis Fly; Heckham Peckham; March Brown with silver body; Ramsbottom's Favourite; and White Tip and Claret. His advice on how to fish these flies was as follows:

Mrs Clapham fishing.   *A basket of trout from a hill stream.*

If you know a place where sea trout or salmon lie, your aim should be when fishing it to present your fly so that it flashes as it swings round in front of the fish. To do this it must come down with the light behind it, and then as it swings round the light strikes it, and there is a flash from the body and the wings.

With regards to a rod for fly fishing for sea trout, he preferred a 10-foot split bamboo or steel fly rod. He believed that faith in the fly being fished is more important than the fly itself, 'one pattern of fly is as good as another if you have faith in it'. However, he did believe that size of fly was important and that, in a big water, a larger fly should be used.

Although a number of anglers on the tidal reaches of the Leven fished for salmon and sea trout with worm or prawn, Clapham was no great lover of this method:

Personally speaking I am no lover of natural bait fishing in tidal water. Compared with spinning or fly-fishing it is a tedious business with little life about it, and you miss that feeling of exhilaration when a good sea trout or salmon almost pulls the rod out of your hands as it hits your minnow.

As well as fishing for sea trout and the occasional salmon, Clapham also enjoyed fishing for brown trout on Lakeland becks and tarns and even wrote a book outlining his tactics, entitled, *Trout Fishing on Hill Streams* (1947). Rather controversially, perhaps, when fishing for trout on moorland streams he used only one fly, invariably a Black Spinner, otherwise known as Lee's Favourite. It was dressed as follows: Tail – two fibres of black cock's hackle. Body – black silk ribbed with silver. Hackle – black. Wings – snipe or starling. Since trout on rapidly flowing hill streams and moorland becks have little or no time in which to pick and choose their food, he believed that one or two patterns of artificial fly are quite sufficient. However, the flies should be slimly dressed to give an impressionistic idea of living insects.

I have found to my own satisfaction that on rocky, fast-flowing streams the 'one-fly' man can easily kill as many or more trout than the angler with the bulging flybook who is for ever changing his feathered lures.

Clapham came to this conclusion after reading Stewart's *Practical Angler* (1857), in which the author pinned his faith in half a dozen patterns, all of which were lightly dressed. Clapham himself decided to choose a couple of patterns and fish them for a whole season in order to compare the total catch with those of previous seasons. The two flies he selected were the Black Spinner (see above) and the Black Spider, the latter being dressed with the small feather of a cock starling and brown silk. At the end of his first trial season he found he had killed more trout with his two flies than he had caught in previous seasons. He believed that confidence in your chosen flies is more important than the pattern and, following this experiment, he more often than not fished a Black Spinner.

I feel that many of today's fly fishers could take a leaf out of Clapham's book and stick to just a handful of tried and tested patterns rather than constantly changing their flies. I am confident they would be just as successful.

For beck fishing, Clapham believed in fishing 'fine and as near as you can', and, as a result, he liked to use a long fly rod and a short line, while moving stealthily up the beck, casting in all the likely lies. His method proved extremely successful, as the following extract from his fishing diary records:

In 1913 I opened the season on March 5th with 5 trout. Between then and April 9th I had eight day's fishing, and the total ranged from 6 to 32 trout. On April 14th I had a good day and killed 40 nice fish. Four moderate days followed, and then on April 25th I creeled 41 trout. April 29th was not a bad day, total 34 trout. Until May 7th there was not much doing, but on that date I killed 51 trout . . .

And so it goes on. Much of his beck fishing was carried out on Troutbeck near to his home and I wonder whether such baskets of trout would be possible from that stream today? During the months of May and June, when stoneflies are abundant, he liked to use a natural bait. Using a rod of eleven or twelve feet, the natural 'creeper' or stonefly was fished like the upstream worm. At the business end, the natural stonefly was impaled on a two-hook rig, with one hook through the throat of the fly, with the lower one through its abdomen.

To fish the stonefly, choose if possible a day with an upstream wind, and an inch or two of fresh water in the beck. Streams and broken water are likely places, as are the fringes of the gravel beds. Should there be a good breeze you may take some trout from the pools. Having collected sufficient flies, keep them in a box from which you can extract them one at a time.

During the summer months, when the becks were low and clear, Clapham often fished the upstream worm, a method rarely seen nowadays. A great deal of stealth is required when using this method since trout in low water are easily spooked. When employing this method Clapham preferred a long whole cane and greenheart rod that was light and stiff, which allowed him to fish a short line and make a close approach. He liked to bait his

*Above: Up-stream fly fishing
near the head of Lakeland beck.*

Right: Tarn fishing.

worm on a three-hook Stewart tackle, which enabled him to strike at the first touch when the hooks would invariably be found in the trout's mouth. He liked the worm to trundle down the stream at the will of the current and no shot was placed on the cast.

Having cast to a likely spot, or to a fish visible in the shallows, you let the current bring the worm down while you raise the point of the rod, so as to keep the line fairly tight. When a trout takes, the worm stops, and you see a tremor of the line. Now and then the worm is held up by a stone or other obstacles, but experience enables you to decide between such a contretemps and a taking fish.

Using this method, Clapham claims to have taken some of his heaviest baskets in the early morning, although trout can sometimes take well during the heat of the day.

In his *Sport on Fell, Beck and Tarn* (1924), Clapham tells of his methods for fishing the Lakeland tarns. He ventured to the mountain tarns at the height of midsummer when the becks were at their lowest and fly fishing during the day was often fruitless. Occasionally, he liked to set out for a tarn by moonlight, reaching it as the first rays of the sun began to oust the gloom. He is almost moved to poetry in describing the scene:

It is almost unreal in its loveliness, and you pity the poor mortals down below who are still abed, oblivious behind drawn blinds to Nature's splendid handiwork. You reach the rocky rim beneath which lies the tarn, its shining surface dimpled with expanding rings, the sight of which makes you rattle down the long scree-beds in your eagerness to reach the water and begin the day. And how they do rise, those brightly coloured trout!

For fly fishing on tarns he liked to use a light 9-foot rod and the same two flies, Black Spinner and Black Spider, which he used for beck fishing. However, when the bracken clock beetle appeared, he abandoned his principles and fished the natural or an artificial version, the Kennedy's Beetle, which is described as a lifelike copy. In addition to fly fishing, he enjoyed spinning a natural minnow on tarns, a method he found productive and, for this, he used an 8½-foot casting rod and Silex reel. When the weather was right, he would sometimes fish a tarn from midnight till dawn, and claims to have taken some good baskets of fish during this period.

Richard Clapham was clearly a dedicated Lakeland angler and, although some of his methods may nowadays be regarded as unfashionable or unconventional, he was undoubtedly very successful, and today's Lakeland angler could do worse than learn from his books. Clapham was also an angler who believed there was more to fishing than simply catching fish and was captivated by the beautiful environment of the Lake District:

While our main object in angling is to catch fish, we nevertheless admire the beauty of our surroundings, if only subconsciously. It is our admiration of the wild places that takes us far from the madding crowd to some high-lying tarn, among the mountains, a rocky fell beck, or the tidal reaches of the river. Over and above the actual fishing there are so many things to see and hear if only you keep your eyes and ears open. To be alone with Nature, if only for a few hours, is a panacea for most of the ills that flesh is heir to.

23

Arthur Ransome
AUTHOR, ANGLER & JOURNALIST

When Arthur Ransome was a young child, his father, Cyril, dropped him into Coniston Water to see if, like some animals, he could swim naturally. He couldn't, but fortunately his father saved him and he lived to tell the tale. You might think that the young Ransome, after this early submersion in the cold waters of Coniston, would be put off water for life. This was not the case. In fact, Ransome loved to be by the water, especially the waters of his beloved Lake District, and throughout his life, he had a passion for angling and sailing.

Arthur Michell Ransome was born on 18th January, 1884 in Leeds. His father, Cyril, was Professor of History at Yorkshire College, later to become the University of Leeds. His mother, Edith, who enjoyed painting in watercolour, spent her honeymoon painting by the banks of the Eamont, while her newly-wed husband fished. Both his father and his grandfather, Thomas Ransome, were keen anglers whose favourite river was the Bela. Ransome himself, in his autobiography, tells us that his grandfather was an ingenious fisherman who saw the advantage of using shorter, quicker-striking rods over the long whippy rods, which were then in vogue. However, he added a whalebone tip to his rod to add some elasticity and to prevent the horsehair cast from snapping on the strike.

Ransome was the eldest of four children and his father, who had definite ideas about education, was keen that his son should grow up to be fluent in languages. As a result, Ransome was placed in the care of a French nurse, Victorine, who was to tutor him in the rudiments of her language and, almost as soon as he could speak, his father began to teach him Latin. Unfortunately, the Latin language was lost on the young Ransome and he claims to have forgotten what he had learnt almost at once. Cyril Ransome had learnt how to shoot and fish from his father and he hoped, in turn, to pass these skills on to his son. However, the young Arthur claimed that he was a disappointment to his father. When accompanying his father on trout fishing expeditions to the Wharfe, Arthur was not content to watch and learn from his father, instead he preferred to wander down the river and paddle in the stream. As for shooting, after witnessing a wounded hare screaming, he was put off the sport for life.

Although the Ransome family lived in Leeds for most of the year, the long summer vacations were spent at High Nibthwaite Farm, the home of the Swainson family, on Coniston Water. It was here that Ransome's father spent his days fishing and was no longer a professor who fished, but a fisherman who wrote history books in his spare time. Preparations for the summer's fishing began long before the end of term. There would be 'an orgy of fly-tying'. His father tied the delicate Yorkshire wet flies that T.E. Pritt featured in his famous book and he tied them both for his friends and for himself. They were lightly hackled and dressed on short lengths of fine gut or horsehair. His father was one of the first to introduce the methods of Halford to the North and to fish with the dry fly. However, he gave up tying dry flies after a year or so because he apparently had no time to spare for them, preferring, himself, a wet-fly for trout fishing.

For weeks before they left for Coniston Water the wooden candle-sticks in his father's study were festooned with his new-made casts, the rods were in readiness, his landing-net mended, and the children's perch-floats and shotted casts inspected.

At Nibthwaite, the Ransome children lived an idyllic life and were allowed to roam free. However, as soon as they arrived at Coniston, Arthur would perform his own little ritual - dipping his hand into the water and greeting his beloved lake. It was a ritual he was to perform through-out his life every time he

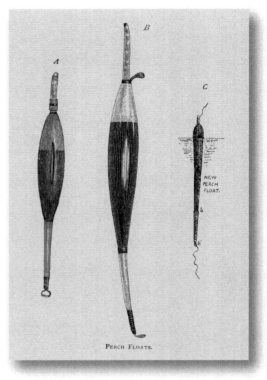

Perch floats from Pike and Perch, *by Alfred Jardine.*

visited Coniston. The Swainsons had a boat on the lake, with oars that worked on pins instead of rowlocks (very useful when fishing) and it was here that Ransome learned to be at home on the water. Days were spent befriending the farm animals, local gamekeepers, charcoal-burners and various fishermen. Haymaking, picking mushrooms and blackberries, turning the butter-churn, tickling trout and walking with their father were some of the other activities enjoyed by the Ransome children. It was fishing for perch in Coniston with his own rod that convinced Ransome there was more to angling than simply watching his father catch trout.

Sometimes, when his father was fishing the lake for trout he would row the whole family up to Peel Island and leave them there while he carried on fishing. The children would spend the

Coniston Water.

day playing savages while their mother sat sketching and painting. Some of their adventures on Peel Island were later to find
their way into his *Swallows and Amazons* series of books. Towards
evening, their father would return for them with trout in the
bottom of the boat for Mrs Swainson to cook for next day's
breakfast.

One of the duties of the Ransome children at Nibthwaite was
to watch for the first signs of rising fish on the river Crake, where
it issues from the lake. On seeing a number of rising fish they
would rush into the farmhouse, where their father was hard at
work writing history books. He would immediately leave his
papers, take his rod, which was always set up in readiness in the
porch, and hurry across the fields to the river. Cyril Ransome
often caught sea trout in the Crake and his son vividly recalled
hearing the sudden scream of his reel when he had hooked a
large fish in the pool below the bobbin-mill. Cyril also enjoyed
spinning for pike on Allan Tarn and on Coniston using artificial
baits, which he made himself and which were painted realistically
by his wife. In his autobiography, Arthur Ransome recalled an
occasion when his father hooked a large pike on Coniston.

It was a pike of about twenty pounds, hooked just off the point by Brown How whilst Arthur rowed the boat for him. It went off at a great pace, taking the boat with it, so his father was unable to make sure it was properly hooked. Despite being told to 'back-water' by his agitated father, Arthur went the wrong way, rowing after the pike as fast as he could. He well recalled the exasperated cries of his father as he did so. However, despite Arthur's 'ineffi-ciency', his father did succeed in catching the pike, 'and a very good one it was'.

At the age of nine and after attending a day-school in Leeds, Arthur Ransome was sent to a boarding school in the Lake District, the Old College at Windermere, to prepare for entrance to one of the great public schools. His father's decision to send him there was partly down to the fact that the school's head-master was Arthur Raikes (1858-1929), a fellow angler on the Bela and a fine carver of fish models. During the summer holidays Raikes would take the sons of rich parents on fishing trips to Norway, which resulted in his book, *Some Norway Tales* (1918). Alas, Arthur Ransome never accompanied him on these expeditions. In fact, despite the headmaster being a keen angler,

The Old College, Windermere.

Ransome was extremely unhappy at the Old College. He was not very good at games and, as a result, was not very popular with his fellow students. It was only after he left Windermere that it was discovered he was so short-sighted as to be almost blind to detail unless very near. The only high point in his time at the Old College came in February 1895, when for week after week, Windermere was frozen from end to end and the boys spent whole days on the ice. He even recalled seeing perch frozen in the ice, preserved as if in glass beneath his feet.

On the evening of 24th June, 1897, the headmaster's wife came into Ransome's dormitory and told him that he would never see his father again. He had died. It was his love of fishing that contributed to his untimely death (he was forty-six). One night, after fishing for sea trout on the Crake and laden with a heavy basket of fish, he was climbing out of a pool when he caught his foot under an old grindstone and fell forward over it. He thought that he had only sprained his ankle and carried on fishing. On the walk back to Nibthwaite he was in agony and the next day his foot was badly swollen. The foot never grew better and eventually his doctors found that he had damaged a bone and a form of tuberculosis had attacked the place. First, his foot was cut off, then his leg at the knee, and finally it was cut off at the thigh. He was never the same again.

Following his father's death, Ransome was sent to Rugby School and, although he was not a scholar, he was taken under the wing by sympathetic teachers and was much happier. After leaving Rugby in 1901, he went on to study science at the Yorkshire College, where his father had taught history. However, he soon found that science was not for him and he left after less than a year and managed to get a job with a London publisher. His publishing career was also relatively short-lived, after which he took up writing full-time. He started out by writing articles for literary magazines, followed by a collection of essays published in 1904. It was around this time that he met W. G. Collingwood, Ruskin's secretary and biographer, and over the next few years he spent many happy holidays with the

Collingwood family at their home at Lanehead, not far from Brantwood. Ransome's first successful book was *Bohemia in London,* published in 1907.

In 1908, he met and fell in love with Ivy Constance Walker whom he married in March 1909. However, in spite of the birth of their daughter, Tabitha, in May 1910, the marriage was not a happy one. In 1913, Ransome went to Russia to work on a collection of Russian folk tales, which was published in 1916 bearing the title *Old Peter's Russian Tales.* Apart from brief visits to England, he remained in Russia throughout the First World War, working as a correspondent for the *Daily News* and, from 1919, for the *Manchester Guardian.* He covered the Russian Revolution of March 1917 and met regularly with Trotsky, Lenin and other leaders. It was around this time that he met and fell in love with the woman who would become his second wife, Evgenia Petrovna Shelepina, who was working as Trotsky's personal secretary. During his time in Russia he continued to fish but mainly for food. He also became acquainted with the fishing memoirs of a nineteenth century Russian nobleman, Sergei Aksakov. He translated these memoirs and they were included in the original version of *Rod and Line*, published in 1929.

At the end of 1919 he took Evgenia with him to Reval in Estonia, where Ransome continued to report on Russia. It was here that he built his first boat, sailed around the Baltic and wrote *Racundra's First Cruise* (1923). Following his divorce from his first wife in 1924, he immediately married Evgenia and brought her to live in England. In March 1925 they bought Low Ludderburn, a small cottage near Windermere, overlooking the Winster valley. He continued to work as a correspondent for the *Manchester Guardian* and was commissioned to write a regular fishing column under the heading of *Rod and Line*, which appeared most weeks between August 1925 and September 1929. A selection of these articles was published under the title *Rod and Line* in 1929 and Ransome dedicated the book to 'the most long-suffering of fishermen's wives'. The book was eventually turned into a

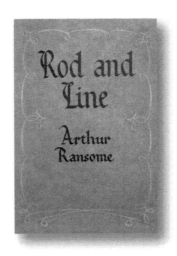

television series in the late 1970s, with Sir Michael Hordern playing the part of Arthur Ransome. A further selection of these articles was published posthumously by Jonathan Cape in 1994 under the title, *Arthur Ransome on Fishing*.

While living at Low Ludderburn, Ransome formed a friendship with Colonel Kelsall, a neighbour who lived at Barkbooth across the valley. They regularly fished the Winster and, since neither of them possessed a telephone, they devised a signalling system, which enabled them to arrange their fishing outings. Ransome used black signals on his white-washed cottage, and Kelsall used white on his dark grey barn. They used different shaped signals to mean different things - triangles, squares and diamonds - and were able to say anything they wanted on the subject of fishing:

'ARE YOU GOING FISHING?' 'WHICH RIVER?'
and in the depth of winter, going to fish for grayling,
'HAVE YOU ANY WORMS?'

On one occasion, while fishing with Kelsall for grayling on the Eden at Appleby, they had to break the ice at the edge of the river, go into the water to unfreeze their waders and dip their rods to prevent the fine lines from freezing solidly to the rings. They even managed to catch a respectable basket of grayling!

The year 1928 proved to be an important one in the life of Arthur Ransome. In 1915 Dora, the eldest Collingwood daughter, had married Ernest Altounyan and had accompanied him to the hospital at Aleppo in Syria, which he helped his father to run. They now had five children and in 1928 the whole family returned to England for several months, staying at Bank Ground Farm, near Lanehead. Ransome spent a great deal of the summer teaching the children to sail on Coniston and when it was time for the family to return to Syria, they generously bequeathed their boat, *Swallow,* to him. It was his time spent with the Altounyan children and their adventures on Coniston that inspired him to write his first children's book, *Swallows and Amazons,* which appeared in 1930. A sequel, *Swallowdale,* was published a year later, to be followed by a stream of other children's books. Sailing and fishing feature predominantly in his children's books partly inspired, no doubt, by his own childhood holidays at Nibthwaite. We have already seen in Chapter 2 how one of the children, Roger, hooked a large pike in *Swallows and Amazons.* In *Swallowdale,* the children go fishing on Trout Tarn (a pseudonym for Beacon Tarn, situated in the hills at the southern end of Coniston). Following Captain Flint's demonstration of fly

Beacon Tarn.

fishing, John is allowed to try his luck with a fly rod and presently lands his first trout. The other children, however, decide to float fish at the spot where the beck flowed out of the tarn. Not long afterwards their float disappears amid great excitement and Roger, not wanting to wait for the arrival of the landing-net, goes in after the fish, splashing about in the shallows until he catches it. Then he makes his way, 'splashing worse than ever', to the shore, slips on the way, drops the fish, falls on it immediately and finally brings the big trout ashore just as Captain Flint arrives with the landing-net:

"He's two pounds if he's an ounce," said Captain Flint. "You've got one of the grandfathers. Beaten the lot of us. Float-tackle and all."

At the end of 1934 the Ransomes decided to leave Low Lud-derburn and moved to the east coast where Arthur could enjoy greater opportunities for sailing. However, when war broke they decided to return to the Lake District and in 1940 they pur-chased The Heald, a stone built house on the eastern side of Coniston, not far from Brantwood. During the 1940s Ransome became increasingly interested in salmon flies and devised a new fly, the Elver Fly, in imitation of a small eel. In 1943, while stay-ing at the Park Lane Hotel in London, he had observed a number of American officers chewing gum in the lounge. The thought suddenly struck him that this was exactly what salmon do in fresh water. They do not feed in fresh water but they will toy with a fly or worm in their mouths for some considerable time. His thoughts turned to devising a fly that would not irritate or frighten a salmon but would enable it to recapture a flavour that it could remember enjoying. The last creature a salmon was likely to have fed on before entering fresh water was an elver. His problem now was finding suitable feathers, which could imitate the elver. His problem was solved when an ornithologist friend sent him some Vulturine Guinea Fowl feathers from East Africa and, after some experiments with hook size, he eventually came up with the Elver Fly. According to

Ransome the fly caught fish in a number of rivers including the Leven, Lune and Cumbrian Derwent. As far as he was aware the biggest fish caught on an Elver was a 26-pounder from the Eden. Nowadays, the Elver Fly is still used and is a popular choice in the Hebrides.

In addition to the Elver Fly, he also devised an effective sea trout fly, the Port and Starboard, the body of which is composed of luminous scarlet and green wool. On its first outing in a Cumbrian river in the middle of a July day it accounted for a sea trout of 3¼ lb. The following season it accounted for over sixty sea trout and a number of salmon. During the 1940s Ransome had hoped to publish a lavishly illustrated book on salmon flies and their history, but unfortunately the technology of the time was not up to the challenge. However, many of his thoughts on salmon flies appeared in his last book, a collection of essays entitled, *Mainly About Fishing*, published in 1959. Ransome also wrote a pamphlet, *The Fisherman's Library* (1955), for the

The Elver Fly.

National Book League, in which he reviewed angling literature and recommended his favourite books to the reader.

Not only did Ransome invent the Elver Fly in 1943, he also devised a novel method of fishing for charr on Coniston and Windermere. We have already seen (Chapter 7) how traditional charr fishers developed the plumb line method of fishing. Ransome, however, because of a hernia was no longer able to row and, as a result, devised a method of catching charr by sailing. In the Bay of Biscay he had seen tunny fishers with mast-high rods trolling under sail. The main problem of this method was sailing sufficiently slowly. After a great deal of experimentation, Ransome managed to solve this problem and was rewarded with a dish of charr for supper.

In 1945, the Ransomes moved south to a flat in London but by 1948 they were back once more in the Lake District at Lowick Hall, a large house near Nibthwaite. Two years later they returned to London where they lived for the next decade. During this period they returned to the Lakes every spring and summer so that Arthur could enjoy his fishing. However, Arthur could not bear to be away from his beloved Lake District for long and in 1960 they made their final move north and bought Hill Top Cottage on the northern edge of Haverthwaite. By now Ransome's health was beginning to deteriorate but he continued to fish regularly for the rest of his life, catching his last salmon, a 7lb cock fish from the Derwent at Cockermouth at the age of seventy-six. In the autumn of 1965 he was taken to the Cheadle Royal Hospital where he died on 3rd June, 1967, aged eighty-three. He was buried in the beautiful churchyard at Rusland in the heart of the Lake District countryside, which he had loved and which he had made so much his own.

Fortunately, Ransome left behind a wonderful literary legacy and, as far as the angler is concerned, his *Rod and Line* has few rivals. It is witty and instructive and he is as much at home with coarse as with game fish. Indeed, he was a true all-rounder, whose philosophy of angling is best summed up in his own words:

I think I should say here that I have never claimed to be a good fisher-man, but only one who thoroughly enjoys fishing. Going fishing I have never thought to catch more fish than anybody else, luckily, for I should seldom have succeeded. Then, too, in the matter of enjoyment I am for-tunate in that no sort of class consciousness affects my pleasure. I have had great pleasure for salmon, sitting as it were on the strong supporting stream. But I have also had great pleasure sitting on a wicker basket, one of a row of fishermen on the tow-path beside a still canal, watching for the slight quiver of the float that should signal a roach mouthing my maggot.

(*The Autobiography of Arthur Ransome*, 1976)

24

Tom Davison
ANGLER & RAILWAYMAN

Although Thomas (Tom) Davison was not born in the Lake
District he spent most of his life there, working and fishing. He
was born on 14th November, 1905, at Toxteth Park near Liverpool in what was then Lancashire. His father, also Thomas
Davison (1870-1966) was born in Workington and worked on
the railways as a plate layer. In the 1911 census the young Tom
Davison was living with his parents at his uncle's house in Crosby
Garrett, Westmorland. Not surprisingly, perhaps, Tom followed
in his father's footsteps and spent his working life on the railways as a signalman, mainly in Cumbria. In 1931, at the age of
twenty-six, he married Dorothy Ullock at Sedbergh in Yorkshire.
He is chiefly remembered today for his book, *Angler and Otter*,
published in 1950, in which he recounts his angling and otter
hunting exploits, mainly on the Lune. He was also a lover of the
countryside and regarded the scenery around Low Gill and Tebay
as some of the finest in the country.

He appears to have commenced his angling career in 1926

while living at Low Gill on the upper reaches of the Lune. In fact, most of his angling was carried out on the Lune between Low Gill and Tebay. Davison clearly had a sense of humour and his first attempt at angling got off to a disastrous start:

Whirr, Whirr! Crack! What on earth is happening? Oh no, reader, it is not a big fine trout making my reel whirr, but if you are new to this fine sport of angling, take it as your first lesson, never to lay your rod down on the ground beside the river if there is a dog about, for mine has just fouled my line, drawn a hook into her tail, and off she has gone as though she had sat and wagged her tail too hard on a wasp's nest. What now have I for my carelessness but a broken rod, a cast of flies gone, and the trout just coming on to rise. What would you do? Don't accept defeat. I examined the rod and discovered that it had broken half an inch above the top ferrule.

While he was dealing with this incident, his friend cast in his spot and promptly hooked and landed a fine three-quarter pound trout. Not long afterwards, however, after making a hasty repair to his rod and putting on a cast consisting of a Dark Snipe and Purple, and Woodcock and Orange, he landed his first fish, a trout half an inch under the limit.

Like many anglers of his generation Davison was no purist when it came to fishing, and by the following year, 1927, he was sufficiently confident to try his hand at fishing the natural stone fly. At his very first attempt, fishing the Lune upstream to the Long Dub and on to the Fairmile, he soon had five nice trout and by the end of the day he returned home with a basket of eleven trout.

Although otters are now making something of a comeback, in the 1920s and 1930s they were a relatively common sight on many of our rivers. One night, while fishing a cast of bustard flies, Davison hooked what he thought was a salmon. The salmon, however, turned out to be an otter and it almost put him off night fishing for life! Terrified having hooked it, he made for the safety of the nearest bridge and in his desperation to get away

broke his line and then fled. The next day he returned to recover his line and to revisit the scene – 'the river looked innocent of the startling adventure of the night before'. Thereafter, the event came back to haunt his dreams and if he went night fishing at all, he tried to make sure he had company.

About three weeks later the Kendal and District Otter Hounds were hunting in the district around Low Gill when they put up an otter. After a skirmish between the otter and one of the hounds, the otter headed upstream. The hounds eventually tracked it down and pounced upon it. Davison was convinced it was the same otter that he had hooked.

Most anglers, I suspect, never forget their first capture of a salmon. It is almost like a rite of passage in a game angler's career. I vividly remember catching my first salmon, a beautiful bar of silver weighing six pounds, caught on the Aros, a small spate river on the Isle of Mull. Tom Davison, too, gives a vivid account of the capture of his first salmon. It was during the first week of September following several days of rain. Davison had been fishing the river without a salmon licence when he promptly hooked and lost a fine fish. This prompted him to buy a licence and the next day he was on the river early, equipped with his trout rod (he did not yet own a salmon rod) and a couple of small *Silver Doctor* salmon flies. After trying several dubs (pools) he arrived, accompanied by a local boy carrying his gaff, at Carlingill Dub where the height of water seemed just right:

I never saw or felt anything, but on attempting to take off my line after about half a dozen casts, my rod bent and my line stayed on the river, and then there was a splash and boil. This really was my first salmon, and I thought there was no need to strike, as I had done so in my attempt to take off. It was a good thing I was handling my rod inexpertly or I would have given a harder lift to my rod for a long cast, and would have broken with the sudden stop of hooking the salmon. As it was my first fish, I handled it very gently indeed, and I had no unexpected incidents with it. It put in a few queer moves that made me feel worried with the thought that it would get away. However, I was at a good place to land it, and after taking about twenty-five minutes, considerably longer than I know is necessary, I brought it to the side. I tried to tell the boy how to gaff it, and then run clear back on to the gravel. He put the gaff over and then ran back, the point just entered the fish, and he got it clear of the water. Then I dived on it, hit it on the head with a stone, and my prize lay before me. It was a cock fish, none too clean and fresh run, and weighed seven and three-quarter pounds.

On another occasion, after catching an 8lb salmon, he encountered a fellow fisherman staying at Kendal who had had no luck. The fisherman offered to buy the salmon and Davison reluctantly agreed. That same evening Davison paid a visit to his girlfriend in Kendal (it was before he was married) and while drinking in a hotel bar, the fisherman to whom he had sold his salmon walked in. On being asked by a couple of people standing at the bar how he had got on that day, he entertained them with the story of his capture of a fine 8lb salmon. Davison was not pleased!

Apart from fishing the Lune, Davison occasionally fished elsewhere. In 1927, his job on the railways entailed a temporary transfer to Ingleton in Yorkshire where he fished the Greta, a tributary of the Lune, and had a certain amount of success using natural stone-flies. Killington Lake and its service area will be

Angling on the Lune at Kirkby Lonsdale.

familiar to travellers on the M6 on their way to and from the Lake District. For a number of years Tom Davison and a group of his friends paid a visit to Killington Lake, which once served as a header for the now disused Kendal to Lancaster canal, to fish for its perch, pike and trout. According to Davison, the lake was reputed to have been stocked with bass although he never saw one. He and his friends would hire a boat and float fish with worms. Although they enjoyed watching a float bob up and down and took home some good baskets of perch, they rarely caught anything above six or seven ounces. However, on one occasion, a lovely quiet evening, one of their party, a young lad, saw his float disappear and struck. As he was reeling in the fish, his rod suddenly bent double and he found himself attached to something much bigger than a 6oz perch. The fish headed towards the boat and then under it and round the other side. They finally got a glimpse of the fish - it was a pike, 'a monster'. Three minutes later it broke surface but then dived down deep again. It was the first time the group had caught, or even seen a pike. Unfortunately, after watching it surfacing and diving a few more times, they lost it. They estimated it at twenty pounds. However, all was not lost as still on the line when they retrieved it was a perch.

The pike had obviously seized the perch as it was being reeled in, a scenario that will be familiar to many anglers. In March 1930, before the official start of the trout fishing season Davison longed to be at the river and, after digging a few worms, fished up the Westmorland side of the river:

Halfway up the Long Wood I did have a small quiet tug, and I thought the fish had become disinterested and had left my worm, so I lifted quietly up to see if the worm had gone. Lo and behold, I could feel a fish. I broke my rod in attempting to land it, and when it was eventually landed, it was a good size, but in poor condition, and weighed one pound fifteen ounces. That incidentally was the biggest trout I ever got on worm.

In the early 1930s Davison was transferred to a signal box at Clifton, near Penrith, where he spent four years. Whilst there, he managed to obtain a permit to fish for trout on a fly-only stretch of the Lowther. The stretch was one and a half miles long and heavily fished. As a result, Davison found it difficult to connect with any trout of a decent size and he decided to stretch the rules a little and fish the natural stone fly. After collecting a tin full of stone flies, he started to fish just below the Lowther viaduct. The trout seemed to be partial to the natural fly and it wasn't long before he landed several good fish. While he was busily engaged in fishing he was spotted by one of the estate keepers who suspected him of fishing the worm. The keeper came over and, after asking to see his ticket, wanted to know what was in his tin, thinking he would find worms. Davison promptly opened his tin and out flew a stone fly. After giving the keeper a demonstration of his technique, the keeper seemed satisfied and handed him back his ticket!

In March 1938, Davison was transferred to Tebay just in time for the opening of the trout season. On his first outing at Tebay, in the midst of falling snow, he managed to take eight nice fish.

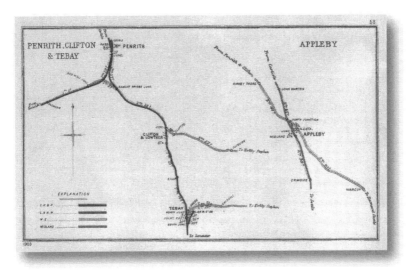

Map of the Eden valley railway, showing Clifton and Tebay.

When he first came to Tebay it seemed that few anglers fished for salmon with a fly, preferring instead worm, spoon and spinner. Davison, with his salmon fly rod, was regarded as something of an oddity. However, that soon changed when, at his very first outing with the salmon fly, he grassed a fine 14lb spring fish at Blamire's Pool, followed several days later by two other spring salmon.

During the Second World War, long hours at work combined with service in the Home Guard, meant that Davison had little time for fishing. However, in 1944, while fishing at the Trough Dub he managed to hook a very large fish. After a tremendous fight lasting over forty minutes, during which the fish headed nearly seventy yards downstream and back up again, he managed to put his handkerchief over the fish's tail and haul in a magnificent 21½-pounder - the biggest he had ever landed. The following season, the last to be recorded in his book, he landed a fine 18½-pounder from the same pool.

Not only was Davison a fine angler, he was also a skilled fly dresser and tackle-maker. In the Appendix of his book he gives the reader detailed instructions on how to dress the wonderful North-country spider patterns, which he dressed without the aid of a vice. He was also critical of pristine-looking shop-bought patterns and advised the reader to dress flies with dirty hands:

So before you start dressing flies, see that your hands are dirty, and in need of a wash (not greasy). Your flies may look dirty and grubby, but they will catch fish.

Although the last entries in his book refer to the 1945 season, Tom Davison lived on for another forty years, dying at Ulverston on 13th July, 1987, at the age of eighty-one. It is a matter for much regret that he never wrote a second volume covering his angling exploits after the Second World War.

25

Hugh Falkus
THE SEA TROUT GURU

With the exception of Izaak Walton's *Compleat Angler*, few angling books have stood the test of time as well as Hugh Falkus' *Sea Trout Fishing*, first published in 1962 and in print ever since. A revised and enlarged edition was published in 1975, with a further revision in 1981 to include colour plates. The book serves as a lasting testimony to one of the greatest, if not *the* greatest, sea trout anglers of all time. Its author, Hugh Falkus, was a complex character who had an extremely varied career as a pilot, mink farmer, writer, film maker, television presenter, casting instructor and angler. He is best known today for his books on angling and his films on natural history.

Although not a Cumbrian by birth, Hugh Falkus spent almost forty years of his life living at Cragg Cottage, near Ravenglass in the beautiful Eskdale valley. Hubert (he preferred Hugh) Edward Lance Falkus was born on 15th May, 1917, during a Zeppelin raid on London. Shortly afterwards, the family moved to Essex where they lived on a converted Thames barge, the *Neptune*. At

Above: Falkus with a sea trout (from A Life on the Edge *by Chris Newton).*

[277]

some point during the mid-1930s, James Falkus, Hugh's father, decided to retire from his job as a banker manager and devote his time to sailing, fishing and shooting. Hugh seems to have had an idyllic childhood accompanying his father on his fishing and wildfowling outings. By the age of six Hugh had learned how to handle a shotgun and would often retrieve the wildfowl shot by his father. He seems to have had few friends of his own age and spent a lot of time in the company of a one-eyed former sailing-barge skipper named Puggy Dimmond who lived on an old houseboat in the Essex marshes. According to his autobiography, *The Stolen Years* (1965), long summer days were spent fishing for flounders and eels with Puggy from a duck-punt. Puggy was 'a wizard at catching flounders' despite using crude tackle - for a rod, a bamboo pole with a length of thick line tied to the end, and for a float, a net-cork. He was a skilled angler and at the end of a fishing trip the floor of his punt would always be covered with fish. His technique was simple - he would cast in his bait (usually ragworm), lay the pole in the rowlocks and then squat motionless:

> . . . *his single misty blue eye steadily watching the big cork that floated on the tide a yard or two away.*
>
> *Suddenly, he would sit up straight and gently lift the rod.*
>
> *"Watch out, boy! They're here. I c'n smell un!"*
>
> *Sure enough, this was a signal for his float to bob. A short pause. Then a chuckle of delight as he heaved up a flounder and swung it flapping into the punt.*

In 1927, at the age of ten, the young Falkus was sent as a boarder to the East Anglian School in Bury St Edmunds. Although he did not particularly enjoy his schooldays, he excelled at sport, especially swimming and in 1931 he performed in a school pro-duction of *As You Like It*. At the age of nineteen Hugh joined the Air Corps and by the beginning of the Second World War he had held a pilot's licence for over a year. Not surprisingly, perhaps, he joined the RAF and became a fighter pilot. His first flying job, however, was with the Met Flight in Northern Ireland gathering data for weather forecasting. It was here that he met Atlantic Sam, his angling mad Commanding Officer, who first introduced Falkus to the delights of sea trout fishing. During their free time they would drive to various Ulster rivers: the Foyle, the Bush and the Bann, in search of their quarry. Before war was declared in September 1939, Falkus married (on 11th July) Doris Marjorie Walter whom he had met two years previously while helping out at his brother's shop in Old Leigh. In January 1940 Doris gave birth to twins, Christopher and Malcolm. Hugh, however, had little time to spend with his new family. On 1st June, 1940, on a fighter sweep over Dunkirk, Falkus' plane was hit by flak and then shot down. He crash-landed in a field near Calais but was captured and spent the next four years and eleven months as a German prisoner of war. While serving as a POW, Falkus was involved with several unsuccessful escape attempts. At Stalag Luft III, Falkus and a friend, Bill Fowler, stole the Kommandant's well-fed cat, put it to death and served it up in a casserole. With its skin Falkus even made himself a pair of mittens! He was eventually liberated by the British Army, arriving home on 6th May, 1945, nine days before his twenty-eighth birthday.

The immediate post-war years proved a difficult period for Hugh Falkus. He remained on the Reserve of Air Force Officers and in 1949 he returned to flying as an instructor with the Volunteer Reserve. He officially retired from the RAF in 1959. His marriage to Doris broke down and he abandoned her and the twins. They divorced in 1947. However, in July 1945 he was introduced to the beauty of Eskdale by his POW friend Bill Fowler whose family lived at Long Yocking How. On 15th July, Bill took Falkus sea trout fishing on the Esk. They fished with Norwegian spoons and Bill managed to catch two small sea trout while Falkus was unsuccessful. The following week, however, he caught his first Esk sea trout while fishing the Borrowdale Pool, near Eskdale Green. From then on Falkus became a regular visitor to Eskdale and during the summer he and Fowler would fish for sea trout and in the autumn and winter they would go wildfowling on the Esk estuary.

In between his fishing and shooting exploits, Falkus developed his acting talent, which he had nurtured during his time as a POW, and found work with a number of repertory companies. In 1950, he secured a regular slot, reading stories on BBC *Children's Hour*. That same year he married Diana Vaughan, the young editor of *Argosy* magazine. Tragically, on 12th May, 1951, she drowned in a boating accident off the coast of Achill Island in County Mayo, while they were making a film about the local shark hunting industry. Falkus, a powerful swimmer, managed to swim over a mile to the shore and raised the alarm, but it was too late.

In 1952 he married Lady Margaret Vane-Tempest-Stewart, daughter of the seventh Marquess of Londonderry, but the marriage was short-lived and by 1955 Falkus had returned to Eskdale and moved in with Bill Fowler who was now living at Knott End Farm. Hugh and Lady Margaret were divorced in 1958.

It was at Knott End that Bill and Hugh set up a mink farming business. Fur was very much in fashion in the mid-1950s and they hoped to cash in on the demand. Other people, too, had a similar idea, and before long the price for mink pelts fell and the business was relatively short-lived.

While he was living at Knott End, Falkus met and fell in love with Kathleen Armstrong, the daughter of a local farmer. Two months after his divorce came through he married Kathleen at the Register Office in Whitehaven. Together they bought and renovated Cragg Cottage where they ran a bed and breakfast concern and for a short time Falkus worked at Windscale (now Sellafield) as a health physics monitor. His job entailed patrolling the plant with a Geiger counter to check on radiation levels. Cragg Cottage had the advantage of access to a superb stretch of the Esk, which in those days was brimming with sea trout. Not surprisingly, perhaps, Cragg Cottage soon came to the attention of anglers and over the years was frequented by some of the angling greats: Arthur Oglesby, Fred Buller, Reg Righyni, Richard Walker and the actor, Sir Michael Hordern, himself a keen angler. It soon became known as 'Falk's Club', where many anglers and friends went to relax, fish for sea trout and drink copious amounts of whisky. Kathleen herself described life at Cragg Cottage during the sea trout season:

At this time of year, everything revolves around the fishing. The sitting room looks like a tackle shop. In the kitchen there's a jumble of wet boots beside the stove; trousers hang dripping from pegs - someone's always falling in - clothes, nets, bags, stockings, lines and rods are drying; the precious fish hang in the larder, away from the cat, waiting to be cooked for breakfast - but not until they've been carefully weighed, of course!

Hugh is on the river day and night looking for poachers, or fresh-run salmon and sea trout; helping the guests to catch fish, or fishing himself.

(From Chris Newton's, *Hugh Falkus - A Life on the Edge.*)

It was on the Esk that Falkus studied the sea trout and its curious ways and it was on the same river that he developed his strategies for catching these wily fish. When he started fishing the Esk, the fish were plentiful and there were few anglers, and even fewer anglers who fished at night. The anglers who did fish the Esk at that time included Falkus' father-in-law, Benny Armstrong, George Jackson, Brian Heath who had lived at Cragg Cottage before Falkus moved in, Geoff Rivaz and several members of the Woodall family, the well-known bacon curers. The fish were mainly caught using conventional wet-fly patterns, dressed on larger hooks

Falkus preferred to fish alone and, when he did have guests staying, they were positioned well away from one another and were expected to fish quietly. The Esk is a relatively narrow river and its water gin clear. He liked to rely on his natural hunting instinct and he seems to have had the uncanny ability to sense when a fish was about to take. During those early years at Cragg Cottage his rod accounted for a large number of sea trout, including some large specimens. In July 1957 he landed a magnificent fish of 15lb 6oz, a record for the Esk. The story of its capture is told in Maurice Wiggin's, *The Angler's Bedside Book*

(1965) and also in a slim limited edition volume entitled, *The Sea Trout*, published in 1987 to commemorate the author's seventieth birthday and the twenty-fifth anniversary of the publication of his book, *Sea-Trout Fishing* (1962).

The story of its capture is very dramatic. Falkus had spotted the fish that afternoon lying above a rock at the head of a pool and it was the biggest sea trout he had ever seen. It was ten minutes to midnight when he commenced fishing, wading in well above the fish's lie. After making one or two practice casts to ensure that his line and fly were sinking he moved slowly downstream to find the spot that he had marked that afternoon. With great anticipation, he sent the line singing through the air into the 'bushy darkness' under the opposite bank. The fly had scarcely touched the water when he felt the line tighten and then pull. Then 'all hell broke loose' and the fish rose to the surface 'lashing in a boiling ring of foam' before torpedoing off down the pool.

After a tremendous fight, Falkus managed to bring the fish into the shallows but, even then, all was not straightforward:

Sweating, I managed at last to pump him up. He came into the shallows on his side, a swathe of silver in the moonlight.

As he touched the stones, the hook flew from his mouth into the bushes behind me.

For a terrible moment I stood paralysed, while the great fish splashed violently in a cloud of spray. Then, dropping the rod I plunged in and seized him by the tail. He writhed from my grasp and skidded away towards deeper water. Again, my fingers slipped on his slimy flanks. Now he was nearly able to swim. Almost demented, I fell on hands and knees beside him, got both arms underneath and heaved him up on to the shingle. He began to flop back towards the river, but I stumbled forward and flung myself on top of him.

The outline of the fish was traced on a stone slab, which for many years was on display at Knott End.

During the early years of the 1960s Falkus often fished with Brigadier (Briggy) George Wilson from Keswick, whom he had met while salmon fishing on the river Derwent. Briggy was treated as a guest of honour at Cragg Cottage and was always put on the best pools on the river. In his later years Falkus admitted that he had learned a lot from Briggy. It was also during the early 1960s that Falkus wrote a series of articles on fishing for sea trout for the *Fishing Gazette* in which he outlined his strategies for fly fishing at night. These articles were the prelude to his book, *Sea-Trout Fishing, A Guide to Success*, which appeared in 1962. In the book, Falkus set out his philosophy of sea trout fishing. He believed that sea trout were very different from salmon and brown trout and need to be considered in their own right. He maintained that mature sea trout do not normally feed after entering the river and they should be fished for with large lures resembling the prey they pursued at sea. He also regarded night fishing as the principal means of fishing for sea trout and not a minor branch of the sport.

When Falkus fished for sea trout at night he invariably took two rods with him to the river, one equipped with a floating line, the other with a sink tip or fully sinking line. He divided his night into three separate periods during which he employed different strategies. The first period, from dusk until approximately midnight, he referred to as the 'first half'. The second period from midnight until around 1am was known as 'half-time', and the third period from then until daybreak was the 'second half'. During the 'first half', when sea trout take best of all, he normally fished a floating line. After anything from half an hour to an hour and a half, the sea trout stop feeding and go down. This is the start of 'half-time', a period when the fisherman might as well fish in his bath! Many anglers go home at this point. However, Falkus believed that it was during the 'second half' that most of the bigger fish were taken and to catch them he either fished a sunk fly or a surface lure dragged across the surface of the water.

Falkus developed a number of fly patterns to tempt the sea trout during these different periods including: the Medicines, Surface Lures, Sunk Lures, and the Secret Weapon, which included a flying treble hook for fish that came short. Despite the claims in his books, these patterns were basically adaptations of existing patterns. During the 1980s Falkus came to an arrangement with Riding Brothers of Preston to supply both his sea trout and salmon flies in presentation boxes. They sold extremely well.

His book has had an enormous impact on sea trout fishing and has encouraged many more anglers to venture out at night. However, despite winning high praise, the first edition of *Sea-Trout Fishing* sold relatively slowly, the original print run of 1,500 copies taking eight years to sell out. It was reprinted in 1971 with a much enlarged and revised second edition coming out in 1975. Since then the book has never been out of print and has sold over 20,000 copies.

In addition to sea trout fishing on the Esk, Falkus enjoyed sea fishing and often accompanied Paul Pedersen, a professional fisherman who owned a small vessel working out of Ravenglass. He would join Pedersen for a day or two at a time and bring back a supply of fish for the freezer at Cragg Cottage. On one occasion Falkus and a friend, Frank Plum, took a rowing boat out from Ravenglass to go plaice fishing and nearly lost their lives. Frank was hauling up the anchor when the boat overturned and both men ended up in the water. Fortunately, they managed to drift to safety.

Some Falkus sea-trout flies.

The 1970s was a fruitful decade for Falkus. In addition to the enlarged and revised edition of *Sea-Trout Fishing*, which came out in 1975, that same year witnessed the publication of *Freshwater Fishing*, co-authored with Fred Buller. Buller, who for a time worked for the Freshwater Biological Association on Windermere, formed a friendship with Falkus in the late 1960s, a friendship which was to last until Falkus' death. *Freshwater Fishing* is a magnificent book and is one of the most authoritative books on fishing ever written. It deals with all the species of freshwater fish that the angler is ever likely to encounter and is a mine of fascinating historical information. It is a book that I consult frequently. As well as writing, Falkus also produced a number of films during this period including *Self Portrait of a Happy Man* (1976), a celebration of his life and of nature in Eskdale, and *Salmo the Leaper* (1977), a tribute to the salmon.

During the 1980s Falkus increasingly turned his attention to salmon fishing and to another man's wife. Romille Booth entered Falkus' life in the spring of 1982 when she attended one of his casting courses at Boat of Garten on Speyside. The following July, she enrolled on his sea trout course based at the Riverside Inn at Canonbie on the Border Esk. At the end of the course the couple stayed on at the inn and began looking for a house where they could live together. They eventually found a cottage near Eskdalemuir in the valley of the White Esk. By now Falkus was sixty-six and in declining health, while Romille was a good looking woman in her mid-thirties. It was Romille who helped him to complete his book *Salmon Fishing*, published in 1984. Falkus was a very experienced salmon fisherman and for many years had a rod on the Derwent as well as helping out at Arthur Oglesby's salmon fishing courses on Speyside. In the book, Falkus puts forward his own take on salmon fishing although the book contains few original ideas. It was, however, enormously successful, the first print run of 5,000 copies selling out within months, and like his *Sea-Trout Fishing*, is still in print today.

In 1985, Falkus and Romille moved to a house in Pembrokeshire. Their relationship, however, was not to last and in June 1986 he returned to Cragg Cottage and Kathleen. In 1982, Bill Arnold, a keen shot and angler had bought Knott End Farm and a year later constructed a 3½-acre tarn on some boggy land between the farmhouse and the river. Falkus became friendly with Arnold and the two fished together on many occasions and in January, 1989 they opened the Knott End Academy of Speycasting and Game Fishing. Over the years the Academy introduced hundreds of anglers to the delights of speycasting. To help their pupils with the complexities of this style of casting, Falkus and Arnold developed a series of training devices, one of which was known as the Hugh Falkus Figure-of-Eight Speycasting Simulator. Made out of plywood, it was shaped to define the movements of the rod during a correctly-executed cast. Other devices included the Casting Corset and the Crucifix, which were strapped to the student's shoulders to prevent upper body movement. To show how the upper body should remain still while executing a cast, Falkus would balance a glass of whisky on the peak of his cap and cast without spilling a drop! A number of angling celebrities passed through the Falkus Academy, including David Swift, David Beazley, Fiona Armstrong, Ed Koch and Roman Moser.

In addition to teaching his clients to cast, Falkus was not slow in extracting money from them by selling them signed copies of his books or even Hexagraph rods, made by Bruce and Walker and endorsed by Falkus. Malcolm Greenhalgh, a close friend of Falkus in his later years, relates a number of such incidents in an article he wrote for *Waterlog* magazine (Oct/Nov 2003). On one occasion, when a distinguished surgeon turned up for casting lessons, Falkus took one look at the rod he had brought with him and suggested he took it down to Ravenglass and use it to catch crabs. He promptly sold him three brand new Bruce and Walker rods, complete with reels and lines. On another occasion, a Welshman turned up at the door of Cragg Cottage to ask Falkus if he would sign his copy of *Sea-Trout Fishing*. Falkus readily agreed and invited the man in. Ten minutes later, the man departed laden with signed copies of *Salmon Fishing, Spey Casting, The Stolen Years* and *Freshwater Fishing* but tens of pounds lighter!

The success of his casting courses at Knott End led Falkus to put down in writing his idiosyncratic ideas on speycasting. The book *Speycasting a New Technique*, which appeared in 1994, was the last book to be published during his lifetime and sold extremely well.

In 1992 Falkus was diagnosed as suffering from colonic cancer but, in spite of the pleading of his friends, refused surgery for his condition. Hugh Falkus passed away peacefully at Cragg Cottage on 30th March, 1996, aged seventy-nine. He was cremated at Distington Hall Crematorium, near Workington, and his ashes were buried near the grave of one of his beloved dogs by the banks of the Esk.

Hugh Falkus was a complex and sometimes contradictory character. He was dashing, daring, courageous, witty, charming,

and a brilliant communicator who could hold an audience spell-
bound. However, he did not suffer fools or dissenters gladly and
he could be rude, arrogant, unfeeling and offensive. He fell out
with most of his friends at one time or another, often after heavy
bouts of drinking. In a short chapter such as this it is difficult to
do justice to a character who led such a varied and interesting life
and, for the reader who would like to learn more of this intrigu-
ing man, I wholeheartedly recommend Chris Newton's brilliant
biography, *Hugh Falkus - A Life on the Edge* (Medlar Press, 2007).

APPENDIX

A NINETEENTH CENTURY LIST OF FLIES
FOR THE LAKE DISTRICT

While carrying out research for this book in the Museum of Lakeland Life at Abbot Hall, Kendal, the author was shown a box of fishing tackle containing the fly wallet of George Foster Braithwaite (1813-1888), together with another wallet, which may have belonged to a member of the Braithwaite family. In the back pocket of this wallet was a yellowing piece of paper folded down the middle containing a hand-written list of flies for use throughout the season, together with a section on hints for fishing upstream, downstream and lake fishing.

The list was clearly not intended for publication but was more likely to be an aide-memoire for the angler himself. As well as a list of flies for various months, written in red, the document also contains a number of annotations, written in black ink, giving further details of their usage. Whoever wrote the list had clearly fished in France since the writer stated that the Brown Silverhorns fly was excellent in the north of France. The list itself is not dated but was almost certainly written during the latter half of the nineteenth century. The front of the list is divided into two. The left-hand side contains hints for fishing, while the right contains a list of flies for use during the months of March and April. The reverse contains a list of flies for the months May-August, together with a list of Lake Flies. Both pages are transcribed overleaf.

HINTS

Up-stream fishing to be preferred when river has run down fine, that is, if the water be moderately clear. When, on the contrary, water is coloured then
Down-stream fishing may be indulged in as the fish will then most likely be searching for food all over the water. In up-stream style cast first quite close to the bank, allow the fly to come almost to one's feet then cast again a little more into the stream, and the next yet a little more towards the centre, soon finishing by casting right to the opposite bank if possible; then advance a little farther upstream and repeat. Casting the fly on to the opposite bank and allowing it to drop into the water will often prove a killing method – cast under overhanging boughs or bushes when practicable.

Lake-fishing by the leeward shore, unless it be too rough, as in the very curl of the wave and in the streak of foam the very best fish are often found. Don't pass any islets without giving them a try. Fish the edges of weeds or reeds very carefully making the Drop-fly "skim" the surface. If trees or bushes overhang the lake throw under them. Where rivers or brooks join the stream are generally to be found plenty of fish. Wade if possibly to be done but be very careful of the footing.

MARCH

BLUE DUN
Of darker or lighter shade according as weather is cold or mild.
MARCH BROWN
The female is of a greenish tinge; use both in cast.
COW DUNG
Use if a strong wind blowing.
NEEDLE BROWN
Vary in size and shade. Very useful.
PALMERS
Coch Y Bondu

PEACOCK FLY
RED SPINNER
Sometimes, but seldom, seen in the day. Slight showers or rain good.
GREAT RED SPINNER
Useful if March Brown has been on thickly.

APRIL

YELLOW DUN
In warmer weather than the Blue Dun – middle of day.
IRON BLUE
On sunshining days.

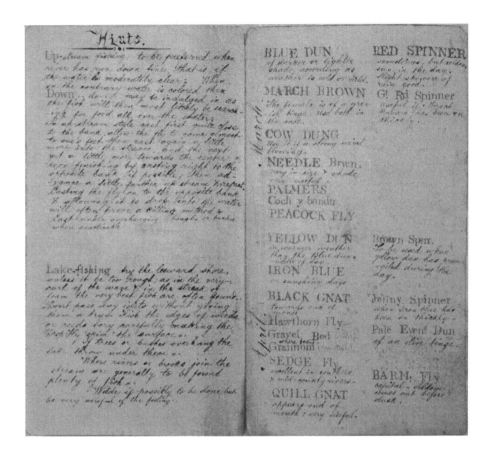

BLACK GNAT
Towards end of month.
HAWTHORN FLY
GRAVEL BED *(spider)*
Where found
GRANNOM *(Greentail)*
SEDGE FLY
Excellent in southern and mid-county rivers.
QUILL GNAT
Appears end of month; very useful.

BROWN SPINNER
To be used when the yellow dun has prevailed during the day.
JENNY SPINNER
When Iron Blue has been on thickly.
PALE EVENING DUN
Of an olive tinge.
BARM FLY
Capital - seldom comes out before dusk.

MAY

STONE FLY
"Work" the imitation; for dapping.
CAPERER
Large fly; comes out towards evening.
OAK FLY
Windy weather.
SKY-BLUE
ALDER
Excellent; for dapping.
LITTLE YELLOW MAY
Good; also for dapping.

JUNE

GREEN DRAKE
Imitation to be used in morning early or late in evening.
FERN-FLY
YELLOW SALLY
FRANCIS
Dressed small (day), dressed large (evening).
COACHMAN
Dressed small (day), dressed large (evening).
GOVERNOR
Dressed large.

JULY

ANT-FLIES
Viz., red and black.
MOTHS
Small moths "might" be used during day - evening best time.
HOUSEFLY
WRENTAIL
Fine summer weather.
MIDGES
Fine warm evenings.
GREENWELL'S GLORY
On very hot days - dressed small.
LARGE YELLOW DUN
BLACK SILVER HORNS
BROWN SILVER *HORNS*
Excellent in north of France.

RED SPINNER
To be generally used in the evening on account of several flies changing to spinners much resembling the blue duns.

AUGUST

AUGUST BROWN
Capital, very general fly. Somewhat like March Brown.
COWDUNG
Dressed small.
CINNAMON
Capital fly - also for lake fishing.
NEEDLE BROWN
HOFFLAND's FANCY
Useful on account of resemblance to many small flies.
EMPEROR - WELLEINGTON
WHIRLING DUN
Noted fly.
WILLOW FLY
On warm days

LAKE FLIES

To be used instead of local monstrosities.

SOLDIER PALMER
RED SPINNER
MARCH BROWN
AUGUST BROWN
MOTHS
CAPERER
CINNAMON
SMALL DRAKES
GREAT RED SPINNER

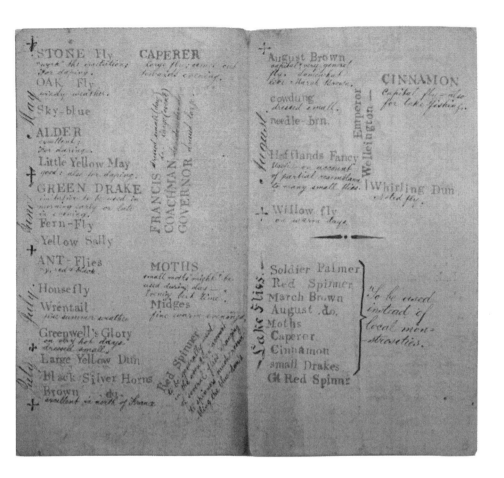

The flies in this list are common North-country patterns and the list itself appears to come from Francis Francis', *A Book on Angling*, first published in 1867 and running to several editions. The idea of casting the fly on to the opposite bank and allowing it to drop on to the water also comes from Francis. The flies in Francis' book are taken from a number of sources dating as far back as Charles Cotton (1630-1687) who added a section on fly fishing to the fifth edition of Izaak Walton's *Compleat Angler*, published in 1676. Amongst the patterns in the list which ultimately derive from Cotton are: the Barm Fly, Blue Dun, Whirling Dun,

Black Gnat, Peacock Fly, Yellow Dun, Fern Fly, Green Drake etc. Many of the flies on the list are also recommended by John Kirkbride, a Carlisle fishing tackle maker, who wrote *The Northern Angler*, published in 1837. Before returning to Carlisle to set up in business, Kirkbride had been principal fly-maker for Ustonson's, a famous fishing tackle maker of Temple Bar, London.

Clearly this list of flies must date to the latter half of the nineteenth century following the publication of Francis' list and, although most of the flies it contains are tried and tested North-country patterns with a long pedigree, there are one or two more recent patterns, which include the Greenwell's Glory and the Francis. The Greenwell's Glory was invented by Canon William Greenwell of Durham while fishing the Tweed at Sprouston in May 1854. The pattern, designed to imitate one of the olive duns, is now a very popular pattern in the fly fisherman's armoury. The Francis, as its name suggests, was invented by Francis Francis around 1858 and, with its peacock herl body, was regarded as a good all-round fly. Francis himself claimed that in its larger sizes it was responsible for the capture of many sea trout, salmon and even mahseer in India! The Hofland's Fancy (spelt with two 'f's in the manuscript) was the invention of another nineteenth century angler, Thomas Christopher Hofland (1777-1843), author of *The British Angler's Manual*, published in 1839. The fly itself was invented around 1830 and was designed in imitation of a small spinner. Even today it is considered a good general purpose fly, especially when fished in the evening.

The only enigma in this list of flies is the Emperor-Welleington (which presumably should be Wellington without an 'e'). I can find no trout fly bearing this name and can only assume it is an oblique reference to a fly known as the Waterloo, a fancy fly with a body of crimson silk and kingfisher wings, designed for lake fishing, which appears in Kirkbride's *Northern Angler* (1837). Another fly bearing the same name appears in Hutchinson of Kendal's trade list of flies thought to date to the late nineteenth century (see Chapter 8). However, the dressing given for this fly, with its blue silk body and heron wings, is completely different from Kirkbride's pattern.

Together with his list of lake flies the writer has made an interesting comment, 'to be used instead of local monstrosities'. Alas, he does not say what those monstrosities were!

The list itself is an interesting document and the flies mentioned would certainly serve the late nineteenth century Lake District angler well. Indeed, many of the flies listed have stood the test of time and can still be found in the fly boxes of many of today's anglers.

(List reproduced by courtesy of the Museum of Lakeland Life, Abbot Hall, Kendal.)

BIBLIOGRAPHY

Armistead, J. J., *An Angler's Paradise and How to Obtain It,* The Angler, 1894.

Beazley, David, 'The Saga of the 'Snecky-Limerick', *The Flyfishers Journal,* Vol. 84 Nos. 299 & 300, 1995.

Braithwaite, George Foster, *The Salmonidae of Westmorland,* Hamilton, Adams & Co., 1884.

Brogan, Hugh, *The Life of Arthur Ransome,* Jonathan Cape, 1984.

Buller Fred & Falkus, Hugh, *Freshwater Fishing,* Cresset Press, 1992.

Cholmondeley-Pennell, Harry, *The Modern Practical Angler,* Frederick Warne & Co., 1870.

Clapham, Richard, *Sport on Fell, Beck and Tarn,* Heath Cranton, 1924.

Clapham, Richard, *Trout Fishing on Hill Streams,* Oliver & Boyd, 1947.

Clapham, Richard, *Fishing for Sea Trout in Tidal Water,* Oliver & Boyd, 1950.

Clark, Len, *On and Off the Rails,* Helm Press, 2003.

Davison, Tom, *Angler and Otter,* Nicholas Kaye, 1950.

Davy, John, *The Angler and his Friend,* Longmans, 1855.

Davy, John, *The Angler in the Lake District,* Longmans, 1857.

Falkus, Hugh, *Sea-Trout Fishing,* H. F. & G. Witherby, 1962 and later editions.

Falkus, Hugh, *The Stolen Years,* the Museum Press, 1965 and later editions.

Falkus, Hugh, *Salmon Fishing,* H. F. & G. Witherby, 1984.

Falkus, Hugh, *Some of it Was Fun,* published posthumously, The Medlar Press, 2003.

Gordon, Mrs, *'Christopher North', A Memoir of John Wilson,* Thomas C. Jack, 1879.

Hart-Davis, Rupert (editor) *The Autobiography of Arthur Ransome,* Jonathan Cape, 1976.

Herd, Andrew, *The Treatyse of Fyshynge wyth an Angle,* A New Translation, The Medlar Press, 1999.

Herd, Andrew, *Angling Giants,* The Medlar Press, 2010.

Herd, Andrew, *The History of the Fly,* The Medlar Press, 2011.

Hills, Rt Hon John Waller, *My Sporting Life,* Philip Allan & Co, 1936.

Holgate, James, *Reflections Upon Lakeland Angling,* Cast Publications, 1989.

Houghton, Rev. W, *British Fresh-Water Fishes,* William Mackenzie, 1879.

Keen, Peter, *Fly Fishers of Fame,* The Medlar Press, 2009.

Kipling, Charlotte, *The Commercial Fisheries of Windermere,* Transactions of Cumberland and Westmorland Antiquarian and Archaeological Society, Vol. LXXII - New series, 1972.

Le Cren, David, *The Windermere Perch and Pike Project: An Historical Review*, Freshwater Forum, The Freshwater Biological Association – Vol. 15, 2001.

Maxwell, Sir Herbert, *British Fresh Water Fish*, Hutchinson & Co., 1904.

Mitchell, W. R., *The Eden Valley and the North Pennines*, Phillimore, 2007.

Nelson, William, *Fishing in Eden*, H. F. & G. Witherby, 1922.

Newton, Chris, *Hugh Falkus, A Life on the Edge*, The Medlar Press, 2007.

Newton, Chris, *The Trout's Tale*, The Medlar Press, 2013.

Niven, Richard, *The British Angler's Lexicon*, Sampson Low, Marston and Co, 1892.

Oliver Stephen, *Scenes and Recollections of Fly-Fishing in Northumberland, Cumberland and Westmorland*, Chapman and Hall, 1834.

Pickering, A. D., *Windermere, Restoring the Health of England's Largest Lake*, Freshwater Biological Association, 2001.

Railton, Martin and Davies, Gareth, *Archaeological Evaluation of the Salmon Coops, Corby Castle, Cumbria*, Transactions of Cumberland and Westmorland Antiquarian and Archaeological Society, Vol. VII – Third series, 2007.

Ransome, Arthur, *Rod and Line*, Jonathan Cape, 1929.

Ransome, Arthur, *Mainly about Fishing*, A & C Black, 1959.

Richardson, Sheila, *Tales of a Lakeland Poacher*, Red Earth Publications, 1993.

Savage E. U. (editor), *The Watcher by the Bridge*, Titus Wilson, 1937.

Swift, Jeremy, *Arthur Ransome on Fishing*, Jonathan Cape, 1994.

Thompson, Ian, *The English Lakes - A History*, Bloomsbury, 2010.

Watson, John, *The Confessions of a Poacher*, The Leadenhall Press, 1890.

Watson, John, *Sketches of British Sporting Fishes*, Chapman and Hall, 1890.

Watson, John, *The English Lake District Fisheries*, Lawrence and Bullen, 1899.

West, Thomas, *A Guide to the Lakes*, J. Richardson, 11th edition, 1821.

Wilson, John, *Recreations of Christopher North*, William Blackwood, 1864.

INDEX